Composing Arguments

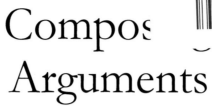

Jared K Miller

ISBN: 1533090386
ISBN-13: 978-1533090386

DEDICATION

I dedicate this book to every coach and instructor who has to struggle to provide the activity of debate to their students. As a student, I had no idea the resistance that my teachers encountered just to create a safe space for me to debate. People inherently prefer agreement to conflict, but debate instructors know that learning means challenging ideas. It is uncomfortable. Sometimes, it is ugly. Perhaps this is why it is not more popular. But, the benefits are undeniable. Find any way you can to make people debate. In any forum.

CONTENTS

ACKNOWLEDGMENTS

I would first like to acknowledge the contributions of Matt Shapiro. You have jumped into this project with both feet and have been a great motivator. With continued drive, and determination, I know that we are going to be instrumental in delivering quality argumentation and debate instruction to many people.

For my children who have accepted when I need those few hours alone in the garage to get down my ideas on paper, you are why I even have the motivation to continue working after I put you to bed. I know that this book is not you idea of "fun" reading, but I look forward to the day when it might help you along in your academic pursuits.

For my wife. This project has taken up a lot of my free time. I value the investment that you have put into me. I could not do this without your support. I could not imagine a better partner, a better colleague, or a better person than you.

Foreword

I wrote this book because I think that we are on the verge of a new age in competitive debate. The technology that has developed in the last ten years has been underutilized when it comes to facilitating civil argumentation. Too often there are bald assertions that go unchallenged. This book is my humble effort to combine traditional argumentation theory, common debate practice, and contemporary technology. I encourage instructors to contact me with criticisms, or even requests. I look forward the the possibility of creating custom versions of this manual that borrows from multiple approaches to argumentation and debate instruction.

This textbook is organized into two sections. The first reads like a traditional argumentation text. There, I cover ancient and contemporary theorists, as well as appropriate concepts that help to frame the complexities of argumentation into manageable lessons. The second section focuses on technology that uniquely facilitates computer-mediated debate. It is the second section that motivated me to put in the tremendous effort to compile what I have learned about asynchronous debate. It is an approach that, I believe, will be vital to reaching a whole new audience of students.

It is not necessarily required that you read it in the order that it was written. You may find that your first debate you are assigned the negative side. In that case, you may find it best to jump to the sixth chapter. Perhaps you are debating online, using video recordings. Then you should start with the eighth chapter. You might need to jump back-and-forth between different chapters of the book to garner all of the information that you need for any given debate assignment. Consider the book to be a modular design, where all the parts come together to form my vision of debate instruction, but there are other approaches that are equally beneficial.

Chapter One
Fundamental Concepts

Communication
Apprehension
- Glossophobia
- Effects on the body
- Overcoming fear

Communication
Model
- Linear
- Interactive
- Transactional

Language
- Theories
- Properties

An Ancient
Approach
- The syllogism
- The enthymeme

An Informal
Approach
- Performance
- Audience

Introduction

You may not know it, but by reading this book you are learning a new art form. Not everyone automatically identifies argumentation as an art form. Many self-identified debaters might not even consider themselves artists, but public argumentation and debate is an art as old as human language. And, like learning any art form, your first attempts at it are likely going to feel awkward and unrefined. Perhaps you have tried learning a musical instrument once in your life, or lived with someone who was learning. If so, then you know that picking up a musical instrument takes more than just raw talent; it takes hours of dedicated practice, and a willingness to makes mistakes several times over. The same is true for learning a new language, a new type of dance, a new medium, and so on.

The similarity between music and argumentation is going to be a theme throughout this text. The overlap between these two fields of study is so vast that it is difficult to see where one ends and another begins. One especially strong similarity between the two is how people learn each art form. Bass guitar virtuoso, Victor Wooten, articulated this idea well.

Argumentation is an exercise in language with rules and expectations that improves the skill levels of everyone involved. It builds and evaluates knowledge. It is an art form that requires several people interacting with each other with some type of synchronicity. When people agree to argue about a central topic, and commit to a formal procedure with equitable distribution of time, the educational benefits are remarkable.

One of the more common outcomes that new debate students express is that they never knew how enjoyable it would be. Even when tasked with a side with which they disagree, on a topic for which they don't care, students regularly report that

> "Although many musicians agree that music is a language, it is rarely treated as such. Many of us treat it as something that can only be learned by following a strict regimen, under the tutelage of a skilled teacher. This approach has been followed for hundreds of years with proven success, but it takes a long time. Too long. Think about the first language you learn as a child. More importantly, think about how you learned it. You were a baby when you first started speaking, and even though you spoke the language incorrectly you were allowed to make mistakes. And the more mistakes you made, the more your parents smiled. Learning to speak was not something you were sent somewhere to do only a few times a week."
>
> -Victor Wooten

they liked being a part of a debate, despite making occasional mistakes during the round. Entering into a formal, academic debate is like entering into a practice area where one should feel free to explore and present ideas that they may be unfamiliar with. Test the beliefs of your opponents, as well as your own. It is not easy, and there will surely be times where you will be less than articulate, but in the end you will develop a skill that many people are afraid to even practice.

This first chapter will cover some fundamental concepts that are essential for anyone that has decided to undergo argumentation and debate instructions. First, it is important to face the fear that a vast majority of people have with public speaking. Second, debate is a communication activity, so one must learn the model of communication. Third, every artist must get familiar with their medium, and for argumentation and debate, that is language. Finally, students greatly benefit from learning a little history of how argumentation has been taught to past generations in order to understand how we got to where we are now in the subject.

Communication Apprehension

There is a natural and predictable reaction that most people have to stressful situations, scientists have dubbed this response as the fight or flight response. Meaning that if you're presented with a stressful situation, or a dangerous situation, your body's automatic response is to *fight* that danger or to take *flight*, to run away from it. For most people, public speaking is not just *a* stressful situation; it is the *most* stressful situation that they can think of. In fact, glossophobia, or speech anxiety, is consistently rated as people's biggest fear. People even rate their fear of public speaking as being greater than their fear of dying. This "fight or flight" response to public speaking situations goes by a particular name in communication studies: communication apprehension. Since communication apprehension is often the most difficult barrier to becoming a great public speaker, it is important that we understand what it is. So, in this lesson we are going to explore the affect that communication apprehension has on the body, and then suggest ways to better manage communication apprehension.

MINI GLOSSARY

Glossophobia: speech anxiety, or the fear of speaking in public.

Apprehension and the Body

Anybody that has participated in public speaking is likely aware of when they are experiencing communication apprehension, but it is important to realize that this phenomenon is not just happening in one's head, it affects the entire body. We can now measure, very accurately, the hormones that are released when you are presented with a potentially dangerous or a stressful situation. There are two primary stress hormones: adrenaline and cortisol. It is worth it to think for a second about this as it relates to what we were just talking about with fight or flight. When you're really excited, or even a little scared, that excitement is your body getting itself ready for something. Adrenaline increases your blood pressure and your heart rate to make you more alert, and is literally preparing your body for a physical event that you might need to do. When you're in a fight or flight response, the hormone cortisol is also released into your body. Cortisol affects on the critical thinking parts of your brain in a few specific ways. First, Cortisol lowers electrical activity in your brain. Secondly there's lower neural regeneration, so less total brain cells are being remade over and over again. And third there's a decrease in efficiency, which means the learning and the critical thinking parts of your brain are less engaged.

The analytical parts of your brain are inhibited by cortisol and adrenaline because your body, from an evolutionary standpoint, wants you to prepare yourself for some physical action; the fight or flight from your threat. This makes sense because if someone thinks too long about an imminent threat, they stay in harms way for a longer period of time and increase the chances of being the target of bodily injury. In fact, it is pretty likely that anyone living amongst our ancestors, that did not possess this particular evolutionary ability, didn't live long enough to pass on that particular trait to any offspring. In short, communication apprehension is not only a normal bodily reaction, it is a common trait that is widely found among all people across the globe, and throughout history. You should consider yourself in good company if you experience any level of speech anxiety.

The release of cortisol and adrenaline is beneficial from an evolutionary standpoint, but there's a tradeoff in stressful situations between getting your body ready for a physical altercation and your ability to critically think. It makes sense that our bodies react to things that present an immediate threat to our person, but what is interesting is that when people are in public speaking situations, they tend to react with the same sort of fight or flight response as if they were in dangerous life or death situations. This is a little bizarre considering that they are not under that same threat as if they were confronted with a vicious animal, but it is the same fight or flight response, and the same hormones. As far as your body/brain are concerned: public speaking is a threatening situation.

Coping with Apprehension

There are many great suggestions for coping with communication apprehension, but it is worth taking a moment to recognize that this section is not called "eliminating communication apprehension." That is because even the best public speakers function while they are experiencing speech anxiety. For beginning speakers, the goal should never be to completely eliminate apprehension, because that is setting oneself up for failure. Instead, the goal of individuals that want to improve their public speaking abilities is to function *despite* the feeling of communication apprehension. The following five suggestions are a helpful starting point to give you ideas for approaching the problem of speech anxiety.

1. **Fake it.** This might seem counterintuitive at first, because most people think that they must first have the right attitude, and then they can act accordingly, but the opposite is actually true. People can act as if they are confident, even when they are not, and eventually reduce communication apprehension. And it is easier than it sounds. Harvard professor, Dr. Amy Cuddy, suggests things called "power poses." A power pose is a way that you would stand and/or hold your body if were in a powerful situation. One of the more common power poses is to stand with your feet apart, and your hands on your hips. Another way to appear confident, even if you don't feel it, is to choose clothing that indicates self-assurance. Shorts, and an ironic printed t-shirt do not convey a sense of professionalism and credibility to an audience. Think about the clothing that other people wear that strike you as powerful, confident, and professional. Emulate those choices.

Dr. Cuddy demonstrating a power pose.

2. **Identify with your audience.** More than likely, you are using this textbook in a class with other students that are in the same situation you are. They are given the same assignments, and they probably have very similar levels of experience. Being "in the same boat" helps to reframe this speaking situation. Most of the time, the speaker doesn't have the benefit of knowing their audience. But, the most successful speakers put in a great deal of energy trying to find out as much information about the crowd they are speaking to before the event arrives. A classroom setting comes with the benefit of being able to observe your fellow classmates, and pay attention to the things that interest them. Use this to you advantage. Note the things they react to. Their likes and dislikes. But, above all, realize that they are probably just as scared as everyone else in the room.

3. **Build a knowledge base.** This should go without saying. People who know about the subject they are debating have a greater ability to recall appropriate and relevant information when it is time to speak. One of the most common sources of communication apprehension is the fear that you won't know what to say. Building a knowledge base means collecting more information than you will likely use in a debate, researching common arguments that your opponent might make, and categorizing the information you collect. People who prepare just enough to fill their allotted time are often disappointed with their performance because they feel under prepared. Knowing more information than you can use in a debate is not rated energy; it is necessary for you to be able adapt to the many possible issues that might arise.

4. **Match the conditions.** This means to practice in an environment that is as close to what the actual event will look like. Check to see if the room you are to debate in is available for a practice round. If not, find a room that is of similar dimensions. Practice at the same time of day, with the notes you plan to use, with the same outfit you plan to wear. There are some people who think they are better off "winging it." Most people do not have this skill. Even if you feel that you have some special ability to speak with little preparation, you can still improve your chances of a successful speech by taking extra time to prepare.

5. **Set reasonable goals.** Your first is not going to be perfect. You will likely have verbal fillers, awkward pauses, and/or forget some argument that you were prepared to deliver. Demanding perfection is a sure way to disappoint yourself. Instead, set achievable goals. These could include making sure that each section in your speech is numbered, or speaking for the entire allotted time, or that every source citation includes a date, or to limit the number of verbal fillers to three. Focus on one goal every time you practice, rather than all of them. You may have to work on things that come naturally to others, like eye contact and vocal variety. Don't overwhelm yourself with unreasonable expectations. Debate is something that everyone has to practice regularly if they want to get good.

Communication apprehension is not just your mind playing tricks on you, there are significant physiological factors at work when anyone experiences speech anxiety. Your body is releasing hormones, whether you like it or not, and those hormones have a measurable effect on your mood and cognitive abilities. Fortunately there are methods that deal with, and even overcome those barriers to performing in front of an audience. Physically manipulating your body into power poses, preparing well, and reframing the public speaking event have shown to be effective ways to manage communication apprehension. Consider utilizing these strategies the next time cortisol and adrenaline start coursing through your body.

Communication Model

It would be easy to assume that communication has been the subject of study for hundreds of years, and in a general sense it has if you count language studies like rhetoric or english. But, communication, as its own academic field of study really got its start in the early 50's. The advent of technologies like the telephone and television gave rise to new ways of thinking about the act of communication itself, prompting thinkers like Claude Elwood Shannon and Warren Weaver to develop new theories and models to help better explain how it is that human beings share information. Another easy assumption would be that these theorists got these ideas right the first time, but a model for how humans communicate has undergone revisions ever since it was introduced. Therefore, the focus of this section is to understand the communication model by following its evolution from its origins in the linear model, to the development of the interactive model, and finally visit the concept of transactional communication.

The Linear Model

When building a model, for anything really, the person doing the building is essentially trying to represent one thing for another. When the thing being modeled is a concept, like say communication, then the model builder is trying to simplify something that is very complex. The first attempts to model communication were very simple indeed; in fact, a little too simple. The models consisted of little more than a sender, a message, a channel, and a receiver. You see, Shannon and Weaver were primarily interested in communication through the telephone, and developed their model around its parts. The sender included the person on one end, the receiver included the person on the other, and the channel was the telephone itself. This model provided the beginning that would take on several evolutionary stages. For instance, Shannon and Weaver identified an element that they called noise, or anything that impeded the signal itself. The strength of this model lies in its simplicity, but that turned out to also be a weakness. The complexities of communication were not captured by this model, so other elements were added to the model for the purpose of accuracy. One complexity that is omitted from this model is known as feedback. Some might think of this as that loud annoying buzz that you get when you put a microphone in front of a speaker, and technically it is, but feedback includes anytime when a receiver returns their own message in response to information from the receiver. Even simple nods of the head, or confirmation from the receiver counts as feedback. Communication models that lack feedback as an element are generally referred to as linear models of communication, and for many communication scholars this was unacceptable.

> **MINI GLOSSARY**
>
> Noise: in communication studies, anything that impedes the transmission of a message.

The Interactive Model

Thus, the next evolutionary stage of the communication model is commonly referred to as the interactive model. Some refer to this as having two linear communication models layered on top of each other in order to represent the element of feedback. There are generally seven parts to this model. The sender, message, channel, noise, receiver, feedback, and situation. Let's address each element in order.

1. **Sender**. We can understand the sender by understanding their credibility. Regardless of who is the sender of information, or what the context, there are some assumptions about a person's credibility that arise from whoever the audience is. One way

you can improve your credibility is by practicing their speech and organizing it well. The sender sends a message.

2. **Message**. A message is anything that the sender communicates. Notice that the message is not always what the sender intends to communicate. Unintentional messages are sent all the time, especially nonverbal messages. A speaker could come across as nervous when they are actually confident, angry when they are calm, and ignorant when they are intelligent. Everyone should be familiar with the idea of saying one thing when you meant another. The next element is the channel. Messages must be sent through channels, sometimes multiple channels simultaneously.

3. **Channel**. A channel is the medium that the sender choose to send the message through. It could be face-to-face, through the television, text, the phone, a billboard, skywriting, interpretive dance, and the list goes on. The interesting part about the channel, in the communication model, is that which channel one chooses can greatly affect one's message. Have you ever sent a text message that was meant to be sarcastic, but the person who received the message took it literally? If you would have said the exact same message, but face-to-face, there probably wouldn't have been the same misunderstanding.

4. **Noise**. The channel isn't the only thing that distorts a message, as mentioned before, noise, or interference also distorts a message. Interference can be internal or external. External interference are things that impede a message that originate from outside of the communicators, like the room temperature, loud noise, the weather, etc. Internal interference is anything that impedes communication and originates from within the communicators, like a bad night's sleep, or communication apprehension.

5. **Receiver**. If the sender is able to transmit a message, using an appropriate channel, and through the noise, only then can someone receive that message: the receiver. One complication that receivers bring to the communication model is that every human being has their own frame of reference. A frame of reference is the totality of a person's experiences that shape the way they view the world. This includes a person's culture, religious and political views, gender identity, age, race, sexual orientation, as well as innumerable others.

6. **Feedback**. Receivers also send messages of their own, and this is known as feedback. Just like any other message, feedback is delivered through channels and affected by noise. Feedback is also affected by the receiver's frame of reference.

There are certain behaviors in one culture that are completely acceptable forms of feedback that would be inappropriate in other cultures.

7. **Situation**. Finally, the situation is the time and place where communication occurs. Examples of situations include the different expectations that people have at a funeral versus a wedding. While both situations might take place at the same location, and even have the same family members in attendance, it would be inappropriate to deliver a eulogy during a wedding toast.

The Transactional Model

All of these elements are helpful ways to conceptualize all communication phenomenon, but there is one reality that complicates things even further. It is that people tend to send and receive messages simultaneously. The reason that the interactive model of communication, described just earlier, fails to account for this is that one subject is labeled the "sender" and the other the "receiver." These labels oversimplify the roles that each individual is playing in the communication act. It is for these reasons that transactional model of communication has become very popular. The transactional model basically does away with the sender/receiver idea and considers all members to simply be "communicators" that are encoding and decoding messages simultaneously. If you think about it, it is really astonishing that we are able to transmit even the simplest of messages between people, yet the vast majority of human beings are able to communicate simple ideas with relative ease.

The communication model is still undergoing evolution as we discover more about this complicated, yet ever-present phenomenon. From the earliest attempts of the linear model, to the interactive model, to the transactional model, modeling communication has been a helpful way to understand one of the most basic of human behaviors.

Exercise: Activity

The Classic Telephone Game
Purpose: To demonstrate the communication model.

1. Arrange the class into a circle.
2. Select a sentence and quietly whisper it into the ear of someone sitting in the circle.
3. The first person now whispers the message into the ear of the person sitting next to them, the second person whispers the message into the third person's ear, and so on until the message comes back to the starting point.
4. Compare the received message with the original message.

Variation 1: Message Overload.

Purpose: To demonstrate how the complexity of a message affects communication.
1. Select 2 messages and whisper each into the ears of people sitting next to each other.
2. Have each message go in opposite directions around the circle. Eventually the two messages will cross and the people will have to negotiate how to communicate both.
3. Compare the results

Variation 2: Musical Telephone Game.

Purpose: To demonstrate how the messages can be affected by noise or interference.

1. Play music and allow the class to speak quietly as a new message is passed around the circle.
2. Gradually increase the volume of both the music and the class conversation while the new message is passed around.
3. Compare the results

Koko the gorilla is famous for being able to understand and use over 1 thousand words in American Sign Language. She was exposed to spoken and sign language at a young age, and has received intensive training for the vast majority of her 44 year life. In contrast by age six the average human child understands over 2,500 words without even any special training. This difference is not insignificant. The ways that humans use language is unique to any other species on the planet that has ever existed. To study language is to study what it means to be human. So we would like to use this lesson to explore the fundamental nature of language. First, we will cover a couple of language theories, and then some essential properties of language.

Language Theories

It would be impossible to cover all of the language theories that have ever been written, so we will cover two. The first is from Noam Chomsky who is a Professor of Linguistics at MIT and an individual that revolutionized his field. Perhaps his most significant contribution is the theory that all humans are born with biological structures in the brain that make us uniquely able to acquire language. What he calls a language acquisition device. Basically he posits that all human beings are hardwired To understand and use language. His theory is not without controversy. The more we are able to measure and analyze the brain, the more it seems that language comes from multiple regions within the brain, not just one. While this doesn't automatically disprove Chomsky's theory, it does make it problematic in order to measure its truth value.

Noam Chomsky

Ludwig Wittgenstein

The second theorist we will cover is Ludwig Wittgenstein, who was an Austrian born philosopher, and taught for many years at the University of Cambridge. He is often credited as one of the most influential thinkers of the 20th century. One of his greatest theoretical contributions to the study of language is the observation that people tend to learn and use language through what he called language games. This is contrary to the prevailing opinion at the time that language was somehow a reverent to some external reality world. Language is an activity that forms relationships and generates behaviors. The best way to understand language is to look at how

12

language is used rather than trying to unearth some sort of meaning.

Language Properties

There's a lot more detail to these theories and other theories that we can't get into right now so let's turn toward the different properties of language. There are three.

1. **Language is ambiguous.** When we say that language is ambiguous, we mean that a single word or sentence could be interpreted multiple ways from multiple people. The word pet might conjure up an image of a dog for one person, a picture of a bunny for another, and a picture of a snake for yet another person. So this means even if your sentences are grammatically well-formed, and the information is accurate, it doesn't mean that your gonna have 100% effective communication with another person.

2. **Language is arbitrary.** When we say language is arbitrary, we mean that there's no inherent relationship between the object being referenced, In the sounds or letters that form the word for that object. This is easily understand by recognizing that many different languages have their own words that sound very different from each other even if they are referencing the same object.

3. **Language is abstract.** When we say language is abstract, we mean that it can refer to things that don't actually physically exist. For instance, the word "please" is very common but it doesn't reference anything in the physical world. There are levels of abstraction that communicators can use making their messages more concrete or more abstract. For instance rocky road is comparatively concrete than a word like ice cream. A lot of people assume that language is some perfect representation of their beliefs and observations, but these three properties seem to indicate otherwise.

From Formal to Informal

Argumentation studies, at least in Western society, can be traced back to some of the first civilizations to begin recording knowledge. Aristotle is one of the best known and referenced figures in all of academia. Aristotle developed two important and inter-related concepts, one known as the syllogism, and the other known as the enthymeme. He presented such a comprehensive version of the syllogism that another famous thinker, Immanuel Kant, declared logic to be "completed." The syllogism and enthymeme, for a very long time, were the only ways of appreciating the nature of arguments. Ultimately, understanding the syllogism and the enthymeme means understanding two of the most fundamental and dramatic advances in human thought.

Syllogisms

A syllogism is a method of reasoning where a conclusion is derived from two given or assumed premises. Therefore, a syllogism is comprised of three parts: a major premise, a minor premise, and a conclusion. Both premises are built upon prior observations. If both premises are true, then the conclusion is necessarily true. A long-standing example of the syllogism is shown below.

All humans are mortal (major premise).
Socrates is a human (minor premise).
Therefore, Socrates is mortal (conclusion).

Notice how this syllogism is built upon universal, or absolute, premises. For that reason, syllogisms are often treated as more scientific than the enthymeme. So, syllogistic logic is more likely to be used in the fields of math and science than in English or Communication. The syllogism has dominated the way people have studied arguments, but Aristotle also offered a variation of the syllogism called the enthymeme.

MINI GLOSSARY

Syllogism: a method of reasoning where a conclusion is derived from two given or assumed premises.

Enthymeme

Aristotle described enthymeme as a syllogism based on probabilities. Over time, the enthymeme has taken on a broader definition. Contemporary thinkers have explored it as a description of an 'incomplete syllogism.' Argumentation theorists have struggled with a way to describe exactly what it means to be incomplete. The incompleteness of a syllogism could be from a missing premise or conclusion, or it could be a result of one of the propositions being probabilistic rather than absolute. And since few things in life are ever absolute, enthymemes are better suited to everyday affairs and practical decision-making.

Despite the fact that the enthymeme allows for the use of probabilities and incomplete arguments, the use of absolute premises has dominated the study of argumentation for literally thousands of years. It wasn't until very recently that there have been methods to analyze

MINI GLOSSARY

Enthymeme: an incomplete or probabilistic syllogism.

arguments as they naturally occur during discourse. The closest thing to studying informal logic was studying informal fallacies (Johnson). It is important to note how a recent turn toward informal logic has blossomed in recent history and how that affects the content in this chapter and this textbook.

Understanding natural arguments means understanding the difference between formal and informal logic. In the 1950's and 1960's, there was an up swell of demand for practical uses of logic. Students felt that syllogistic logic fell short of explaining how people react during argumentative situations, and lacked effective strategies to improve one's performance during argumentation. This demand resulted in several theorists developing a new approach to arguments from an informal perspective; for example, Perelman and Olbrechts-Tyteca explained the importance of invention and being conscious about the role of the audience, and Toulmin accounted for the implied nature of some components of arguments, as well as offered a common language for examining arguments across spheres.

Syllogism Game.
Take note of how the premises
interact with one another.

Premise   (Humans are smelly.)
Premise   (Socrates was human)
Conclusion   (Socrates was smelly.)

Variation 1

Use the Premises provided in the
bank to the right to create formal
syllogisms. Each set of syllogism
will have a total of nine (9) separate
conclusions.

Variation 2

Create your own set of major
premises and minor premises about
one topic. Allow your imagination
to take over and compose premises
that are unique and unconventional.
Follow the premises to their logical
conclusion.

Premises Bank

Human Syllogism
- All humans are mammals.
- All humans need air to survive.
- All humans age horribly.

- I am a human.
- Our teacher is a human.
- (_NAME_) is a human.

Reptile Syllogism
- All reptiles are cold blooded.
- All reptiles need heat to survive.
- All reptiles are scary and gross.

- Snakes are reptiles
- Our teacher is a reptile.
- Matt is a reptile.

Soda Syllogism
- All sodas contain either sugar or sweeteners.
- All sodas are fizzy.
- All sodas are delicious.

- Coke is a soda.
- Cactus Cooler is a soda
- Our teacher is a soda.

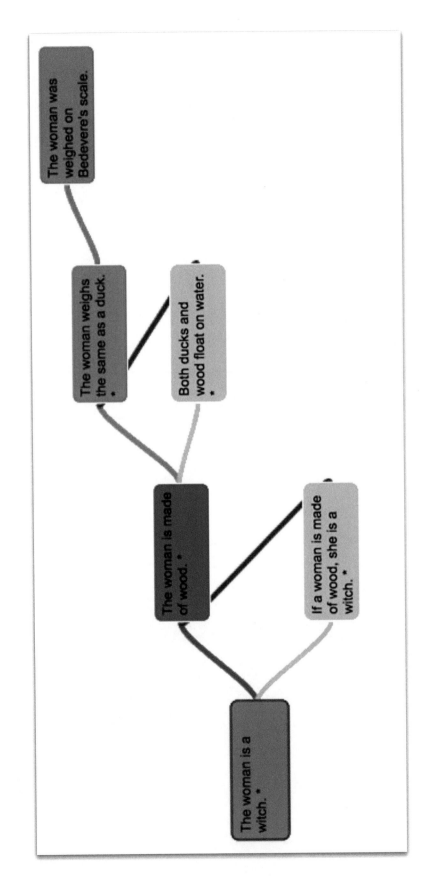

The woman was weighed on Bedevere's scale.

The woman weighs the same as a duck. *

Both ducks and wood float on water. *

The woman is made of wood. *

If a woman is made of wood, she is a witch. *

The woman is a witch. *

17

Example of a syllogism

A conversation between professor and student from "The Great Debaters." The professor of debate asks his student to defend oppose the resolution "Resolved: Welfare discourages hard work." When the student asserts that people will starve were in not for welfare, the professor asks:

Professor Tolson: Who's starving, Miss Booke?
Miss Booke: The unemployed are starving.
Professor Tolson: Mr. Burgess here. (Gestures to a healthy student in the audience) He's unemployed. Obviously, he's not starving. I drew you in, Miss Booke. You gave a faulty premise, so your syllogism fell apart.
Miss Booke: "Syllogism"?
Professor Tolson: Your logic fell apart. Major premise; the unemployed are starving. Minor premise; Mr. Burgess is unemployed. Conclusion: Mr. Burgess is starving. Your major premise was based on a faulty assumption. Classic fallacy. Who's next?

Professor Tolson exposes a fallacy through syllogistic reasoning. The structure is simple, but because the conclusion (at the left) is demonstrably false, the flaw in the major premise (at the bottom right) is revealed.

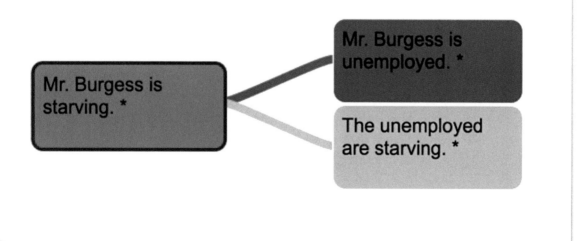

Example of Aristotelian logic gone wrong

A humorous example of Aristotelian logic gone wrong was written into a scene from "Monty Python and the Holy Grail," in which medieval English villagers are trying to determine whether or not a particular woman is a witch. They consult Bedemir for wisdom:

CROWD: A witch! A witch! A witch! We've got a witch! A witch! VILLAGER #1: We have found a witch, might we burn her?
BEDEMIR: Quiet, quiet. Quiet! There are ways of telling whether she is a witch. ...Tell me, what do you do with witches?
CROWD: Burn, burn them up!
BEDEMIR: And what do you burn apart from witches?
VILLAGER #2: Wood!
BEDEMIR: So, why do witches burn? [pause]
VILLAGER #3: B--... 'cause they're made of wood...?
BEDEMIR: Good! So, how do we tell whether she is made of wood? Does wood sink in water?
VILLAGER #2: It floats! It floats!
BEDEMIR: What also floats in water?
ARTHUR: A duck.
BEDEMIR: Exactly! So, logically...,
VILLAGER #1: If... she.. weighs the same as a duck, she's made of wood.
BEDEMIR: And therefore--? VILLAGER #1: A witch!

The argument is really two connected syllogisms (see page 14). The conclusion, "the woman is a witch," is at the top of the illustration and is connected to two premises, forming the first syllogism. The premise that the woman is made of wood is itself linked to two other premises, forming the second syllogism. Obviously, the logic is flawed, but the form is still apparent. You can also see the connections between the warrants in grey and their corresponding data in dark green.

Chapter 2
Arguments

Argument Defined
- -Controversy
- -Adherence
- -Reason
- -Invention

The Toulmin Model
- -Argument Fields
- -Elements of Arguments

Modeling Arguments
- - Order of analysis
- - Method of analysis
- - Modeling Techniques

Introduction

One of the first instruments that I learned was a saxophone. I loved the sound of it, but I eventually realized that there was a limitation to the instrument. Unlike a guitar or piano, you could only play one note at a time on a saxophone. The ability to have multiple notes interacting with each other, creating harmony and dissonance, bring music to another level. Playing multiple notes at once is known as a chord, and there are complicated discussions amongst musicians about composing music with chords.

Arguments are like chords in the sense that debaters use the combination of multiple propositions, whose meanings harmonize with each other to create an idea that is richer and more complex than any single proposition could ever be. In this chapter we are going to cover the essential elements of arguments through the use of one of the most influential thinkers in argumentation studies, Stephen Toulmin. This chapter will define argument, explore the essential elements of all arguments, and finally explain methods for modeling arguments.

The Definition and Context of Argument

By now, the importance of understanding the background of argument studies should be apparent. Knowing the background of argument studies points to a split in the theory of argument: one that attempts to approach arguments from a purely rational perspective (like symbolic logic), whereas the other explores natural utterances, or everyday, rhetorical arguments. It is the desire to study natural utterances that influences how this textbook defines what an argument is. The primary influence can be seen in the two dimensions of argument that shape its definition. One level deals primarily with the structure of argument, and the other describes conditions in which arguments occur. These two levels have long been distinguished between "making an argument" and "having an argument," commonly distinguished as argument[1] and argument[2], respectively. It is important to realize that it is all but impossible to remove one type of argument from the other.

> Example of complicated definition for "argument"
>
> "An argument is a type of discourse or text— the distillate of the practice of argumentation —in which the arguer seeks to persuade the Other(s) of the truth of a thesis by producing the reasons that support it. In addition to this illative core, an argument possesses a dialectical tier in which the arguer discharges his dialectical obligations."
> — Ralph Johnson

Therefore, both are reflected in the treatment of the definition of argument.

Defining an argument is an essential first step in argumentation studies, but this is easier said than done. One thing that complicates the definition of argument is that people use the word to mean different things in everyday discussions. Hearing the word "argument" brings to mind conflicts, bad interpersonal experiences, or worse. Another complication is that there are many different definitions that have been provided in the past. Some of these definitions are so dense that they hardly seem useful for students that are just beginning their education in argumentation studies.

Rather than presenting all of those different definitions for the word argument, I wish to propose a working definition that incorporates all the essential characteristics of an argument. An argument is any combination of propositions aimed at persuading an audience to a particular viewpoint, belief, or action; and, that particular conclusion is claimed to be supported by the other propositions.

This definition explains the core of an argument, but there are additional characteristics of arguments that are worth exploring in more detail if it going to be useful to the study of arguments. Specifically, it is useful to identify the characteristics of the contexts where arguments are made. If someone combines a series of statements and has no intention of defending those statements, then one may question whether an argument was properly made. As a consequence, I identify four characteristics of situations that often are managed with or characterized by arguments: controversy, invention, adherence, and reason

MINI GLOSSARY

Argument: any combination of propositions aimed at persuading an audience to a particular viewpoint, belief, or action; and, that particular conclusion is claimed to be supported by the other propositions.

Controversy

The first thing that the average person assumes about any argument is that the arguer is discussing an issue that has room for disagreement or controversy. In other words, an issue about which there is uncertainty. This assumption is at the root of peoples' common understanding of what it means to "have an argument." Also, when anyone claims to make an argument 'for' something, it is reasonable to assume that there is the potential for someone else to make an argument 'against' that same thing. The definition provided above uses the term 'to persuade,' which implies that there are competing alternatives for the audience to choose from and that the arguer is advocating on behalf of one of those options at the expense of the others. One might describe argumentation as taking place against a background of controversy.

There are topics that pop to mind when thinking about controversy: abortion, the death penalty, immigration policy, etc. But, controversy exists in all sorts of issues that are not typically considered controversial. Even in mathematics, there is controversy. Math is often taught as a universal language; something that "just *is*." But, controversy surrounded the creation of some of the simplest of mathematical terms. Legend has it that when Hippasus discovered the mathematical concept known as the 'irrational number,' he was drowned at sea for contradicting established mathematical principles. Furthermore, there is still controversy amongst mathematicians about contemporary mathematical problems. Other things are not controversial now, but were very controversial in the past. It is not very controversial to say that slavery is immoral, but that was a very controversial statement in America prior to the Civil War. In fact, the issue of morality and slavery were the focus of several debates between Abraham Lincoln and Stephen Douglas in 1858, when both men were campaigning for the same senate seat in Illinois.

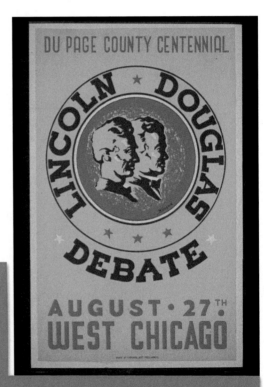

DU PAGE COUNTY CENTENNIAL

LINCOLN DOUGLAS DEBATE

AUGUST • 27TH. WEST CHICAGO

Lincoln Douglas Debates

Abraham Lincoln and Stephen Douglas participated in a series of seven debates that focused mainly on the subject of slavery. It would uncommon to see, in a contemporary academic debate, someone defend chattel slavery outright. But, prior to the civil war, such positions were very common.

Invention

A second addition to this definition is that an argument is made with the goal of creating new knowledge. Acknowledging a controversy is one thing; creating an argument which makes a contribution to understanding, and hopefully decision-making about controversy is another. Without the creation of arguments, there is no way to analyze arguments. An arguer is essentially taking information that was collected prior to the argument and combining it with other information to create something new and valuable. This new and valuable creation is greater than the sum of its parts; in other words, a combination of propositions carries information in the combination which is lost if the statements are separated. Another important factor regarding invention is the concept of uncertainty. Creating new information comes with the risk that you might be proven wrong. Of course, if we only spoke when we are certain about the outcome, then that would eliminate any space for disagreement, and therefore unreasonably constrain arguments.

Adherence

The third contextual element important to realize about arguments is how people and propositions have a tendency to 'stick together.' Adherence can be thought of as the combination of three characteristics: (1) two things are next to each other, (2) they resist being parted, and (3) the origin of the resistance lies within or between them. Adherence emerges in a number of different ways within arguments. First, when arguers adhere to the arguments they are making. Arguments are not neutral like simple observations; arguers take a position and offer an audience direction. There are ways to discuss controversial topics without making an argument. For instance, one could report about issues surrounding the abortion controversy without taking a position (e.g., number of abortions performed per year, average costs of abortion services, etc.). A question is another example of a non-argument. Questions can incite controversy, but the fact that a question requests information rather than directs an audience means that it is not an argument. Second, the goal of arguers is to have an audience adhere to the claims they make. The audience focus of adherence was made popular through the works of prominent theorists Chaim Perelman and Lucie Olbrechts-Tyteca. They even classify different types of adherence based upon whether or not an arguer is intending an argument for a particular or universal audience. But, propositions also stick together to form clusters, making the third type of adhesion. These "clusters" of propositions can be thought of in terms of the Toulmin model articulated later in the chapter.

Reason

The fourth thing to add to this definition of argument is that arguments are supported by reason. This is what distinguishes argumentation from mere assertion or proclamation. Consider when an athletic coach barks commands at their athletes. The coach does not explain why he or she is demanding their athlete perform a particular action, so they are not engaging in an argument. The fact that arguments use reasoning is also what distinguishes them from threats of force. In the definition it states that one of the statements is supported by the others, this means that those other statements

act as the rationale for the conclusion the arguer hopes the audience will reach. If one fails to supply reason for their argument, it is no longer an argument but an assertion.

The Toulmin Model

From the definition of argument we turn to what has become the dominant method of analyzing arguments. This method has come to be known as simply the Toulmin model of argument, named after Stephen Toulmin. In the book, Elements of Argument, Stephen Toulmin outlined some fundamental problems with the syllogism. Additionally, in order to develop an approach toward everyday arguments, he introduced the concept of field logic and proposed a new method of analysis that created the groundwork for a new era of argumentation theory.

1. **Everyday arguments are too complex for a syllogism to describe effectively.** His specific criticism focuses on instances where conclusions are required, but universal knowledge is not accessible. Let's say you were to state as a major premise of a syllogism that "taking the life of another human being is murder." This premise is phrased as if it is universal, which is good when one wants to create a syllogism, but, for many people, if you kill someone through the act of self-defense that does not meet the definition of murder. In many parts of the world there are other exceptions to this rule, including war and capital punishment. A soldier killing another soldier from an opposing army is not considered a murderer. Likewise, others may argue that the death penalty also should not be considered murder. All of these exceptions begin to add up, and it is difficult to allow for all of these exceptions and still have a simple, direct, universal

sentence on which to ground your argument. Furthermore, when you have all the exceptions to your general principle about the definition of murder, a syllogism that allows for all of these exceptions becomes very difficult to write in any convenient sense. Even if your major premise was very detailed and accurate stating that: "taking the life of another human being, except in self defense or when sanctioned by the government, is considered murder," the syllogism starts becoming fairly convoluted and impractical.

2. **The conclusion of a syllogism is redundant.** The second criticism against the syllogism is that the major premise, itself, provides the evidence for the conclusion. Recall the syllogism about "Socrates" in the previous chapter. If the statement "all humans are mortal" is a verified truth, then one must have assessed the mortality of every human on earth. During that verification process, Socrates would be one of those men that was verified for mortality. Therefore, the syllogism's conclusion is really a *foregone* conclusion, regardless of whether or not one includes a minor premise. The truth of the matter is, when we argue, we often speak in probabilities. Toulmin recognized that the syllogism lacked the language needed to analyze everyday argumentation and concluded that there needed to be a model that accommodated for this reality. He crafted a model for studying argumentation that more closely resembled the way people naturally develop arguments.

Argument Fields

Criticizing the practicality of the syllogism required Toulmin to provide an alternative explanation for natural arguments. His approach uses what he calls "argument fields" to describe different social spheres, each with individualized standards for judging good and bad arguments. An easy example of a field is to picture the different disciplines at a university. Biologists have different standards for argumentation than do poets, than do accountants, than do historians, than do philosophers, etc. But this analogy does not capture all of what fields are, because there are many fields of argument that are not academic disciplines. The analogy also fails to show how there may be different fields of argument within academic disciplines.

Regardless of how one decides to identify different argument fields, the major contribution from the identification of argument fields is the concept of field dependency. Field dependency is the idea that certain elements of argument may be considered acceptable for one field, but unacceptable in another. What one field calls valid logic another proclaims to be invalid. Even the meanings of words change from field to field and affect the ability to argue.

The different standards for acceptability also extend to the types of admissible evidence. Take, as an example, a hypothetical argument between a catholic priest and a professor of evolutionary biology. If the priest were to cite scripture as proof against evolution, the professor would likely dismiss the passage outright because she doesn't see the Bible as a credible text on the subject of evolution. In this example, the structure or form of the argument is irrelevant to the professor. It is the difference in argument fields that dominates the discussion.

It is important for arguers to realize, early on, the argument field that exerts the most influence on any discussion in question. Identifying argument fields is useful because it prepares arguers for certain terms and phrases that might otherwise be foreign or misunderstood. But not all analysis of arguments is field dependent; Toulmin also identifies elements of arguments that are field invariant. Field invariant, in terms of the Toulmin model, refers to the components of arguments that are consistent across all fields. Toulmin gives each of these elements a title and description in his model, and the result is the most widely accepted language for analyzing informal arguments.

MINI GLOSSARY

Field invariant: those components of arguments that are consistent across all fields.

The Elements of Toulmin Model Arguments

There are a few things to take note of: one is that Toulmin specifically wanted to focus on the sentence level of argument analysis. He acknowledged that arguments may take a very long time to lay out for an audience, covering several pages in a written work or taking several minutes if verbalized. Let's reuse the music analogy. One could study music by studying entire songs, or take a more detailed approach and study music note-by-note. The model that Toulmin developed takes the latter approach and takes a very detailed, sentence-level view of arguments. His work did not focus on every single utterance that an arguer happens to make. He wanted to focus on those components that were specifically interrelated. This means that when you are reading from the opinion section of a news source, or listening to a politician give a speech, that not every single sentence that is written or spoken is part of an argument. People use style and flair to embellish arguments, and those embellishments do not always factor into the analysis. Additionally, arguers purposefully omit parts of arguments for stylistic purposes. In fact, sometimes a listener or reader must paraphrase, or fill in gaps that are left by the author.

Despite these limitations, the Toulmin model offers the most widely recognized approach for analyzing arguments across the many contexts in which they are deployed. What follows are the six elements of argument as defined by Stephen Toulmin. The first three elements—the claim, data, and warrant—comprise the three necessary elements of every argument; whereas the second three elements—qualifier, rebuttal, and backing—are optional ways to add depth, character, and strength to arguments.

Claim

The central component of any argument is the claim. The claim is the fundamental position (belief, viewpoint, or action) which arguers want an audience to accept. For a syllogism, this is the conclusion, and is simply a byproduct of combining two premises. The Toulmin model, however, treats the claim as central to any argument regardless of where it appears, whether it is before, after, or during the introduction of support for the claim. If you are writing an essay, then your thesis can be considered your claim. However, just like when writing a thesis, when one constructs a claim the level of clarity is of the utmost importance. A vague or convoluted claim is generally considered a sign of poor argumentation. Some arguers might want to elaborate on the central claim through the use of "sub-claims," or additional sentences that offer additional clarification to the central claim, but there is still a single unifying idea that represents the central aim of the argument.

So how do you identify a claim when you see it? There is no easy answer, but a claim is really identified based on its relationship to the other sentences that are part of the argument in question. This mirrors the practice of listening to the different notes in a chord in order to identify the 'root.' In other words, look at the other sentences within an argument, and ask yourself which expresses the central position being advocated. Usually anything that is stated as a matter of fact is not the claim, but is another part of the argument called the data, or support (which I will soon address). The claim should be the part of the argument that fulfills the expectation of invention; some new knowledge you are leading the audience to accept.

Data

The next element of an argument is the data. Data is any research, evidence or other support that is presented in order to support the claim (see fig. 4). Identifying data is usually one of the easier parts of analysis with the Toulmin model, but there are times when the data relies on shared values or beliefs, and is masked in language. In such cases, it can be more difficult to identify the data for an argument. What some people initially think is a requirement of data is that the statement is in fact true, but in reality the statement is really just claiming something *as if* it were true. Some data may require additional backing (discussed below). One important feature of data is to realize that the claim, whatever it may be, is dependent upon the data. In other words, an arguer's claim cannot find agreement with the audience unless the audience agrees with the data. In fact one of the easiest ways to identify the claim is to first look for the data presented in the argument. Then, trace the conclusion from that data. It is good to remember that this data, when analyzed using the Toulmin model, is in the form of a single proposition. It is not, therefore, a complete research project or journal article. Remember, the Toulmin model as a tool for sentence-level analysis. Analyzing entire articles is a complicated undertaking requiring several iterations of Toulmin model analysis.

Warrant

The third element of arguments that Toulmin outlined is the warrant. This element rounds out the three required elements of every argument. The function of a warrant is to connect the data with the claim. Essentially the warrant answers the question of how you came to your conclusion based on the data. Sometimes this connection is self evident, sometimes it is not. In fact, many times an argument is made without an explicit warrant, thereby forcing the audience to fill in the missing component. This common practice mirrors the definition of an enthymeme discussed earlier. A warrant can also be considered the reasoning within an argument. In these cases, the warrant is an implied warrant. The claim, the data, and the warrant all form what Toulmin considers to be the three core elements of every argument. He considers these three to be mandatory whenever an argument is made.

Qualifier

In addition to the three core elements outlined above, Toulmin includes three others as dimensions of arguments that appear in more robust and nuanced controversies. The first of these elements is called the qualifier and is contained within the claim itself. The qualifier effectively modifies the strength of a claim. It might seem counterintuitive to weaken a claim that one is making, but in reality it helps arguers adopt more reasonable positions when they don't try to overstate a claim. Life rarely has universal rules that are unquestionable, so arguers must be allowed to make arguments that are realistic and account for uncertainty. Otherwise, you would be forced to make arguments so absolute there is no amount of evidence that could every support them. Qualifiers also make it impossible for people to make decisions based on probabilities. Without the ability to make decisions based on probability, we would be paralyzed into inaction because we could only act when we are absolutely sure of an outcome. Therefore, often times one decides to write claims that contain the words "sometimes," "probably," "more often than not," and "likely." These, and similar words and phrases, are examples of qualifiers.

Rebuttal

When one clarifies the conditions for a qualifier, they are articulating a rebuttal. This practice, understandably, bothers opponents in a controversy because it is a way for arguers to relieve themselves of defending the most extreme cases that might fall under their claim. The common question that is raised when an arguer includes a qualifier in their claim is for clarification on what those exceptions are. So if you were to say that a "college educated person is more likely to be wealthier than someone who is not college educated," somebody else might ask "what do you mean by more likely." Any response that offers further clarification is the rebuttal.

Backing

The final part of the Toulmin model argument is called backing. Backing is any additional information or evidence that is used to support the data or the warrant. Notice how this fulfills much the same function that the data does for the claim, it is just one step removed from the claim. So yet again, identifying backing really is a matter of identifying the relationship that it has with the claim and the other data. You might now be able to see how an argument can begin to form chains, wherein a claim begins an argument but there is not necessarily any end. There can be an infinite number of backing elements within an argument. Anyone who is ever talked to a three-year-old knows exactly what this is like. Children of this age are very inquisitive, and their favorite question to ask is "why." If you have ever attempted to answer all of the questions as to "why," you would know that a 3 year old can ask you "why" far more times than you can answer their question sufficiently. Every time an arguer introduces new information, he or she increases the complexity of an argument, but not necessarily the strength because not all arguments require lengthy explanations. These elements form a model, or pattern that is repeated with dozens of variations in differing argumentative situations.

Field Dependency Exercise

Often words can mean different things in different situations or contexts. This exercise will demonstrate how there are different expectations within specific fields. Take note of how different fields of study might use the same words, but there are arguments that are common in one field which are not common in the other. Discuss the two examples provided below, then brainstorm two fields of study on your own. You might need to invest some time researching. Use the following discussion items as conversation starters:

- Discuss the differences between the field contexts of family and corporate information sharing.
- What arguments might you expect in one field, but would seem out of place in the other?
- Does the field context substantially change how arguments about information sharing are used?
- How do the ideas conflict with one another?

Sharing

1. In an interpersonal relationship context, sharing is generally encouraged between members of a group. Sharing personal information is often commonplace among close family and friends, and is even considered vital for healthy relationship development.
2. Information sharing on an institutional level is much different. People frequently do their best to keep their personal information out of the hands of corporations and government.

Relativism

1. Einstein's theory of General Relativity has massive amounts of evidence proving over and over again. Many more contemporary physic's concepts have simply built upon General Relativity.
2. Ethical Relativity is known as ethical relativism. The theory holds that peoples actions are only able to be considered morally right or wrong from the standpoint of the culture or society they come from. It is frequently debated and discussed.

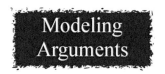

Modeling Arguments

Modeling arguments using Toulmin's approach is useful for two reasons. First, it provides a language with which to inspect arguments, understand how they work, and examine the support used by those making them. In other words, it allows critical thinkers and decision- makers to do more than choose to accept or reject the arguer's position. It allows them to explain the basis for their decision. At the same time, by mapping the components of the argument, the Toulmin model provides a means to identify the components of an argument and assess their strengths and weaknesses. I conclude this chapter by examining a small portion of an argumentative text to demonstrate the use of the Toulmin model.

For some people, simply understanding the characteristics of each of the elements of arguments is all they need to be able to identify those elements in the everyday arguments that they encounter. For many others, analyzing arguments is deceptively difficult. In order to develop the ability to analyze arguments, it helps to begin with written, rather than spoken, arguments. Written arguments are easier because they are —black and white, and you can literally number the sentences for analysis. Spoken arguments can also be analyzed using these techniques; unfortunately, there is far less time to do the same amount of work. Therefore, it is helpful to start with written arguments and to develop a reasonable level of proficiency before attempting to identify the elements of arguments in spoken contexts.

In this section I offer step-by-step procedures that aid the beginning student of argument in developing an "ear" needed for hearing the individual components of argument. Think of it as an exercise that you repeat in order to build proficiency. Of course, in order to demonstrate these procedures, we need an actual argument to work with. The following argument is far from perfect, but natural arguments in the public sphere rarely are. Try to withhold the urge to provide your own opinion about the value of the argument. When identifying elements of an argument, it is not completely necessary to also know the responses. Let's take the argument provided as a case study.

The myth that video games cause violent behavior is undermined by scientific research and common sense. According to FBI statistics, youth violence has declined in recent years as computer and video game popularity soared. We do not claim that the increased popularity of games caused the decline, but the evidence makes a mockery of the suggestion that video games cause violent behavior. Indeed, as the U.S. Ninth Circuit Court of Appeals declared: "The state has not produced substantial evidence that...violent video games cause psychological or neurological harm to minors."
--Gallagher, U.S. News and World Report

1. Take stock of the sentences that make the argument in question.

This is fairly simple, but for the best analysis you should also separate out independent clauses. If you don't do this you risk blending different elements, making analysis difficult. For example, in the above argument, there are four sentences. If you only letter the sentences, you get the following results:

a. The myth that video games cause violent behavior is undermined by scientific research and common sense.

b. According to FBI statistics, youth violence has declined in recent years as computer and video game popularity soared.

c. We do not claim that the increased popularity of games caused the decline, but the evidence makes a mockery of the suggestion that video games cause

d. Indeed, as the U.S. Ninth Circuit Court of Appeals declared: "The state has not produced substantial evidence that...violent video games cause psychological or neurological harm to minors."

Sentence 'c' has two independent clauses. Take the extra step and treat them as separate sentences, it will simplify things in the long run. To keep track of the original structure, use numbered sub-points. For example:

> a. The myth that video games cause violent behavior is undermined by scientific research and common sense.

> b. According to FBI statistics, youth violence has declined in recent years as computer and video game popularity soared.

> c.i. We do not claim that the increased popularity of games caused the decline.

> c.ii. But the evidence makes a mockery of the suggestion that video games cause violent behavior.

> d. Indeed, as the U.S. Ninth Circuit Court of Appeals declared: "The state has not produced substantial evidence that...violent video games cause psychological or neurological harm to minors."

2. Focus on one element of the Toulmin model at a time.

The order of elements that you analyze is important. You can waste a significant amount time randomly selecting elements to analyze. You also risk mislabeling sentences. I suggest the following order of elements when analyzing any argument.

First
Locate the Claim

Identifying claims is comparatively easier than identifying other elements because claims are often (but not always) explicitly included in the text of arguments. Also, identifying claims precedes identifying data because identifying claims is the most important skill a student of argument ought to develop.

Second **Locate the Data**	Identifying data is relatively easier than identifying other elements because data is often (but not always) a product of research provided by the author. Identifying data precedes identifying warrants because data is often (but not always) explicitly included in the text of an argument.

Third **Locate the Warrant**	Warrants are relatively more difficult to identify than many other core elements because warrants are often (but not always) implied by the author of an argument. Identifying warrants precedes identifying backing because it is one of the three core

elements of any argument, whereas backing is an optional element that may not be a part of an argument.

Fourth **Locate the Backing**	Identifying backing is relatively easier than finding the other optional elements of the Toulmin model because backing is often (but not always) a product of research provided by the author. At this point in the analysis,

analyzing the rebuttal may precede the backing if the analyst so chooses.

Fifth **Locate the Rebuttal**	Identifying the rebuttal is relatively more difficult because a rebuttal might be written with a good deal of rhetorical flair.

Finally **Locate the Qualifier**	Identifying the qualifier might happen immediately after identifying the claim because the qualifier often is found within the claim.

3. Compare two sentences from the argument in question.

The element that you selected in step two is the basis for comparison. You are listening for indications that the first sentence more closely resembles the characteristics of the element than the second. Say the two sentences out loud. Write them down side-by-side. Write one on top of the other. Do whatever technique helps you to come to a conclusion. Keep in mind, an argument has several sentences, so there is no requirement that either sentence fit perfectly with the selected element. But that does not prevent you from coming to a conclusion as to which sentence is a better fit.

For our argument, I begin with the claim and compare the first two sentences. Given the choice between these two sentences, I conclude that 'a' is a better candidate to be a claim than 'b' because 'a' asserts a position about arguments regarding video game violence as demonstrated by scientific research and common sense. Whereas, sentence 'b' cites and reports scientific research (FBI statistics) about video game violence.

a. The myth that video games cause violent behavior is undermined by scientific research and common sense.

b. According to FBI statistics, youth violence has declined in recent years as computer and video game popularity soared.

4. Select the next sentence and repeat steps 3 and 4 until there are no more sentences to compare from the argument.

You are now going to take the 'winning' sentence from your most recent comparison and hear how it matches up with the others. Do this a systematically as possible to save on time. 'a' is a better claim than 'c.i' because 'c.i' clarifies what the author is not claiming, rather than what he is claiming.

a. The myth that video games cause violent behavior is undermined by scientific research and common sense.

i. We do not claim that the increased popularity of games caused the decline.

36

Very similar, but 'a' sounds more direct than 'c.ii.' Also, 'c.ii' makes a reference "the evidence," which implies a unique relationship to a specific fact outside of the sentence. 'a' makes a more general statement implying multiple types of support.

a. The myth that video games cause violent behavior is undermined by scientific research and common sense.

~~ii. But the evidence makes a mockery of the suggestion that video games cause violent behavior.~~

'a' is a better claim than 'd' for the same reason 'a' is a better claim than 'b,' because a sounds more "persuading," and 'b' sounds more "matter of fact."
The final result: 'a' is most likely the claim for this particular audience.

a. The myth that video games cause violent behavior is undermined by scientific research and common sense.

~~d. Indeed, as the U.S. Ninth Circuit Court of Appeals declared: "The state has not produced substantial evidence that...violent video games cause psychological or neurological harm to minors."~~

5. Remove the sentence from further analysis and label it with the appropriate Toulmin model element.

There can be many ways of doing this, even as simple as a chart, but there is value in being able to read the original argument as a common paragraph. Therefore, the following formatting suggestions offer a common way to label elements of an argument with the least amount of clutter possible.

Suggested formatting for analyzing arguments using the Toulmin model.

Claim	**Bold**
Data	<u>Underline</u>
Warrant	*Italics*
Backing	<u>*Underlined italics*</u>
Rebuttal	**<u>Bold underline</u>**
Qualifier	***Bold italics***

For this argument, the result at this point in the analysis is:

The myth that video games cause violent behavior is undermined by scientific research and common sense. According to FBI statistics, youth violence has declined in recent years as computer and video game popularity soared. We do not claim that the increased popularity of games caused the decline, but the evidence makes a mockery of the suggestion that video games cause violent behavior. Indeed, as the U.S. Ninth Circuit Court of Appeals declared: "The state has not produced substantial evidence that...violent video games cause psychological or neurological harm to minors."

6. Move onto the next Toulmin model element, and repeat steps 3-6 until all core elements are accounted for.

Consider the analysis of each element to be a "round" of analysis. Therefore, the number of "rounds" ought to equal the number of elements in the Toulon model. It is important to remember that there ought to be a single claim per argument, but there may be multiple of any of the other elements. Therefore, you should check if the author has offered more than one data sentence before moving on to the optional elements of an argument. Unfortunately, there is a higher risk of error during this "double-check" because there is no requirement for additional data for any given claim. Another complication that arises during this step is when a warrant is implicit rather than explicit. There are times when none of the sentences seem to fill the role of warrant for the claim and data. Additionally, if an author offers several different kinds of data to support a single claim, it is likely that there are several warrants that are also part of the argument. For our argument, each round, and its results, would be as follows:

Round 1: The claim

a. The myth that video games cause violent behavior is undermined by scientific research and common sense. claim

b. According to FBI statistics, youth violence has declined in recent years as computer and video game popularity soared.

c.i. We do not claim that the increased popularity of games caused the decline.

c.ii. But the evidence makes a mockery of the suggestion that video games cause violent behavior.

d. Indeed, as the U.S. Ninth Circuit Court of Appeals declared: "The state has not produced substantial evidence that...violent video games cause psychological or neurological harm to minors."

Round 2: Data

a. The myth that video games cause violent behavior is undermined by scientific research and common sense. claim

b. According to FBI statistics, youth violence has declined in recent years as computer and video game popularity soared. data

c.i. We do not claim that the increased popularity of games caused the decline.

c.ii. But the evidence makes a mockery of the suggestion that video games cause violent behavior.

d. Indeed, as the U.S. Ninth Circuit Court of Appeals declared: "The state has not produced substantial evidence that...violent video games cause psychological or neurological harm to minors."

Round 3: The warrant
Remember, that it is possible that the warrant is implied. What to look for is some type of rationale connecting the data to the claim. Since you have already identified both, you should have an idea what it might sound like. Not all warrants are of equal quality.

a. The myth that video games cause violent behavior is undermined by scientific research and common sense. claim

b. According to FBI statistics, youth violence has declined in recent years as computer and video game popularity soared. data

c.i. We do not claim that the increased popularity of games caused the decline.

c.ii. But the evidence makes a mockery of the suggestion that video games cause violent behavior. warrant

d. Indeed, as the U.S. Ninth Circuit Court of Appeals declared: "The state has not produced substantial evidence that...violent video games cause psychological or neurological harm to minors."

Round 4: The backing
This step should only happen when you feel confident that you have all core elements, implicit or explicit. Each optional Toulmin model element is dependent on one of the core elements. You should still focus on one element at a time, but now apply the element to each remaining sentence in order and independently determine if each fits into the element in question.

a. The myth that video games cause violent behavior is undermined by scientific research and common sense. **claim**

b. According to FBI statistics, youth violence has declined in recent years as computer and video game popularity soared. **data**

c.i. We do not claim that the increased popularity of games caused the decline.

c.ii. But the evidence makes a mockery of the suggestion that video games cause violent behavior. **warrant**

d. Indeed, as the U.S. Ninth Circuit Court of Appeals declared: "The state has not produced substantial evidence that violent video games cause psychological or neurological harm to minors." **backing**

Round 5: The rebuttal
A rebuttal defends the reason for qualification of the claim. In this case, the argument preemptively responds to the potential objection that one should not assume that video games decrease violence just because there is a correlation.

a. The myth that video games cause violent behavior is undermined by scientific research and common sense. **claim**

b. According to FBI statistics, youth violence has declined in recent years as computer and video game popularity soared. *data*

c.i. We do not claim that the increased popularity of games caused the decline. *rebuttal*

c.ii. But the evidence makes a mockery of the suggestion that video games cause violent behavior. *warrant*

d. Indeed, as the U.S. Ninth Circuit Court of Appeals declared: "The state has not produced substantial evidence that...violent video games cause psychological or neurological harm to minors." *backing*

Round 6: The qualifier
Remember that the qualifier is part of the claim itself. In this case, "undermined" modifies an absolute claim like "disproven." The final result is an argument with all core elements explicated and all sentences accounted for:

a. The myth that video games cause violent behavior is undermined by scientific research and common sense. *claim*

b. According to FBI statistics, youth violence has declined in recent years as computer and video game popularity soared. *data*

c.i. We do not claim that the increased popularity of games caused the decline. *rebuttal*

c.ii. But the evidence makes a mockery of the suggestion that video games cause violent behavior. *warrant*

42

The myth that video games cause violent behavior is *undermined* by scientific research and common sense. According to FBI statistics, youth violence has declined in recent years as computer and video game popularity soared. **We do not claim that the increased popularity of games caused the decline,** *but the evidence makes a mockery of the suggestion that video games cause violent behavior. Indeed, as the U.S. Ninth Circuit Court of Appeals declared: "The state has not produced substantial evidence that...violent video games cause psychological or neurological harm to minors."*

For this argument, the warrant is explicitly included, but in many cases, perhaps even a majority of cases, the warrant is implied. Do not force sentences into the argument structure, they should naturally resonate with one of the elements more than the others. If you think that there are two claims within the combination of statements you are analyzing, consider treating it as two arguments rather than one. If you can't find a warrant or data, consider the possibility that they are implied. Also remember that there may be "leftover" sentences that don't really add anything to the argument other than style or rhetorical flourish. The modeling process is very long and involved, but the more you practice the easier and quicker it becomes. You begin to be able to identify claims at a rate that makes it seem like intuition or reflex. Once you identify the claim, the data and warrant are simple to sniff out. But just like any skill, it requires practice.

Exercise: Modeling Arguments

Use the method explained above to analyze the arguments provided below. Then, find an argument from a news article and analyze it using the same method.

- There is nothing more American today than a mass shooting, the quickest way for the wicked among us to join the ranks of the reviled. Their motives are many, but their opportunity is limited only by their gun and ammunition magazine brand preference. In this country, the federal government limits duck hunters to weapons that carry only three shells, to protect the duck population. But you can buy an assault weapon in seven minutes and an unlimited number of bullets to fire with it. For every McDonald's in the United States, there are four federally licensed gun dealers and an untold number of unregulated private dealers who can legally sell an unlimited number of guns out of their homes, backpacks, and car trunks without requiring a criminal background check or proof of ID.

  -Boston Globe, June 16, 2016

- The death penalty has been rightly put behind us. The Connecticut Supreme Court on Thursday ruled, for the second time, that the statute prohibiting capital punishment must apply to all, including those already sentenced and on death row. In 2012, the General Assembly abolished the death penalty, but only for future cases. That contortion of the law — banning capital punishment except for those already on death row — had been a way to ensure that Steven Hayes and Joshua Komisarjevsky, sentenced to death for the brutal assaults and murders of the Petit family in Cheshire in 2007, would still face execution.

  -The Hartford Courant, May 27, 2016

Chapter 3
Delivery

Audience
Analysis

Listening
  -Types
  -Poor Listening

Delivery Methods
  -Scripted
  -Memorized
  - Extemporaneous
  -Impromptu

Word Choice
  -Word economy
  -Figures of speech

Introduction

It is impossible to know for sure, but there are probably a lot of brilliant musicians that we will never know about. Imagine all the people that practice, alone in the homes, perfecting their ability to play an instrument, but have no desire to play in front of an audience. What is it about standing in front of an audience that changes people's ability to perform? For some, the thought of performing in front of a group of people is frightening, even intimidating. For others, the thrill of performing in front of an audience is what keeps them coming back. What is interesting is that the activity—playing music—is technically the same. A musician can play the same notes, in the same order, with the same inflection, to make the same song; but, play that same song in front of people and it is an entirely different experience.

> The real test of a musician is live performance. It's one thing to spend a long time learning how to play well in the studio, but to do it in front of people is what keeps me coming back to touring.
> -Neil Peart

In the same way that live performance changes one's experience, live debate is an experience that often exceeds the exceptions of everyone involved. Debaters often report the thrill they feel during rounds. Some even experience withdrawals once their eligibility has expired. It's not that they are not allowed to composed arguments, and even publish them publicly. It is the feeling of having people, even a small audience, listen, and agree, to arguments they prepared. Some have a natural ability to speak in front any sized group, but most people do not. This chapter is going to cover some basic information that is helpful to prepare to deliver a debate; specifically, audience analysis, listening, methods of delivery, word choice, and nonverbal communication.

Audience Analysis

Picture any speaking event in your mind and there is one element that should always be present, the audience. Think about it. A speaker without an audience is just a weirdo talking to themselves in a huge room. That audience without a speaker is a bunch of weirdos sitting silent staring at nothing. A successful public speaker must always consider the audience first. This section is going to cover the essentials of audience analysis. First we're going to discuss exactly what audience analysis is then have a discussion about demographics. Then psychographics, and finally, situational analysis. Let's first get a basic understanding of what audience analysis is.

By definition, audience analysis is the process of discovering as much as possible about your audience, with the purpose of improving communication with them. The reason is that you can't tailor your speech unless you know something about who the audience is. You could think of audience analysis as involving three steps. First, ask to whom am I speaking. Second, ask what do I want my audience to know, do or believe as a result of my speech. Third, and finally, what is the most effective way of composing and presenting my speech to accomplish my goals?

An indispensable tool in audience analysis is called demographics. This literally means "characteristics of people." Some characteristics include the audiences age. You ought to think about people's common levels of age experience. Another demographic to consider is gender. Consider if the audience is composed of predominately males, females, or some other combination. You don't want to make assumptions about gender roles. Ethnicity is another demographic and it refers to people who are united through language,

historical origins and/or cultural systems. Another is religion. You don't want to make assumptions that everyone has the same beliefs. Other demographics include economic status, occupation, education level, physical characteristics But even things like height, weight, style, fitness, gender display, and obvious disabilities, could also factor into your demographic analysis.

In addition to audience demographics there are audience psychographics. And this refers to the attitudes, believes, and opinions people in your audience share. Let's admit it, people are ego centric. And often being ego centric has a negative connotation. In public speaking, it means your audience wants to hear about things that they think are interested in, or apply to their lives. So perhaps it's better to consider being ego centric Just a natural and predictable human behavior. Don't be afraid to include information that would appeal to your audience. Last, let's talk about situational analysis. There are five situational factors to analyze with the purpose of accomplishing your goals.

1. **Audience Size**. The first is size The number of listeners you have impacts many choices you will need to make. You can't have a question and answer period with an arena full of people, and you probably don't need a microphone if you're

only speaking to a classroom. Those decisions are examples of things that come up when you know the size of your audience.

2. **Environment**. The next situation is the environment. Don't be afraid to adjust the environment in your room to suit your goals. If it cluttered with furniture and you need a speaking area you might need to rearrange some of the objects in the room. Perhaps there's noise emanating from outside and you need to shut the window.

3. **Occasion**. The next factor is the occasion. Your audience has an expectation for what type of speech you will be giving and how they want to feel through the experience. Consider for example that people have different expectations for eulogies than they do for wedding toasts. A speaker who confuses those expectations risks social disaster.

4. **Time**. The next factor to consider is time. This could include the time of day as well as how long you have to speak. People's receptiveness is very different in the morning than at night and you can only include as much detail in your speech as time allows.

5. **Importance**. The final factor to consider is importance. This dictates the seriousness, content, and approach to your speech. In a professional setting, you want to rise to the level of professionalism that is expected. Falling short of that and you risk people not taking you seriously. If people aren't taking you seriously, then they're not gonna listen to your message.

A disciplined audience analysis sometimes determines your success as a speaker. Now that we've covered what audience analysis is, and some of its parts, perhaps you can put the essentials of audience analysis into action. The speaker and audience relationship is paramount in having a successful public speaking experience.

Have you ever heard one song over and over again, and go to the point where you were sick of it? And then for no reason whatsoever, you decide to listen to the lyrics carefully. And suddenly, The song has a whole new meaning to you. Active listening is a complex process and it's important to understand this process not just for public speaking but for all of your other relationships as well. This section is going to cover how to understand and utilize active listening. Its important to first discuss hearing versus listening. Then types of listening, and finally ethical listening in public speaking.

Often times people mistakenly think hearing and listening are the same thing. In truth, they are very different. Hearing is the physiological activity that occurs when sound waves hit our ear drums, it's passive. Active listening, is a communication technique that emphasizes concentrating on, responding to, and remembering a speaker's message.

1. **Mindfulness**. The first step of listening is mindfulness. This is the conscious decision to listen Think of active listening almost like flexing a muscle. You're intentionally doing something consciously. It is your decision.

2. **Receiving**. The second step, is physically receiving the message, or hearing. This is why hearing and active listening, are not exactly the same. Hearing could be impeded by certain outside elements, like noise. Or interference could be internal like having high communication apprehension. Or having a bad nights sleep.

3. **Organizing**. Next, is selecting and organizing material. We do not have the capability of taking in all the information that is thrown at us. We attend to things that we like or that stand out then we take that information and organize them into preconceived social constructs or scripts that we have in our mind.

4. **Interpreting**. Next we interpret the information that we have just organized. Two different people can be presented with the exact same information and draw different conclusions. It is because of this stage of the listening process, interpreting communication, that this occurs.

5. **Responding**. The next step of the active listening process is responding. This is where the listener lets the speaker know that they are actively listening. It could be as simple as eye contact or a head nod. Or as complex as asking a question about the material that the speaker is talking about

6. **Remembering**. The final stage of the active listening process is remembering. It doesn't do much good to put a bunch of energy into listening if you're not gonna utilize that information in the future. Remembering sometimes uses devices in order to recall information at a later time. As you can see active listening is a complex process and people just

aren't born good active listeners. It requires practice and a conscience effort to absorb the information that the speaker is trying to convey.

Types of Listening

In addition to the stages of active listening there are types of listening. You can think of a type of listening as being defined by what motivates individual to listen to anything in the first. While there might be several additional ways to describe the different types of listen, it is useful to

1. **Appreciative**. The first of which is appreciative listening. This means listening for pleasure or enjoyment, nearly everyone has some sort of favorite music that they like to listen to and when they do this is a great example of appreciative listening. Another example is when somebody goes out for stand up comedy, people are very willing to be good active listeners if a comedian can make them laugh.

2. **Empathetic**. The next type of listening is empathetic listening. And this is listening to provide emotional support. Everyone has probably gone through an experience where they had a bad day, or a traumatic event happened in their life. And when they sat down and talked to somebody that they trust, they felt better afterwards. Well being the person who can listen in that situation provides a whole lot of support for somebody in need.

3. **Comprehensive**. Next is comprehensive listening, and this is listening to try to understand a message. Students in a lecture should be engaging in comprehensive listening, where every part of the lecture is Being committed to memory, or trying to be understood in some other way. This can be very difficult if the subject in question is complicated. Speakers might overwhelm their audience with too much information, resulting in what we call, Information Overload.

4. **Critical**. The last type of active listening is critical listening, and this is listening to evaluate a message. Movie critics are very good at this. They will watch an entire movie with a very critical eye, looking for things that they like, don't like, that are creative or mundane. And then they will express those ideas in an article that they write. Notice how that approach is very different than say just listening for entertainment. In which the enjoyment of the art form itself is being absorbed by the listener. It's helpful to understand which type of listening is best suited for different events. If you are acting as a critical listener when a family or friend wants emotional

support Then that relationship might be strained because of the improper approach to the type of listening.

Avoiding Poor Listening Habits

Unfortunately, not everyone is a good active listener. And there are some suggestions on how to be a better active listener by following ethical listening practices. And good ethical listening practices means avoiding non-listening habits.

1. **Pseudo-listening.** One type of non-listening is known as pseudo-listening, and this is where one pretends to listen, I'm sure everyone has either done this or experienced this, where somebody is nodding or giving affirmations when you know that they're not actually listening to anything that you're saying.

2. **Selective listening.** Another type of non-listening is selective listening, where this is focusing on only some parts of the message that you feel are important. Selective listening is a an listening habit because you're not really processing any of the other information that the speaker is trying to convey. Perhaps you should be experiencing this in a conversation where somebody seems like they're not listening. As soon as a subject that comes up like sports that they like, they jump in and have a whole lot to say about it.

3. **Defensive listening**. The last type of non-listening that we will cover in this lesson is defensive listening. And this is turning an informative message into a personal attack. For example, if a speaker states that their purpose is to inform, then it is your ethical responsibility to comprehensively listen. Perhaps you have had the experience where you stated something that was just supposed to be a statement of fact, but the person received it as some sort of personal affront. Avoiding these and other types of non listening is a good way to be an ethical active listener.

Now that we have discussed the difference between hearing and listening, you can incorporate the different types of listening and employ ethical choices. Listening is a very active process and requires your effort and focus. It's not just passive. Just as the meaning of a song can change when you start to pay closer attention to the lyrics, so can a speech. There's a lot of responsibility to be an ethical audience member.

Methods of Delivery

One of the more interesting criticisms that people direct towards presidential candidates is how they handle themselves off-script. It is commonplace for candidates to use a teleprompter or a screen that projects a script for them to read to an audience. But the ability to speak without the use of a teleprompter is what many people believe to be the true test of their ability to represent the people and country of the United States.

The words that you use within your speech are incredibly important, but people have constantly reported about how they consider the way people deliver a message to be equally, if not more, important. The choices you make regarding how you plan your speech greatly effect your audiences receptiveness of your message. This section is going to cover the basic methods people use to deliver speeches. We will first look at two scripted methods and then two unscripted methods.

Manuscript

Using scripts to deliver a speech is by far the more popular method that people use. Reading from a teleprompter is a very valuable skill, and it represents the first scripted method of delivery. This is also known as a manuscript or transcript method of delivery. It means having your notes be word for word representations of your speech, and then reading it to your audience. While this reduces the amount of time that you have to memorize your speech, it also has a few drawbacks to it. One of the drawbacks is that it risks sounding flat, because often times when people read to an audience it really sounds like they're just reading to an audience. They don't take the time to put in vocal inflection or to sound conversational. Also, you risk not having a connection with your audience because you're looking down at your script. And you can't make eye contact and therefore it reduces the ability for you to make some sort of emotional connection with them. The exception to this, if you have a well-placed teleprompter that mimics the look of making eye contact with your audience.

Memorized

Another method of scripted delivery is memorizing your speech. In one way this is exactly the same as a transcript method of delivery, because you are Preparing a word for word representation of a speech. And then just reciting it to your audience. The benefits of this is that you can now lift your eyes and make contact with your audience, where you couldn't do that as readily with a transcript. But there are drawbacks to this method as well. Mainly, mental lapses. If you forget part of your speech. Sometimes people react by just blanking and having a big, long, awkward pause. Sometimes people forget a section of their speech and skip, and therefore their speech is a lot shorter than they planned and it doesn't make as much sense, because they've omitted an entire section.

So scripted speeches have the benefit of thinking about every single word that you're going to use prior to delivering it to your audience but that doesn't mean they're fool proof. There are drawbacks that you should really seriously consider. Now let's compare this scripted approaches to the unscripted approaches. Some people think that impromptu and extemporaneous are synonymous. But in terms of planning a speech, there are subtle distinctions.

Impromptu

First, impromptu. This means giving a speech with little to no preparation. While this might sound like a speaker is just making it up as they go along, In reality, the speaker is in a constant state of preparedness, ready to redirect any topic toward a subject that he or she knows a lot about. Then they're able to speak from a wealth of knowledge that they basically carry around with them at all times Again, this comes with draw backs. Even though you haven't wasted a whole lot of energy preparing the speech, sometimes you draw blank as to what direction you ought to go with this topic. Again, people feel that one of the reasons that they have communication apprehension is that they are unaware or feel uneducated on the topic that they are giving. So impromptu speaking might be kind of intimidating for the beginning speaker.

Extemporaneous

Very similarly, extemporaneous speaking is when you are given a little bit of time to prepare But specifically it means giving a speech off of a well organized outline. So typically an extemporaneous speech has more time to prepare than impromptu. The speech is not written out word for word but the speaker has time to collect information and put together some notes. Then, they operate off of the skeleton of an outline in order to deliver their speech. This is really helpful because it is the middle ground between a scripted and unscripted approach to speaking. Since you only have an outline, there's no need for you to constantly look down at your notes because there's very few words that you can reference. But there is just enough of a safety net that if you ever feel like you're going to blank, you could look down in order to get a refresher and find out where you are in the speech and progress forward.

There are a multitude amount of ways to deliver a speech, both scripted or unscripted. Make a conscious decision about how you plan your delivery. Realize that every method that you choose has some benefits and some drawbacks. You should discover which method works best for you, because who knows. You may find yourself running for president one day and people will expect you to be able to speak under a variety of circumstances.

**Word Choice** Haikus have a very specific number syllables that are allowed in each phrase which forces poets to think hard about how to express their observations but with a limited number of words. Debaters typically use the term "word economy" when referring to the art of saying more with less. There are several ways to improve the way arguments are presented in debate so that they are more concise and efficient, while simultaneously making them simply sound better. Every argument could be presented in a number of ways, some more efficient than others. This section will explain several techniques for improving word economy.

Power-tagging

The first one we call power-tagging. Every major argument should have its own label. Think these labels as the titles you give your arguments. If you simply used numbers as titles to your arguments they aren't likely to be very memorable. The tags you choose should contain one, two, or three words which generally explain or summarize the most important part. hope that argument if the argument seeks to show economic benefit to the plan. The advantage tagline should simply be "economics." This may seem obvious repetitive, but simple tag-lines allow the debaters to navigate amongst all of the arguments in a debate. The same argument could also easily be called deficit spending, housing bubble, or second Great Depression; depending on the economic story that you want to tell. A good power tag can bolster any major argument by giving it an identity; thereby, making it more memorable.

Signposting

Closely related to power tagging is a technique commonly known as signposting. This is another way to keep organized while delivering arguments by simply numbering the sections within arguments. Think of this as verbally bullet-pointing arguments. Typically signposting will consistent of labeling major arguments within advantages disadvantages. Debaters literally say "sub-point a," and "sub-point b" throughout their speech. This is incredibly valuable to audience members who are trying to follow the debate, especially debate judges. Judges work really hard to listen, so this technique helps to maintain order. Dividing arguments up to be understood in sequence also makes it very easy to refer back to previous speeches when you find yourself in rebuttals. It is very obvious what you intend to refute if you say "I have 2 responses to some point b of their disadvantage." This technique increases efficiency and also makes clear where you want your analysis to be applied in the debate.

Time Allocation

The next technique to consider is time allocation. First, a very simple goal is to use all of your time, every time. If the speeches are eight minutes, speak for eight minutes. Debaters preparing arguments in should be excited to deliver them. Rarely is a concept or idea thoughtfully discussed in a sentence or two. Slow down your speed to increase clarity, and allow your brain time to think about what you are saying. Second save enough time for all arguments. Every speech has a specific time limit, so it is important not to put more of your effort into one argument because it will reduce the amount of time that you can devote to others. When a speaker spends eighty percent of the time speaking on one argument, but has four to deliver, the speaker will not be able to explain each one adequately. Third don't repeat arguments. Once a point or argument is made there's no need to continue explaining it. Sometimes speakers will get carried away with one argument and repeat the idea three times before moving on. This is risky because your audience might not think that that argument you're devoting so much time to is as good as you think it is. Whenever the audience understands the argument, move on to something new. A good time manager will know how many arguments they plan on making, and how much time they have to deliver them. Some arguments might require more time than others, but don't get carried away. Important arguments central to the debate must be exhaustively refuted. Give as much time to as many arguments as is allowed by allocating time. By, planning ahead speeches will sound much more organized and deliberate; both features a good persuasive performance.

Spreading

The last technique worth covering is a technique that is notorious in the debate community, and has come to be known as "spreading" (short for speed-reading). More simply speaking at an unusually fast pace. Debaters have been known to speak in excess of 300 words a minute, where average conversational speed is about 120. This is not at all common for beginning debaters, but it can still be intimidating to hear somebody speaking like an auctioneer. The strategy of spreaders is to overwhelm their opponents with arguments. Spreading is a numbers game simple math. If I make 10 arguments, and you can only respond to three, then I can argue that the seven dropped arguments should win the round. If you're not the best at speaking fast you can still manage a quick opponent by lumping simple arguments together in answering them collectively without increasing your pace. This is what many debaters call the "lump-and-dump" method. Keep in mind that judging preference is a factor in whether speed will be tolerated. For beginners, speed is something that should only come with practice and a firm understanding of arguments. Simply talking really fast will never win a debate if it's nonsensical and incoherent.

Techniques like these enhance your ability as a speaker. Power tags, time management and speed: all things that can work on to improve word economy. Debate is a language game, so don't be afraid to play with words. There is always another way to represent an idea through other words, just like the challenge of representing complex and sophisticated ideas with a minimal amount of syllables.

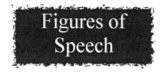

Have you ever seen those word magnets for the refrigerator? You know, those simple black and white magnets that you can move around to make sentences that sound like something out of a poetry book. Or maybe mad libs, where you ask a friend to fill in blanks with nouns verbs and adjectives without knowing what the story is about, and when you read it afterward the story is ridiculous. Most people would easily recognize these as word games, but that doesn't mean that they are insignificant. In fact, Ludwig Wittgenstein, one of the most important philosophers of the twentieth century, proposes that games are the primary, if not only method that we use to acquire language.

Wittgenstein was before refrigerator magnets and mad libs, so he was talking about other types of games. In fact, Wittgenstein proposed that language itself was just a series of games, and that trying to locate meaning within words was futile. The best that we could hope for is to understand how language is used. This is the perspective we are going to take for this section because we are going to explore many uses of language by focusing on figures of speech.

You may be thinking that the term "figure of speech" is only applicable when someone is misunderstood, or when there is confusion about how someone phrases their ides. But figures of speech have a very specific meaning and a long history in the study of persuasion, they are an all encompassing term for what are known as schemes and tropes, and we will discuss as many of these as possible in this video, but keep in mind that there are hundreds of figures of speech and that we cannot cover all of them in ten minutes. In fact, there are entire college courses that have been devoted to the study of schemes and tropes. Schemes are generally known as figures of speech that focus on the sequence of words, or more specifically, how to change the sequence of words in a sentence. Tropes, on the other hand, aren't about the order of the words, but instead changing the meaning of the words themselves.

Schemes

So, let's start with schemes. You are probably familiar with some schemes already. Actually, we already covered one called antirrhesis, but we called it refutation. And that is exactly what antirrhesis is, the refutation of an argument in your speech. But when it comes to really understanding this figure of speech, you need to realize that you can refute arguments that were never made by your opponents. You can use antirrhesis in the first affirmative to undermine arguments that you anticipate your opponents will make. So, antirrhesis is really the refutation of any argument regardless of who makes it. You can refute the author of a piece of evidence that isn't present.

MINI GLOSSARY

Scheme: in language, it is a figure of speech where the arrangement of words are modified for effect.

There are other popular schemes that you are likely familiar with, like rhyme. Something as simple as having words end with the same sound can be profoundly persuasive. In one of the most famous court cases of our generation, the OJ Simpson trial, the lawyer for the defense used the fact that the bloody gloves found at the crime scene were too small for the defendant to create a simple and memorable rhyme; "if the glove don't fit, you must acquit."

You might be familiar with the tongue twister "she sells sea shells by the sea shore." This is an example of another scheme: alliteration. This is where the beginning of words sound alike. You can even have the middle vowels of a word sound alike, and that is known as assonance.

These three schemes are very popular in the English language, but there are some that aren't as well-known, yet still very powerful when used properly in a debate. One very powerful scheme for debate is antithesis. You may know this word to refer to the opposite of something. As a scheme, it is using opposite words in the same sentence for contrasting effect.

> **Famous rap artist Eminem makes constant use of assonance in his Oscar-winning song Loose Yourself.**
>
> Oh, there goes Rabbit, he choked
> He's so mad, but he won't give up that easy, no He won't have it,
> he knows his whole back's to
> these ropes It don't matter, he's dope
> He knows that, but he's broke
> He's so stagnant that he knows When
> he goes back to his mobile home,
> That's when it's back to
> the lab again yo.

Take an example from the movie the Great Debaters. One of the main characters is faced with a problem familiar to most debaters, how to answer the economic disadvantage. He handles is well through the use of antithesis, saying of his opponents: "they would let the unemployed die so the economy can live."

Dying is the antithesis to living, and when placed side-by-side, it makes clear the choice of competing values in the round to the judges. Heck, you could replace "the unemployed" and "the economy" with any two words and still have a profound sentence. Do it well and it may be the most memorable line in the round for the judge.

Another simple and powerful scheme is accumulatio. This is where a speaker reviews the points already made in the speech in a compact and forceful manner. If you place this list in order of increasing importance, then that is known as climax. This is a perfect scheme to use in the closing sentences in your last rebuttal, imagine yourself listing the arguments you are winning "if we don't win on topicality, then we win on the economic disadvantage. And if not that then politics, then the plan flaw, the solvency turn, the uniqueness press." It just sounds like there is too much to overcome. You could also repeat the same word it is known as epizeuxis. Again, the Great Debaters offers an example when, giving her first rebuttal in competition, one of the debaters asserts "the time for justice, the time for freedom, and the time for equality **is always, is always** right now!" None of these schemes requires anyone using them to have any special gift of language. Well, maybe some of the more complicated rap lyrics. But most of these schemes are simple use of repetition, contrast, and comparison.

Tropes

Whereas schemes are the resequencing of words within sentences, tropes modify the meaning of words themselves. One of the most famous rhetorical scholars of all time, Kenneth Burke, identified what he called the four master tropes. Burke considered these tropes to be more than merely word play. He saw the master topes as ways to access and describe the truth. You may be still be asking yourself, "what's the difference between a trope and scheme?" Perhaps an example of one of the more popular tropes would help.

1. **Metaphor**. Metaphor is a trope, and most people are familiar that metaphors make comparisons between things. Notice that this isn't about the order that he put the words, it was about altering the meaning of the words for greater impact through comparison. That difference is what distinguishes schemes from tropes.

2. **Metonymy**. Another trope is Metonymy, where you refer to something associated with a word rather than the word itself.

A simple example is how people refer to journalists as the press, in reference to the printing press. Or the famous phrase: the pen is mightier than the sword. This is helpful is debate because you can reference complicated concepts with simple language. Instead of saying the "United States Federal Government" every time, you can say "Washington." This reduces the chance of stumbles over long titles, and even saves a little bit of time, which could be crucial in close rounds.

3. **Synecdoche**. Synecdoche is a type of metonymy, and Kenneth Burke describes synecdoche as "part of the whole, whole for the part, container for the contained, sign for the thing signified, material for the thing made…cause for the effect, effect for the cause, genus for the species, species for the genus." So, calling a car a set of wheels is an example of synecdoche. But, you could also refer to fossil fuels as coal. In fact, you could refer to the entire process of extracting fossil fuels, burning them and converting the power into electricity as "using coal." This, again, saves time and creates a memorable reference point for your judge and/or audience.

4. **Irony**. The last master trope is irony, and this has a confusing role in debate. Irony is hard to define, but a common, yet overly simplistic definition is that irony is when the intended meaning of your words is opposite of their actual meaning. For instance, if there was a no smoking sign inside a tobacco shop, that would be ironic. But how do you use irony in debate? The way it is most often seen is when opponents "praise" the arguments of their opponents, but they are actually ridiculing. Some people confuse irony with sarcasm, and for good reason. Both are similar and related, but no synonymous. How to use irony, or really whether or not to use irony in debate is a bit of a controversy itself. If done wrong, judges are confused and don't know the point you are trying to make. But if done well, can be tremendously entertaining and greatly enhance the credibility of the speaker. Perhaps the best recent examples of using irony to make socially significant

Al Franken, Senator from Minnesota, used a metaphor to explain the scientists that deny climate change. Say you went to a doctor who told you, "You know, you better start eating more sensibly and start exercising because you are tremendously overweight and I see that your father died of a heart attack at an early age. So you've got to go on a diet and start working out."… If 98 out of 100 doctors tell me I've got a problem, I should take their advice. And if those two other doctors get paid by Big Snack Food, like certain climate deniers get paid by Big Coal, I shouldn't take their advice. Well, 98 out of 100 climate scientists are telling us we've got a problem.

arguments are the Daily Show with Jon Stewart and the Colbert Report. For instance, Stephen Colbert once ironically opposed the theory that global warming is occurring, and cited "noted climatologist" billionaire Donald Trump. Notice how easy it is to discredit a source with ironic qualifications. This one simple way to deploy irony in an argument. But irony could be the basis for entire positions like disadvantages, counterplans, and even affirmative cases. Unfortunately, there isn't much guidance on how to use irony in debate beyond this.

It is easy to see debate as a language game; therefore, you should play with language when you debate. Figures of speech are short and simple ways to play with language that might make the difference between a win and a loss. Figures of speech can be used to justify an unorthodox interpretation of the resolution, giving you access to your favorite arguments. Figures of speech can make your arguments more memorable than your opponents, giving you a slightly better chance of winning a ballot. Figures of speech help you say more with less, giving you more time for arguments. And there are dozens of them. If you want to look up more figures of speech, all you need to do is look it up on Wikipedia. They have a nice long list that will keep you occupied for hours. There is something about a uniquely worded idea that is mesmerizing to humans. Whether it is word magnets, mad libs, scrabble, hangman, or any of the hundreds of other language games you can play, a well worded sentence changes lives.

Vocalics

Have you ever heard of a paralegal? If you have, then you know it is a person that works along with a lawyer to help research and write briefs. What about a paramedic? The people that typically provide medical attention prior to a patient getting into a hospital. These are common terms, but what about paralanguage? Para is originally a Greek prefix that means "next to" or "outside of." So paralanguage are those things that are outside of the words themselves, yet still convey information. Typically, it refers to how a person's vocal tone contributes meaning to speech.

People have reported that if they detect a conflict between the person's words and their tone, the listener is more likely to believe that what they interpret from the speakers tone over the actual words that they use. Vocalics is a nonverbal type of communication that refers to the tone of a person's voice when they are speaking, and it is vitally important that we examine the many ways that the voice adds meaning to messages. So in this lesson, let's focus our attention first on common properties of vocal delivery, and second give special attention to fluency and verbal fillers.

Vocal Tone

There are many different properties of vocal tone, but we're going to cover five in this lesson. The first property is pitch, and it refers to how high or low the tone of voice is of the speaker.

1. **Pitch**. Speakers with lower pitch voices are generally perceived as more credible than those with high pitched voices. One of the most famous examples of a public figure who purposefully lowered the pitch of her voice is Margaret Thatcher, the former prime minister of England. At the beginning of her career, she had a much higher pitched voice then at the end of her career. In fact, she went through intensive speech training in order to lower the pitch of her voice and make her appear to be more of a leader.

Margaret Thatcher

2. **Rate**. The next vocal property is rate, and it refers to how fast you speak. Conversational rate is typically one hundred fifty, to two hundred words per minute, but you might want to purposefully increase the rate to connote excitement or decrease the rate for deep thinking. Competitive debaters are notorious for speaking exceptionally fast in rounds in order to make multiple arguments. They sound kind of like an auctioneer at an auction trying to get bids from people that are betting on certain items for sale.

3. **Volume**. Another important vocal property is volume, and it refers to how to how loud you speak. People tend to think that important moments ought to be marked with increased volume, but lowering your volume in front of an audience is a great way to add drama to moments in your speech. In fact, when you all of a sudden lower the volume in front of an audience, it seems like the air gets sucked out of the room and it increases drama for whatever you're saying at that moment.

4. **Articulation**. The next vocal property we will talk about is called articulation and refers to how clearly you say words. Slurring and mumbling are examples of poor articulation. In order to improve articulation there is a little trick of that speech practitioners tend to use. You put a pen or pencil sideways in your mouth, and then deliver your speech. The obstruction in your mouth forces the muscles in your lips and your tongue to work around the object. Once you remove the

pen or pencil and deliver your speech again, you are now over articulating and it seems much more clear to your audience.

5. **Pronounciation**. The final property for this lesson is pronunciation, and pronunciation refers to the sounds that you choose to verbalize words. There are many examples of words that have multiple accepted pronunciations: tomato and tomato, potato and potato, aluminum aluminum, Caribbean Caribbean, Caramel caramel etc. Make sure you practice unfamiliar words, and have a consistent pronunciation if you're not entirely sure how to pronounce words. Oftentimes the pronunciation of people's names that might seem foreign or unfamiliar to you are offered. In fact many websites offer pronunciations for hard to pronounce words, and you could find these in video productions.

Fluency

Let's transition from verbal properties to verbal fluency. The first step that people usually have to make in order to become a more fluent speaker is to recognize how often they have verbal fillers. Once you recognize the problem. Then you could try one of these three techniques in order to reduce verbal fillers.

1. **Slow down.** First technique is to use your rate to reduce verbal fillers. In other words slow down and use what's known as your mental speed to your advantage. Mental speed is the difference between how fast you talk and how fast you think. People typically think a lot faster than they talk, so slowing down allows many of your different thoughts in your head to occur without necessarily getting in the way of your pronunciation or articulation.

2. **Use pauses.** You can also use pauses to reduce fillers. Oftentimes, replacing a filler with a pause is the best way to eliminate fluency problems. Pauses imply that you are thinking carefully about your next word, which you are, and increases your credibility in the process.

3. **Use conjunctions.** Finally, you can use conjunctions to reduce fillers. Saying "and" or "but" instead of "um" or "uh" forces you to insert another clause, but it also eliminates the fillers. Don't obsess about what follows the conjunction. Keep it simple. Keep it going.

Vocal properties and verbal fluency are two important aspects to know if you want to understand vocalics. Mastering vocal variety can add or reinforce the message in your speech. So it's something you should absolutely practice. This is why vocalics is considered a language in and of itself, also known as a paralanguage.

Kinesics

People readily draw interpretations of your expressions and body movement regardless of what your intention behind that movement was. And while people may focus on each other's faces, our entire bodies communicate messages all the time. This section will cover the concept of kinesics, defined as the study of non verbal communication that transmits messages through the use of body movement. We commonly refer to this as Body language. There are many facets of that you can focus on, but we're gonna focus on four. First the eyes and face, then gestures, then body movement, and finally attire.

Eyes and Face

As stated earlier, people give special attention to the face and eyes. Eye contact is critical in public speaking. It has the power to influence how people think of you and the topic that you are discussing. The size of the audience determines how much direct eye contact you can make. With an audience of about 30 people such as a class, It is important to make eye contact with every audience member at some point in your speech. Think about keeping eye contact with one person for a complete thought. Jumping your eye contact from person to person too quickly makes you look skittish. Holding eye contact for too long Starts getting a little creepy. For people with difficulty making eye contact, looking at a person's tip of the nose or at their forehead is close enough to their eyes that often times they can't tell that you're not looking at them directly.Facial expression is also important. Forehead and mouth, communicates to the audience how we feel. If our facial expressions do not match our vocals, the audience will not believe the vocals alone. Since getting our audience to feel something as a result of our speech, facial expressions are critical. If we do not feel something for our speech, our audience never will.

Gestures

Gestures add an important element to any speech. There are different types of gestures, like illustrator gestures. When was the last time you read a book with pictures in it? When you were a kid? Hopefully it was within the last couple of days when you read your textbook. What goes through your mind when you look through a textbook for the first time and you see there are absolutely no pictures in it? Is it "oh my God, this class is going to be awful?" Did you consider dropping the class? We as an audience consider illustrations very important. In public speaking, there's no difference. Your hands and arms become the illustrators to your message. Practice some. Use your hands to show the size of something, the speed of something. Your hands can also illustrate how you feel about something. Straight fingers and sharp movement can illustrate anger or frustration or a serious message. Loose fingers and fluid or circular movement can illustrate a more relaxed or happy feeling. Also consider gestures having the same function of highlights. When we gesture, we're highlighting the words we are saying. Therefore, communicating to your audience this is something important for you to pay attention to.

The next type of gestures are called adapter gestures. Anyone who has traveled a bit knows that they have to bring on electrical adapters if they go to certain other countries. This is kind of the same thing, that you need to adjust your environment in order to adapt to the situation. Both make sense. Like the electricity running through the wires in our walls, we have energy in our bodies. When in a new and sometimes frightening situation like public speaking, we generate more energy than usual. Our body must release this energy and therefore we move in ways we are unaware of, that also communicate our nervousness.

Body Movement

Gestures are just one type of body movement that adds meaning to your speech. Another way to move your body is what you do with your entire body during a presentation. Namely where you stand at any given point during the speech. Now the environment helps determine what type of movement is best, transition walks, leaning forward, etc. Try to avoid full body movement adapters like pacing. This is where we talk a little bit about what's called the speaker's triangle. It's called a triangle because that's the shape that it makes on the floor if you're looking form a bird's eye view. All speeches should start with an even number of audience members on the left and right. Once a person starts speaking, they get through their introduction if they're following a linear organization. Then they walk. They take four or five deliberate, confident steps to the left or to the right. The meaning behind this is to indicate that not only is your speech transitioning verbally, But non-verbally. The reason why it is called a transition walk is because you commit yourself to walking during the transitions for every transition. This means between the introduction and first body point, the first and second body point, the second and third body point, In between the third and conclusion. Plan it out so that when you transition walk into your conclusion you end up back in the center of the room. Aside from these transition walks your feet should always be planted.

Attire

Finally let's discuss attire. Now we've all been told not to judge a book by its cover, but that doesn't mean you can't have a good looking cover. Your physical appearance can make all the difference in public speaking situations. It is often how you communicate your very first impression. People make judgments on your clothing choices. It communicates how important you consider your message to be. Wearing clothing that is appropriate to you, your audience, the occasion, and your topic. Don't wear clothing or jewelry, or style your hair in a way, that is distracting for the audience. Don't deliver speeches with sunglasses or hats on. Make sure you don't have things hanging out of your pockets, like keys or lanyards. And always be aware of the situation in which you're being asked to speak. Is it professional or is it more celebratory?

Kinesics is one type of non verbal communication that has many parts. Some of those parts including the eyes and face, gestures, body movement, and attire. You can now incorporate effective nonverbal communication into your presentations. Make conscious decisions about when you are going to use gestures. Practice the transition walk. Make sure you've chosen out your outfit for the day of the speech.

Televised Debates
The first televised presidential debates showed the importance of appearance in debate. There were two distinct audiences: radio listeners and television watchers. Those listening to the radio version of the debate generally concluded Nixon won, but television watchers said Kennedy won!

Chapter 4
Preparation

Research
-Finding, Evaluating, and Citing Sources

Understanding Burdens
-Presumption, Proof, Rejoinder

Fiat
- Natural, Artificial

Questions and Cross-examination

Malcolm Gladwell famously postulated that anyone can achieve mastery in a field of study, if they are willing to put in 10,000 hours. One of the more famous examples that support this conclusion was the practice habits of great violinists. While great violinists all had a similar practice schedule to many others at a young age, it was those that put in 10,000 hours by their twenties that were recognized as the best.

Malcolm Gladwell

10,000 hours is an intimidating number, but the thing to learn from this is that nothing comes without practice. Debate is no different. Anyone who thinks that they are good at speaking "off-the-cuff" is usually in for disappointment. While someone might be able improvise large sections of a speech, they usually aren't able to maintain that illusion for the entirety. Practice is important to achieve proficiency, so this chapter is going to cover some of the information that is most helpful during the preparation phase of debate. These things include researching properly, understanding burdens in debate, understanding fiat, and how to question and cross-examine your opponent.

Research

It is so common a for each generation to think that they have had it harder than the new generation that clichés have come about because of it. Perhaps the best known one being how adults would talk about how they would have to walk to school in the snow, uphill, both ways. I find myself sounding like this when I talk about research techniques. You see, I grew up in a time when research had to be done in a library, but right now, research can be done at home at any hour of the day. And, you can find any information that you want. This is obviously convenient for many people. But there are some ways in which it is harder to do research than it used to be. Therefore, in this lesson we are going to account for the information age that we are living in and cover some of the basics of quality research. First, we'll talk about finding sources, then how to evaluate evidence quality, and finally citing sources in speeches.

Finding Sources

So let's start with how to find information in go toward the source that most people are familiar with the Internet. The internet is great. It could retrieve any information you want, at any hour of the day. This is great for convenience, but the unfortunate side effect is that you don't know what information is necessarily dependable. In fact, any term that you put into a search engine will retrieve any information that you want. Do you want to find an article that says the earth is flat? You can find it. So the internet increases convenience, but it decreases dependability and quality of information. Perhaps the most famous search engine is Google, but there are others like Bing and Yahoo. Instead of just going for the results that you get off of a search engine query, perhaps you should go towards the news sources that they have, like in Google News, because then at least those sources have some sort of editorial board that tends to look over information and--at the very least--spell check it before it gets published.

Another excellent area to find sources is an oldie but a goodie; the library. It's not as convenient as the Internet, but the reason why the library is still relevant when doing research is that the librarians that work in these buildings are actually trained to find information. In fact, they might be able to find information better and faster than you can on the internet. Regardless of whether or not you go to a library or on the internet, we suggest that you search out databases. There are databases like Ebsco-host and Lexis Nexis. What they do is that they compile dependable information from academic journals. Not everyone has access to these databases, so check what databases your school provides, or you could visit a local university library. They'll let you use their databases as long as you were inside the library itself, on their computers.

Evaluating Sources

But let's be honest, finding information in this day and age, isn't the difficult part. The difficult part is finding quality information. So here are a few simple suggestions for when you find information in order to evaluate its quality.

The Flat Earth Debate

In one sense, online research easier than more traditional methods. In another sense, research is much more difficult because of the abundance of information online. There is no greater example of this than the resurgence of the belief that the Earth is flat. The amount of information online claiming to prove the Earth is flat has increased steadily to the point where celebrities are willing to publicly defend such arguments.

1. **Primary sources**. The first one is to know the difference between primary versus secondary sources. A primary source is one where the research, and the analysis is done by the author themselves, versus a secondary source which uses other people's information and just sort of regurgitates it or reformats it. One of the most famous secondary sources out there is Wikipedia. This is the primary reason why teachers don't want you to use Wikipedia in your work cited pages because it is a secondary source. Always put the effort into finding primary sources. If only one source cites another, it's the researchers responsibility to verify the accuracy.

2. **Identify bias**. The second suggestion is, be very critical about identifying bias. The only way you could really do this is to compare your source against other sources. Do a quick check of the publication and see if there are any reviews talking about the bias of that particular publication. Bias is something that could really undermine any type of research that you were doing.

3. **Publishing standards.** The last suggestion when evaluating evidence is to select sources with some sort of an editorial process. Make sure that the author's name is on the evidence. Don't cite anything that doesn't have an author. Avoid sources without an editorial board like blogs. The more rigorous the editorial process the more credibility the source. Generally has.

Citing Sources

So you have found information and you are satisfied as to the quality of that information. How do you cite it in your speech? Perhaps the two most common questions I get about citing sources are when to cite sources, and what to include in a source citation. Knowing when to cite sources is a little bit more difficult than it seems.

1. The first thing is to avoid citing sources for common knowledge. You don't need and piece of evidence to explain that the sky is blue, or that the earth is round. That's commonly known.
2. Also, sources are not a numbers game so don't think that more sources is better. You want to have a good amount of sources but you still want to include your voice in your research.
3. Cite sources any time that you are declaring something as a fact that isn't common knowledge, or isn't intuitive.

Ultimately, If you feel that any of your audience members might doubt the veracity of your claims, that's when you want to cite a source.

4. You should always include the name of the publication, and the date. This is not optional.

5. If the publication date includes the day…include the day in your source citation. Including the time might be a bit overkill. But if the date is only a year without a month or a day, then just include the year of the publication.

6. Whether or not to use an author's qualifications is kind of up to the person doing the source citation. If you feel that the authors qualifications will boost the credibility of your evidence, go for it. If you think that it will just distract your audience, go ahead and leave it out.

7. Speakers should consider the language they are going to use when citing sources. If every single time they say: "According to," "according to," "according to," it starts getting a bit repetitive. Think about other ways to introduce it as like, "as noted by," "reported in," "as stated by." There are many different ways to introduce or citations, and adding variety helps your audience to follow your speech.

So we briefly touched upon how to find sources, how to evaluate that evidence, and how to cite them in speeches. Keep in mind that these are just basic techniques, and as you practice you will find more and more ways to increase the quality of your evidence and find new and better sources. Research takes time and practice. People forget that the Internet and the information age are a relatively new phenomenon within our culture. Who knows what advancements in technology are going to take place over the next few years. One thing you can be sure of is that this generation will make sure that the next generation knows how easy they got it.

Exercise: Evidence Evaluation Exercise

All data brought into an argument is founded in some form of evidence, but not all evidence is treated equally. The purpose of this exercise is to familiarize students with different levels of credibility when evaluating evidence.

1. As a class decide on a resolution offered below.
2. Split up the class into four groups.
3. Find one piece of evidence to bring to a discussion and be ready to defend why it is good. Use the Internet, library, databases any resource to get evidence.
4. Put all evidence in your group into a packet and make sure no names or group numbers are on the packet it needs to remain anonymous.
5. Allow all groups to review all packets.
6. Each group must submit a rank of which packets had the best and worst evidence. Rank 1-4.
7. The group packet with the lowest score wins with the most credible evidence.

The United States should accede to the International Criminal Court (ICC).
The United States should agree to the Transpacific Partnership (TPP).
The United States should remove Common Core.
The United States should abolish the Electoral College
The United States should raise the minimum wage.
The United States should lower the drinking age.
The United States should legalize marijuana.
The United States should ban college football.
The United States should implement free preschool.
The United States should implement free college.
The United States should reform social security.

Understanding Burdens

Consider a very strange question: who is winning before a debate starts: the affirmative or the negative? This might sound like a trick question, that neither side should be considered in the lead until at least one argument is made. But, people have strong opinions about which side has the burden to prove. Or in terms of debate theory, who is presumed to be winning at any given moment in the debate. Most people are familiar with the term presumption. Also, most people treat presumption as synonymous with the word assumption. But, within the field of argumentation we treat these two terms slightly different. An assumption is some sort of fact that is taken for granted, but a presumption is different in that it does not necessarily take anything to be a fact.

A presumption is the psychological predisposition of the listener that tends to favor one side during a debate. A person can be completely aware of her presumptions and ready to change their mind when presented with the right evidence, but when it comes to her assumptions, she believes there is no evidence that can disprove them so it is harder to overturn. So, in this lesson we are going to learn all about presumption as it relates to debate theory. We are going to cover the origins, the different types, and how to use presumption strategically in a debate.

Presumption

Archbishop Richard Whately is widely credited with being the individual that introduced the concept of presumption into argumentation studies.

He was a 19th century rhetorician, logician, economist, and theologian. He served as the Archbishop of Dublin in Ireland. In the 200 years since he published his work there have been a lot of articles written about presumption, but it is helpful to understand the origins as well.

Whately described presumption as the preoccupation of ground. You see, he saw arguments akin to military maneuvers on a battlefield, and in many battles there is one side that occupies ground and the other is trying to gain that ground. In other words, a debate is rarely ever completely equal before it starts; one side or the other enjoys presumption. In fact, there are times where one side of a debate enjoys so much presumption that they do not need to even their own side is right, just that the other side has not proven their arguments true.

Whately extends the previous analogy about preoccupied ground to an invading force

Archbishop Richard Whately

72

trying to take a castle. It is up to the invaders to successfully seize the castle, those inside the castle have no requirement to lower the drawbridge and charge their enemies. They can merely take a defensive posture and ward off any assaults. Therefore, in a debate it is important to identify who has presumption. This evaluation could be a little tricky since you can't read minds, and people have many different beliefs on different topics. How can you predict who has presumption? First it is important to know different types of presumption.

Artificial Presumption

There are two very helpful ways to subcategorize presumption, and that is into artificial presumption and natural presumption. Let's start with the easy one: artificial presumption. This is sometimes known as legal presumption, and that's because our legal system consciously uses presumption in due process. Artificial presumption is a presumption whose force is derived from a law or legal rule.

In fact, you are probably familiar with one presumption that our legal system uses, which is the presumption of innocence. People brought before a judge in the US judicial system are presumed innocent until proven guilty. You may have heard this phrase before but never really contemplated it. The presumption of innocence does not mean that the government makes any assumption about the likelihood that a defendant is guilty, they merely grant the defendant presumption and put the burden of proof on the State (but we will talk about burden of proof more in a little bit).

Presumption of innocence is one of the easiest examples of not just artificial presumption, but any presumption in general. There are other types of artificial presumption, like how children under a certain age are presumed incapable of consenting to sex, or similarly how children under a certain age are incapable of committing a felony. The point is that artificial presumption something that is codified, it is written and an individual can research and find the law in question.

Natural Presumption

Natural presumption isn't as well defined. Natural presumption does not get its force from law, but from the predispositions that the audience brings with them to the debate. This type of presumption is difficult to identify, but it is an important part of audience analysis. High level debaters often keep track of judging philosophies and voting record in order to anticipate which arguments are likely to be most successful. There are a few typical natural presumptions that are worth understanding because they are widely applicable.

1. Presumption in favor of existing institutions. One is what Whately called a presumption in favor of existing institutions.

An institution could be a system of education, religion, governance, etc. The point is that any established institution is typically presumed to be worth preserving until sufficient evidence is presented to the contrary. There seems to be a simple rational to this, that the time, energy and resources needed to remove an existing institution are tremendous, so we need to be absolutely convinced if we are to take action.

2. Presumption against paradox. A similar type of presumption is the presumption against paradox, and by this Whately meant that there is a presumption in favor of prevailing opinion. You may think to yourself that basing your beliefs on popular opinion is a fallacy, and you are right, but remember that presumption isn't necessarily what people believe to be true, but is what people accept as true until sufficient evidence is produced to prove the contrary. So there is still a rational to the presumption of prevailing opinion. It is reasonable to presume that prevailing opinion is based on some type of some broader social experience, but don't forget that popular opinion is often wrong. We understand that debaters do not often feel a need to follow popular opinion, but it is still important to honestly asses what presumptions are popular in order to anticipate arguments and adapt appropriately.

Burden of Proof

Finally, let's talk about some specific strategies that you can use in debate rounds that are based specifically on the concept of presumption. There is a classic rule in argumentation that "whoever asserts must prove." This pithy comment is purely derived from presumption, but gives rise to another invaluable concept; burden of proof. We have alluded to the burden of proof before, but haven't defined it. In Latin, burden of proof is known as onus probandi and it is the obligation on a debater to provide sufficient data and warrants for their arguments. Burden of proof is helpful to both the affirmative and negative sides of a debate. On the affirmative, is helps debaters know what the minimum amount and type of evidence ought to be needed to build a compelling case. Specifically, the affirmative has the burden to prove each of the stock issues at least once in order to be considered to have a sufficient case (see stock issues lecture). Inversely, this means that the negative should be able to disprove one or more stock issues in order to convince a judge to vote against the affirmative. Think about it, if the unwritten rule is that "whoever asserts must prove" then the first person to assert anything is the affirmative because they speak first.

Therefore, they have the burden of proof. There may be specific resolutions that complicate this logic, but this generally a good rule to follow.

Burden of Rejoinder

Let's say that the affirmative meets their burden of proof and supply sufficient evidence for a case. There now arises a new burden, and that is the burden of rejoinder. In debate, judges are discouraged from inserting their own presumptions into the round as much as possible (and removing all presumptions is impossible). So if an affirmative presents reasonable evidence, it is considered sound unless the negative responds to it. So the burden of rejoinder is basically the obligation for a debater to respond to any and all arguments from their opponent. Any type of refutation meets the burden of rejoinder, including identifying fallacies, presenting contrary evidence, and criticizing fundamental assumptions. Regardless, every argument made is a potential reason for a judge to vote, so meet your burden of rejoinder by answering any and all arguments from your opponents.

Dropped Arguments

Failing to meet your burden of rejoinder on any argument in the round is known as dropping an argument in debate. Dropped arguments are one of the most important elements in contemporary debate practice. The highest level debaters focus largely on dropped arguments in rebuttals. Whether or not you support you stock issues usually revolves around which arguments are dropped rather than whose evidence is best (even though evidence battles are still fairly common). But just pointing out a dropped argument in rebuttals is not enough. When debaters simply list dropped arguments without explaining their importance, judges often get frustrated by the lack of critical thinking. Therefore, a good way of explaining the importance of a dropped argument is to phrase it in terms of presumption. Take the following example: the affirmative argues that we ought to invest in more technology for education because it will prepare the youth for a future that is sure to require technological literacy. The only argument from the negative is that technology is expensive. Notice, the cost argument does not refute whether or not technology is required knowledge for the future. The affirmative has the opportunity in rebuttals to point out that the literacy argument was dropped and therefore presumed to be true. But the affirmative has the added bonus of providing evidence why technology is cost effective; furthermore, the affirmative can put forward that even if technology is costly, that we as a society have a responsibility to educate children so that they can be productive members in their culture. Ultimately, the moment that the case is dropped by the negative, the affirmative gains a significant amount of ground, so much ground, in fact, that the negative might never recover. So, in short, do not drop significant arguments.

Presumption is a staple in debate theory, but is too often overlooked. This 200 year old concept is the cornerstone to legal due process and audience analysis. Presumption can be artificial or natural. It is the foundation of other important concepts like burden of proof, burden of rejoinder, and dropped argument. And it is often use interchangeably with the word assumption. Just remember, a presumption does not take a fact for granted. It is simply a default position used when there is an absence of evidence. An assumption typically takes certain facts for granted. These are two subtly different, yet interrelated ideas. This lesson may not have definitively answered who is winning before a debate starts. But at least you know that it is rare that debaters are considered by their audience to be completely equal before they begin. Talk to judges and other competitors to get a sense of the presumptions of your judge before a round. Or identify common presumptions in the debate community. Or perhaps, ask what are your personal presumptions. How do they shape your approach to debate topics. You might be surprised.

Have you ever watched a science fiction movie with a friend that would criticize the believability of the story? "Light-sabers would never work in the real world" or "Warp speed is impossible because nothing can go faster than the speed of light." Or maybe you watched a movie about a character with super-human abilities, and someone said "that could never really happen." This person is known as a skeptic, or someone who is prone to doubt what others claim as knowledge or facts, and the debate community is full of them. One might say that debate is an exercise in skepticism because participants are required to find fault in another's arguments. Therefore, when one debater advances an argument about how to fix a problem, and they call upon the judge or audience to imagine a world where a law is passed that addresses the problem in question, it is a common reaction for your skeptical opponent to answer much like they would when watching a science fiction movie…"that would never happen." This argument is so common that debaters developed a concept to deal with the believability of a debate case, and it has come to be known as fiat. In this section we are going to learn what fiat is, how to use it appropriately on the affirmative, and how to prevent others from using against you abusively.

What is Fiat?

You might have already heard of the word fiat, but thought that it only referred to really small foreign cars. In debate theory, fiat refers to a very specific concept. Let's start with the literal definition. Fiat means "let it be done" in Latin. It is a way of imagining that a plan is passed

Using Fiat

in the real world in order to debate the advantages and disadvantages in a round.

But why is this concept even needed? To understand the answer to this question you need to, coincidentally, imagine that you are listening to a debate. Let's say that the resolution is "The United States Federal Government should significantly increase the use of technology in public education." There are innumerable cases that a person could choose, but for this exercise let's say the affirmative wants to provide iPads for all high school students in the country. Obviously, this plan would meet significant resistance from fiscal conservatives in Congress, so much so that they might find any number of ways to prevent the bill from even coming up for a vote. The opposition decides to point out this likely scenario by arguing that the judge shouldn't vote for a plan that would never pass the Congress.

This is the scenario where fiat becomes useful. In this situation, the opposition is side-stepping the central issue in the debate; whether or not more technology is good for education. Whether or not Congress would agree to more technology in education is really beside the point. There are many things that congress would never agree to that would be beneficial to the country, and if we only debated things that might actually happen in the real world, then we wouldn't be allowed to discuss issues that are really important.

Another reason fiat exists is that is prevents the same debate from happening over and over again. Imagine that there was no concept like fiat in debate. Opposition debaters could simply research which way every politician would vote on any given issue and argue in every round that this plan has no chance of existing in the real world. Debate would cease to be an activity that promotes critical, outside-of-the-box thinking. There would be no imagination to arguments, only stale political calculations. So fiat is a way of letting certain topics into debate rounds that would be considered completely unrealistic in the real world. And there you have it, fiat is a way of promoting critical thinking, creative thinking, and preventing debate from devolving into a type of vote-counting paradigm. This is not to say that fiat is universally accepted as a legitimate concept in debate. There are plenty of criticisms of fiat that are outside the scope of this video. For now let's just focus on appropriate and inappropriate uses of fiat.

Knowing what fiat means conceptually is important, but knowing how to use it to your favor in a debate round is another

MINI GLOSSARY

Fiat: latin for "let it be done," it is used as a technique in argumentation and debate to advocate for a plan of action by imagining that plan being adopted in a real-world situation.

thing. Beginning debaters sometimes use fiat in a way that completely defeats its purpose, and we are going to cover that in a bit, but first let's talk about how to use this concept properly.

Ironically, the best use of fiat is when it never becomes an issue in debate. An affirmative team should be able to deliver the first affirmative constructive without ever uttering the word. So how do you do that? Fiat is really an issue that centers around your plan text. Therefore, you need to evaluate whatever you want to advance for your plan in terms of fiat and ask yourself a few questions.

1. **Is it possible?** The first question you ought to ask is whither or not the plan is technically possible? Fiat is not magic. It doesn't let you propose stopping time or reversing gravity, it is a concept that allows debaters to focus on substantive issues rather than petty politics. But there are more subtle plan texts that are not technically possible. For instance, "The Federal Government, through an act of congress, will properly install solar panels on every home in America." Not only does this plan suffer from a horrible amount of vagueness, it assumes that there are enough solar panels that exist to execute the plan. Remember, fiat doesn't magically make impossible plans possible, so make sure that your plan is technically possible.

2. **Does solvency rely on fiat?** The other question you need to ask in order to use fiat appropriately is "does your solvency depend on fiat, or is it a natural outcome of the plan?" The phrasing of this question might be a bit confusing, but it is easily seen in the previous example. A logical solvency argument for the solar panel case is the reduction of CO_2 gas in the atmosphere, but that only works if you install a massive amount of solar panels, and people actually use them. Therefore, an affirmative cannot rely on the line "well, since we fiat solar panels, them people will use them and that solves for CO_2." The affirmative team ought to explore the details of how capable we are of installing solar panels, for how many people, and how likely people are to use them. In other words, don't use fiat in order to be a lazy debater. You still to put the effort into arguing solvency. If you are attentive to these two questions then you should be able to develop a solid plan text that is fair and defensible.

But that doesn't mean that your opponents will just accept the feasibility of your plan without objection. The second affirmative needs to be prepared to defend the use of fiat if challenged. Remember, fiat is meant to be a response when the opposition argues that politics will prevent the plan from passing. So, if you hear this argument, here are some things you can say in response.

1. First, explain what fiat is to your judge. Use some of the language that we have used in this video to summarize what the concept means. This argument establishes fiat as an accepted convention in debate, and sometimes this is enough to overcome the opposition's objections.
2. Second, explain that using fiat creates a better debate than not using fiat. This should be easy enough if you have put in the appropriate effort into establishing harms and solvency. Point to substantive arguments and compare them to petty political arguments.
3. Finally, explain that if the judge votes against the use of fiat that it could affect how debaters in general approach debate. Word spreads fast in debate, and other debaters are likely to follow suit, writing opposition arguments about which politicians will vote this way or that. This argument broadens the scope of fiat from a single round to the entire activity. Often times, this perspective appeals to the important role that the judge plays in the activity of debate.

Defending Against Fiat Abuse

These are the ways to use and defend fiat appropriately, but what happens if someone else uses fiat inappropriately... what do you say? We are going to cover two common areas where debaters often argue that the use of fiat is being abused, but both of them follow the same pattern; first you explain the purpose of fiat, then you explain the way your opponent is abusing this purpose, then argue why that is bad for debate, and finally what the consequence ought to be.

1. **Fiating solvency.** The first type of abuse is fiating solvency, which is usually the result of a debater who doesn't understand fiat. Fiating solvency means that a debater is using the fact that the passage of plan is fiated means that the plan automatically solves. Recall the "properly install solar panels for everyone" plan. Let's say that the opposition argues that such a large undertaking will result in installers cutting corners and taking shortcuts in order to meet installation deadlines. While this argument doesn't generate a lot of offense for the opposition, the affirmative ought to answer it. If the affirmative were to answer "well, plan text says that the government will *properly* install solar panels, and since we get to fiat this plan text, then there will be no cutting-corners or installation mistakes." This answer is an example of fiating solvency. Nobody has the power to ensure that a plan will be executed properly just because it is worded properly. And it's like the old saying, that the road to hell is paved with good intentions. Debaters don't get to win because they intend for their plans to be executed properly, they need to show that there currently exists a way to making the plan into reality,

even if the plan won't really happen. Another common example fiating solvency is when debaters fiat the agent responsible for the harms. For instance, saying that North Korean nuclear proliferation is harmful, therefore North Korea will unilaterally dismantle there nuclear program and all existing weapons. This plan does nothing to acknowledge the complicated nature of international relations that has been at the center of the North Korean proliferation. This use of fiat is just a way of avoiding a debate that one ought to engage. Notice, both of these uses of fiat are ways of avoiding arguments that should be legitimate. If you find yourself on the receiving end of a debater fiating solvency, call them out on it. Start by reminding your judge the true purpose of fiat, then assert that fiating solvency should be considered abusive, follow that with a concise explanation of why fiating solvency is bad (for instance it is bad for education because it teaches debaters that passing a plan is the same as solving a problem, and it is unfair because it takes away legitimate opposition ground), and finally argue that unless the affirmative has real-world explanations for solvency that the opposition arguments should stand. If your solvency press is strong enough, that last argument could actually be a reason why you win the round.

2. **Utopian fiat**. Another common type of fiat abuse is known as utopian fiat. This type of abuse is contentious in debate, but we don't have the ability to get too far into the advanced arguments about utopian fiat, so this is just going to be a quick primer. Utopian fiat abuse is when a debater argues that fiat allows them to pass a plan that is impossible or exceptionally improbable. One

of the more common types of utopian fiat abuse is when debaters argue that multiple actors that typically have a history of animosity all of a sudden just work together. A very popular example would be fiating that Israel and Palestine will stop fighting and be allies. This plan ignores deep seeded animosity that has developed over centuries. A more contentious example is the 50 states plan (usually framed as a counterplan). This is actually a popular type of plan, and whether or not it is an example of utopian fiat usually depends on the topic, but here is the situation. A debater argues that all 50 states will simultaneously adopt the same plan and pass it through their respective legislatures. The states do not have the best track record of agreeing on what laws to pass; for example, segregation, gay marriage, medicinal and recreational marijuana, environmental protection, abortion, minimum wage, and the list goes on. There is very little chance that all 50 states will agree on the exact same plan simultaneously. But the real abuse emerges when an opponent tries to argue that there will be backlash to the plan. Imagine the "Palestine and Israel will now get along" plan. It seems likely that the people of these countries are not ready for this, even if their governments acted in such an unlikely manner. Or for the 50 states plan. Isn't it likely that a handful of states will resist and pass their own version, or none at all? Well, the abusive utopian fiat response would be that because these plans were passed by elected representative, then that means the voters are in favor of it too and won't backlash. This might sound mind-boggling and circular, but it happens. The response is similar to the fiating solvency response earlier. Start with an explanation of what fiat should be, then assert that your opponent is engaging in utopian fiat. Follow that with an explanation of why utopian fiat is bad (like it is unfair because there is no opposition research on utopian plans, thereby limiting ground, and that utopian fiat is infinitely regressive. Why can't I fiat that everyone joins hands, shares resources, and denounces violence forever?). Finally, explain the impact; namely, that the use of fiat ought to be rejected, and without another argument explaining how the plan functions in the real world, the affirmative team's plan ought to be rejected.

Fiat is a relatively new concept in the world of debate, but it is very useful. Unfortunately, as with every good idea there are ways to use it inappropriately. Remember to keep the fundamental purpose of fiat in mind when constructing cases. It is meant to aid debaters to focus on the substantive issues in the round. With that in mind, you should be able to use fiat appropriately without the need to get into a fiat abuse debate. Fiat is a powerful tool that allows debaters to imagine a world where proposals are voted up or down based on rational consideration and not political games. It may feel unnatural to some to momentarily suspend disbelief to the benefit of having a debate, but it's kind of like suspending your disbelief when watching a science fiction movie. Sure, lightsabers will probably never exist, but if you imagine that they could then it opens up a rich environment for entertainment. Likewise, politicians will continue to fight, but if you imagine that they briefly came together to pass a plan, we can explore the merits of that plan without letting pettiness get in the way.

Exercise: Story Telling Exercise

Fiat is a concept that haunts some new debaters. The purpose of this exercise is to familiarize yourself with how fiat functions and its limitations. Fiat is only to be used in ways that can be founded in some sort of reality. It cannot be used for claiming anything at anytime can happen. Follow directions below.

1. Pick a resolution to advocate or argue for.
2. Develop two plans as to how to carry out the resolution.
3. 1st story, try to be reasonable and paint a realistic picture of how the plan will be carried out.
4. 2nd story, try to be as ridiculous as possible and paint an unrealistic picture of how to implement the plan.

Example:

1. (Plan Selection) The USFG should develop the moon.
2. (1st Story) The United States will fund 10 lunar landing missions to develop a lunar colony.
3. (2nd Story) The United States will befriend an extraterrestrial ally and have them use their sophisticated technology to develop a lunar theme park.

Use a resolution below to get started. Feel free to come up with your own resolutions.

The United States should raise the minimum wage.
The United States ought to abolish the electoral college.
The United States should reform social security.
The United States should remove Common Core.
The United States should go green.
The United States should force food to be labeled with genetically modified organisms (GMO's).
The United States should reform education.
The United States should modify its funding of the arts.

When I was a kid my grandmother loved to watch TV legal dramas. What I remember most about those shows was how lawyers acted in trials, specifically what technical things they did to gain an advantage or nullify a threat. One of the things that both good lawyers and debaters understand is that asking questions is one of the most useful and powerful tools at your disposal when dealing with arguments and exposing weaknesses in your opponent's strategies. In this lesson we'll be covering: types of questions in debate, and strategies for utilizing question in rounds.

Types of Cross-examination

At a fundamental level, questions clarify the debate for everyone involved, and at a more sophisticated level questions advance the debate and are an integral part of a strategy you should be using in debate rounds. In debate and in legal communities question asking is called "cross-examination." This is telling because the role of a question is to further examine something. Because debaters like to sound cool, Cross Examination is also called cross-x or CX. There are generally 2 types of CX.

1. **During an opponent's speech**. In one style of debate you're able to ask questions during your opponent's speech, this is most commonly done in Parliamentary and BP or British Parliament debate. Cross-examination in these formats are known as POI's or points of information. Part of the power of CX in formats where you're asking questions during your opponent's speech is that you're intervening in your opponent's thinking along with their strategies; done well, questions undo what your opponents have worked so hard to create. Direct refutation happens while your opponent's are constructing their case, and these questions are actively reframing the debate. You get to

Points of Information

In parliamentary debate, the typical method used to ask questions of one's opponent is known as a "point of information." This happens during a speech, and an opponent may raise their hand, or stand up to indicate their desire to ask a question. Once recognized by the speaker, they as a question. There are no follow-up questions.

insert ideas or thoughts into the debate interrupting the logical flow your opponents have created, it's pretty cool.

2. **Between speeches**. In other styles of debate, instead of asking questions during your opponent's speech there's a dedicated amount of time, usually a few minutes, specifically for question asking. This is done in Public Forum, Policy and Lincoln Douglas debate. This is intense too because a skilled question asker has several minutes to bombard you with difficult questions. It's just as important to learn how to answer questions as it is to ask them. It's an important part of thinking about how a debate round is going to go and what questions you need to have in the debate to advance your arguments. When teams are preparing for a debate round, I often coach them to prepare questions, or what they should anticipate from their opponent's questions. The strategy for asking questions is even as specific as thinking who be the one who asks the question, more on that in the section on strategies.

Cross-examination Strategies

So, what are some strategies when asking questions? First things first, if you don't understand what's going on in the debate it's likely you are losing. So if you find yourself confused, a good place to start is asking questions is about the plan text or the specific advocacy that your opponents are defending.

1. **Ask about your opponent's plan or thesis**. If it's a policy case, consider asking questions about the how the plan text will accomplish the solvency story your opponents are constructing. Ask questions to better understand what mechanisms of the plan text are actually doing. Similarly, if you're debating a value think about how your opponent's advocacy works as it relates to their criteria, do their examples, their contentions, and their narrative make sense through the lens that the criteria established in the round. Hopefully, the debate is clear enough that you can use questions more strategically but sometimes you have to ask a question to have a foothold in the round.

2. **Ask questions to eliminate "bidirectionality."** Bi-directionality is the ability for an argument to do two or more things to harm you. Let's use chess as an analogy, if your opponents have a powerful piece like the Queen or the knight in the middle of the board it's generally considered dangerous because these pieces can attack in any direction. In this situation you would potentially be in a strategically disadvantageous situation. In the hands of a skillful chess

player, the strategy is dangerous but with practice you learn to both defend against it and expose its weaknesses. The trick then is to see the trap coming, as much as possible avoiding dangerous situations.

3. **Ask questions to disrupt your opponent.** In formats of debate competition where you ask questions during your opponent's speech, questions function in their own unique way. Think about how important it is to slow your opponents down during their speech. Similarly think about how useful it is to force your opponent to stop their discussion and start again. It's difficult to regain your momentum, and many teams use questions to trip up their opponents not by doing anything particularly strategic but by simply recognizing that getting on a roll and developing momentum is a difficult thing to stop and start again.

4. **Ask questions to give your partner extra time**. In an event like parliamentary debate or British Parliament there's no preparation time between speeches and where the next opposing speaker is expected to stand up and start speaking within seconds of the previous speech. This is an incredibly difficult task, and requires that many strategic decisions are made early on in the preceding speech. Then, consider how useful questions would be to allow your partner to have a moment to think, focusing their attention if only for a moment on how they're going to construct an offensive strategy for your team.

5. **Consider who should be asking questions**. This is really only an issue in team debating, not one-on-one debating. There aren't any rules about who should ask questions per se, but some strategies are stronger compared to others. For example, the 1st negative speech is a notoriously difficult speech in formats that do not have preparation time between speeches. Questions are useful because the 2nd negative speaker can learn to engage in the debate and protect their partner by asking questions. The second negative speaker should be participating in the debate as much as possible to allow their partner to breathe, think and make good choices. Refer to the video on communication apprehension and how the fight or flight response and stress influence your ability to critically think, sometimes all you need is a few seconds of quiet to think and a better response becomes apparent.

So when you're answering questions, it's important to respond strategically but also authentically and candidly. Transparency should be rewarded, and most importantly it demonstrates that you believe in your strategy. Trust your preparation, trust your ability to think on your feet, trust your coaching, and most importantly trust yourself. It's an awesome feeling knowing that you understand the case or an argument so well that you can withstand multiple rounds of CX, it's a strong indication that you are probably on the right track. In this section we covered the types of questions in debate, as well as some ways to strategically use questions in the debate. So, the next time you're in a round, consider how you're going to use this powerful tool to help you and your partner get ahead. Perhaps, you might even copy some of the strategies that you see television lawyers use when questioning witnesses.

Chapter 5
Affirming

Policy Stock Issues
-Harms -Inherency -Solvency

Values Stock Issues
-Justification -Objection

Criteria
- Background - Value - Policy

Introduction

If you were to study an instrument by hiring a musician to give you private lessons, you would find that each instructor has their own personal approach to leaning music. Learning to debate in front of an audience is similar. No two debate coaches emphasize the same thing. In order to account for the many different concepts that coaches have when teaching theory, I have treated this chapter as a survey of common theoretical issues that are important to the creation of an affirmative advocacy.

Imagine that you were tasked with watching hundreds of debates. Luckily, you do not have to endure such a task, but you might imagine that after a few dozen debates you would start to see similarities amongst the arguments. Scholars of ancient rhetoric studies explain that ancient students were able to identify recurring arguments, and that those recurring arguments are what we now call stock issues. So, in this section we are going to cover the common stock issues in contemporary debate. First we will explore some background information on stock issues, cover the stock issues for policy debates, and then discuss stock issues you find in value debates.

Stock Issues

Let's start with what stock issues are not. They are not, as some people treat them, absolute rules about how to organize cases. The concept of stock issues means different things in different debates. The two most common forms of debate are policy and value. But regardless of what type of debate you participate in, you are going to experience what Aristotle called *stasis*. Stasis is the rest or halt which occurs between opposing arguments. It is likely that you are already personally familiar with this phenomenon. Think to the last time you were asked what you wanted to eat, or what you would like to do over the weekend. Did you spit out an immediate response? You probably took a little bit of time to weigh your options. Well, this happens several times in debates. But not only that, these moments of stasis often revolve around similar issues regardless of the topic. For instance, what to eat

MINI GLOSSARY

Stasis: the rest or halt which occurs between opposing arguments

and what to do both require contemplating how much each option costs and the time involved. Therefore, time and money would be issues common to both questions. Common questions are the foundation of stock issues. In fact, the most inclusive definition of stock issues is that they are the questions which occur with frequency in the course of argumentation. Luckily, people have been having structured debates long enough to record the common questions in debate and have noticed some pretty clear patterns that you would benefit from knowing. For instance, one common question that arises in many debates is "How do we determine which arguments win the debate?" This question is at the root of the criterion stock issue. But beyond this similar stock issue, the patterns are different, for policy cases and value cases.

Policy Stock Issues

For policy cases there are three stock issues that debaters generally recognize (except for the criterion which is covered in another seminar) and the first is called harms. What are harms when we talk about stock issues? Imagine again you are in the ancient academy, where a type of question/answer approach dominates learning. If someone stands up and makes a proposal to levy a tax on citizens, what do you think the most common questions an opponent would have for the speaker? I think it is safe to say that one common question would be "what's the problem?" In fact, that question is asked so often, that it would be smart to just assume you're your opponent is going to ask the question, and include your answer in your first speech...right? Well that line of reasoning establishes our first stock issue.

1. **Harms**. The harms stock issue is an argument, or a set of arguments that attempt to persuade an audience that there are problems with the status quo. Status quo refers to the current state of affairs. I like to think of it as "status now," just because it helps me remember. There are a couple of ways to show harms in the status quo, and a good debater employs the use of both tactics. Those tactics are quantitative and quantitative. Quantitative harms are based on data of particular people and events. They go into detail about the individuals that are currently suffering hardships: whereas, qualitative harms rely on statistical data to articulate the extent of human suffering. Both are compelling to audiences and should be use during the construction and delivery of your affirmative case. For instance, let's say I wanted to articulate the harms of global warming. I could talk about how many inches oceans are set to rise because of melting ice caps, and that is a compelling story, but including information about specific cultures that live on low-lying islands and how they could be wiped out is also compelling to audiences. The first piece of data is quantitative, and the

89

second is qualitative, but when they are used together they create a narrative that is greater than the sum of its parts.

2. **Inherency**. One of the most common questions of an affirmative proposal is "what's the problem," what is another? Can you think of another? You might be asking "is there a solution?" But before that question, there is a prior question that you ought to ask; "what is causing this problem?" This question establishes the stock issue of inherency. The inherency stock issue is an argument, or a set of arguments that attempt to persuade the audience that a problem will persist if no action is taken. I like to think of inherency in terms of the phrase "the harms aren't going to fix themselves." There are two types of inherency, structural and attitudinal.

   1. Structural inherency argues that there is a law, or policy that is creating the harms. For the global warming case, an argument could be made that the subsidies that are given to companies for fossil fuel extraction, and that the use of those fossil fuels contribute to global warming because of carbon emissions.
   2. Attitudinal inherency is the type of inherency that argues that there is a common behavior or attitude that perpetuates the harms. So, for the global warming case, one could argue that people generally prefer fossil fuel sources of energy because it is cheaper and more reliable. I would suggest having one focused, well-researched inherency story. Exploring every single cause to the problem begins to imply that your plan will address all of them, which is an unnecessary burden to take on. To firmly establish inherency, do it with depth rather than breadth. What I mean is, if my plan were to eliminate fossil fuel subsidies, I would focus on the structural inherency of subsidies and only subsidies. Talk about the history. Give figures about how significant the subsidies are. But there is no need to go into the popular attitude toward fossil fuel use because your case doesn't deal with that issue. Remember, you are not obligated to fix all of the world's problems, only to make the world better than the status quo. Inherency is your chance to focus your case on one thing that can be fixed.

3. **Solvency**. Finally, we can ask why the proposal will solve the problems. This question gives rise to the solvency stock issue. Solvency is an argument, or set of arguments that the proposed plan will solve the harms. While this sounds easy, some debaters take this stock issue for granted. As if identifying harms and inherency is all you need in order to justify a plan, but many plans with the best of intentions fail. In fact, solvency arguments are one of the most popular on-case arguments in debate, so put some energy into this stock issue. There are a couple of things an affirmative can do to craft a good solvency argument.

MINI GLOSSARY

Solvency: an argument, or set of arguments that the proposed plan will solve the harms

1. First, you want to make sure that the solvency links to the plan. The link story should explain how the plan creates a series of effects. For instance, eliminating fossil fuel subsidies will cause companies to find ways to supplant that lost revenue, and they will seek renewable energy subsidies. Notice that your plan does not force the companies to seek renewable energy subsidies, but you can still argue that such behavior is likely if this plan were to pass. You might think that this logic is debatable, and you are right...it is.

2. The second thing that affirmative debates can do to craft a good solvency argument is include a significant impact. In other words, there should an explanation that you solve for a significant amount of your harms. You might ask, "what is significant?" That is a good question without a good answer. What is or is not a significant argument is something that is often disputed in debates. My only piece of advice is to defend as much solvency as your research supports and no more. Do not make empty promises of a utopian future, those tend to bite you later in the debate. Use your judgment and argue for reasonably significant impacts.

Value Stock Issues

The stock issues for policy cases do not automatically translate into value cases, so debaters need to follow a different pattern. Furthermore, the stock issues for value debates are not as well-established as the stock issues for policy debates, so they are a little more abstract. Other than criterion, there are two stock issues for value cases, and the first is the value justification.

1. **Value justification**. A value justification simply means that the affirmative side warrants the value criterion in the debate. Remember, stock issues are derived from recurring questions, so one question that commonly arises in value rounds is "In what ways does the affirmative meet the value?" For example, if the resolution is that "Nuclear energy is better than renewable energy," and the affirmative has argued in favor of a value criterion of quality of life, then any argument that nuclear energy improves the quality of life meets the value justification stock issue. These arguments could include how nuclear energy provides a stable source of energy for things like medical institutions and heating during cold seasons. For the same resolution, but a value criterion of security, typical arguments that meet the value criterion would be about how nuclear submarines are effective at repelling hostile attacks.

2. **Value Objection**. The second stock issue in value debates is the value objection. This stock issue answers the question "In what ways does the negative side fail to meet the value?" In this stock issue, the affirmative can debunk arguments that the negative might bring up against the affirmative, and show how the negative does not warrant the value criterion. Remember, you want to filter everything through whatever the value criterion is. For the nuclear energy resolution example, if the value is quality of life the affirmative could explain the unreliability and environmental harm of renewable energy. If the value is security, the affirmative could argue that there are currently no ways to power sophisticated naval vessels with renewable energy. Each of these arguments, of course, require research and evidence for support, but you can see how stock issues helps you frame the arguments you are going to develop even without evidence.

There are more stock issues that correlate with other debates in science, history, and other fields that are outside of the scope of this textbook. But at least you know the two most common sets of stock issues in order to help you plan a general strategy for most debate topics. Following stock issues is more than just abiding by debate rules; you are following a very long tradition in the study of argumentation and debate. You are answering common questions before they are asked. You are covering as many bases as possible before you opponent gets up to speak.

Exercise: Stock Issues

Stock issues are arguments, or sets of arguments, that address issues that tend to recur in debate. They are discussed as principle points to answer typical questions before they are even asked. The purpose of this exercise is to develop your ability to identify stock issues on a variety of topics. You might need to take extra time to get the hang of it, but as you push through these you will become quicker. Answer these questions using the 3-bullet format as written below in reference to the following issues one sentence per bullet:

The United States should go to space.

1. (Harms) Scientific innovation in the US is stalling.
2. (Inherency) The budget for the National Aeronautics and Space Agency (NASA) has been drastically cut.
3. (Solvency) Increasing NASA's budget by 50% would trigger greater technological development.

The United States federal government should raise the minimum wage.

1. (Harms) What is the problem or harm you want to focus on in this debate?
2. (Inherency) Why will the problem persist if no action is taken?
3. (Solvency) How do you plan on solving the problems or solving for the harms?

The fashion industry should promote a healthier body image.

1. (Harms) What is the problem or harm you want to focus on in this debate?
2. (Inherency) Why will the problem persist if no action is taken?
3. (Solvency) How do you plan on solving the problems or solving for the harms?

We should abolish the Electoral College.

1. (Harms) What is the problem or harm you want to focus on in this debate?
2. (Inherency) Why will the problem persist if no action is taken?
3. (Solvency) How do you plan on solving the problems or solving for the harms?

Criteria

Let's imagine a debate round: the resolution is that nuclear energy is better than renewable energy. The affirmative argues that nuclear energy is the least expensive energy in the world. The negative argues that renewable energy is the safest energy in the world. Who wins the round in this hypothetical example? In a previous video we talked about how stock issues are questions that tend to recur is debate, but by far the most common question in debate is "How does the judge determines who wins?" The answer is that a criterion determines who wins. In this sense, a criterion is kind of like the one stock issue common to every type of debate. But, there are still differences in the way that criteria are advanced in different types of debate. And a quick side-note; criterion is singular and criteria is plural. So in this video we are going to explore criteria from the perspective of the first affirmative speech. We will start with a background of criteria in general, then focus on value criteria, and finally policy criteria.

Background

There are a lot of metaphors used to explain what a criterion is and how it functions in debate. One is that the criterion the lens through which a judge ought to view the round. The implication is that the round is fuzzy and complicated, but when viewed through the criterion things come into focus and a judge can see things clearly. Another metaphor is that the criterion is a filter through which arguments are processed. The arguments that meet the criterion are allowed to passed through and count toward the ballot, whereas arguments that don't meet the criterion are withheld from counting toward the ballot. Both of these are helpful visuals of the function of a criterion, but the one that I like to focus on is the metaphor of a criterion as a weighing mechanism.

Imagine a machine that is capable of literally weighing arguments. The heavier the argument the better, and at the end of the round, if all of your arguments outweigh all of you opponents arguments, you win the round. But the tricky part is that criteria determine the weight of arguments based on how they are calibrated. What this means is that there are different settings that you can choose as a debater that will change the weight of arguments that are evaluated by the criterion.

OK, let's use the example from before: which argument is better, cheap energy or safe energy? Hopefully you can come up with several arguments for each. So let's say that before we made the argument that nuclear energy is inexpensive, we argued that the debate ought to be evaluated purely through an economic cost-benefit analysis. The result might be that inexpensive nuclear energy carries more weight than costly renewable energy. But if we instead advanced the criterion that energy production ought to be measured in terms of preserving human life, renewable energy might be favored over nuclear. This is not to say that either outcome is guaranteed, instead this just illustrates how a criterion might affect an entire debate. So, don't overlook the important of explaining and defending a criterion for every debate in which you participate. But, even though a criterion is one issue that ought to be a part of every debate, there are some differences between how they are presented in value rounds versus how they are presented in policy rounds.

Value Criteria

There is far more literature regarding value criterion than policy criterion, so we will deal with it first. In a value debate, there is not necessarily a well-defined plan with predictable consequences; instead, the debate revolves around more general themes and research. As a result, the value criterion wields a great amount of influence because it can add clarity to debates that are typically vague. A value criterion is also different from a policy criterion in the fact that it typically involves two things: the thing that is being valued, and the criterion itself that provides a mechanism for achieving the value.

The example used thus far is a typical value resolution: two things are listed are pitted against each other and debaters are charged with defending one or the other depending on which side of the debate they happen to be on. In this case, the two things being compared are methods of energy production. In this case, debaters have more latitude in deciding the value. Energy itself could be declared the value. This would be an example of an *instrumental value,* or a value that leads to other values. For instance, energy is instrumental for providing people with medical care through technology, preventing death from exposure by providing people with warmth, and maintains economic activity through transportation and communication. It is far more common for debaters to defend a *terminal value,* or something considered value in and of itself. Common terminal values are life, justice, and freedom. But debaters could literally choose anything as a value in debate as long as there is some type of mechanism that can achieve it.

That brings us to the criterion. The criterion is precisely that mechanism which

Debate Societies

The University of Cambridge boasts the longest running debate society in the world. The chambers pictured here have hosted heads of state as well as pop-culture icons. The Cambridge Union, as it is known, was the model for other well-known debate societies in Oxford and Yale.

arguably meets the value. What do we mean by this? If we were to extend the example used thus far about nuclear energy, the affirmative team could advance a value of life and make many of the same argument already articulated, but if the criterion is deontology (a philosophy that requires the means of achieving goals be moral, not just the consequences) then the debate changes. A deontological approach to energy production would look at all stages of energy production, not just whether or not the outcome is less expensive. This would mean that every meltdown, every uranium mine, and all the nuclear waste would now be given weight with this criterion. The likely result would be that much weigh would be given to an argument that it is unethical to risk the lives of some to save the lives of others. A consequentialist approach, on the other hand, would place equal or greater weight on the outcomes of an action to determine its value. This would value the lives lost through production equally with the lives saved through inexpensive and reliable energy. This line of reasoning might result in the opposite conclusion of a deontological approach.

Policy Criteria

A policy debate treats the criterion in a slightly different manner. One noticeable difference is that it is uncommon for a policy debate to declare a single thing to be valued. It is considered the job of debaters to hash out the different impacts in the round. For this reason it is common for criteria to come from economic schools of thought. Economics is very good at analyzing the value of all things. Therefore, the following criteria come from economic origins.

1. **Net-benefits.** The first is one of the most popular, if not the most popular. It is net-benefits. Simply put, a criterion of net-benefits simply calculates the benefits, or advantages, of a plan and subtracts the costs, or disadvantages of the plan. There is another term to describe this method, and that is cost-benefit-analysis, also known as "CBA." Debaters typically prefer the term net benefits, and the reason why is debatable, but CBA typically implies that everything is evaluated in monetary terms. Debaters typically weigh arguments in more humanist terms, so net benefits allows for debaters to defend impacts that are not put into dollar figures. Some benefits to using net benefits as a criterion are that it allows for any impacts to count in a judges decision. This avoids over-limiting which arguments are and are not allowed in the round. But the disadvantage to such a criterion is that it doesn't offer much clarification about how to weigh impacts. In fact, net benefits is such a standard criterion that even if no debater articulated a criterion, it would be the default. Still, disciplined debaters should spend enough time in the first affirmative to articulate a criterion, even if it is as broad as net

benefits in order to avoid an opponent arguing for an alternative criterion that undermines the case.

2. **Risk analysis**. Another criterion that is very popular in the insurance industry is known as risk analysis. This criterion not at all common in debate, but it meets the definition of a criterion, and I think that it could prove very useful. Risk analysis differs from net benefits because it includes probability in the weighing mechanism. In other words, nobody ever truly knows the absolute costs and benefits of any plan, those are all possibilities that may or may not happen upon passage of the plan. Risk analysis accepts this element of decision making and includes it in the weighing of impacts. So, even if an impact is large in magnitude, if it is small in probability, then doesn't outweigh a moderate magnitude impact with high probability. There are volumes of work written about risk analysis and risk management that can help you understand this criterion that are beyond the scope of this video. But the reason that I offer this as a possible criterion is that debaters are known for making arguments on the negative that have impacts that are very large in magnitude, but low in probability. With a CBA criterion, judges typically categorize arguments into costs, and benefits, without paying much attention to probability. Risk analysis reminds judges that all decision carry risk with them, but choosing not to act because of an unlikely disadvantage is not the best use of reason. Instead, people should face risks consciously and make decisions accordingly.

3. **Utilitarianism.** The last criterion I will cover comes from philosophy and is known as utilitarianism. This approach was popularized by John Stuart Mill and argues that we should act in ways that provide the greatest amount of good for the most amount of people. Some benefits of this approach are that it accepts the reality that no debater is ever going to solve all of the world's problems. Providing the greatest amount of good implies that 100% is not necessary to act. This is similar to both of the previous criteria. Another benefit of this criterion is that it makes people the measure of benefit and avoids monetizing people and their suffering. This differentiates it from the previous two criteria which are notorious for quantifying harms into dollar amounts. One particular drawback to utilitarianism is that smart opponents can argue that they have a proposal that provides greater good to more people than the affirmative. NB and RA are moderate in the sense that they simply strive to make the world better than the status quo, even if it is only marginally better, whereas utilitarianism for the "*most* amount of good for the *most* people." Does this mean that if a negative debater identifies a proposal that the affirmative didn't advocate which provides

more good to more people that they win? This question can only be answered in a debate round, but it isn't even a question in rounds with net-benefits or risk analysis criteria.

There are additional criteria from which you can select, but these few that I went over provide a good starting point. People experiment with criteria from time to time, but just because someone argues a criterion that that you are unfamiliar with doesn't mean you need to oppose it in a knee-jerk reaction. Criteria are meant to be neutral weighing mechanisms that can be accessed by either side of a debate. Agreeing to a criterion from your opponent is not, in and of itself, a reason why a debate wins or looses a round. I do suggest taking the initiative to explicate a criterion in the first affirmative because it signals to the judge that you understand the common burdens in a debate round, that you have thought them through, and that your case meets those burdens.

Exercise: Criteria

A Criterion is used to weigh arguments against each other. This exercise will sharpen your ability to recognize how different criteria can be utilized to your advantage. Use the following short list of criteria and discuss which would be best for different resolutions.

Criteria:
- Risk analysis
- Net benefits
- Human survival
- Quality of life
- Human life

Resolutions:
- The United States should raise the minimum wage.
- The United States ought to abolish the electoral college.
- The United States should reform social security.
- The United States should remove Common Core.
- The United States should build a settlement on the moon.
- The United States should force food to be labeled with genetically modified organisms (GMO's).
- The United States should reform education.
- The United States should increase its presence in the Middle East

Chapter 6
Negating

Direct Refutation
- -4 Point Refutation
- -"Take outs"

Indirect Refutation
- -Disadvantages
- -Counterplans
- -Kritiks
- -Topicality

Introduction

Concerts are generally considered events where the audience expects to see a particular musical artist perform a set of songs. But there are some concerts where two or more bands compete against each other, with the goal of getting greater audience reaction, by playing their best songs. Typically, a battle of the bands, as they are known, are judged by a panel of judges. The criteria by which they judge the battle may or may not be explained before hand, so which band prevails could be very subjective. If a band finds itself playing second, they are going to need to prepare a song that can follow their opponent.

In much the same way, when a debater finds themselves the second speaker in a debate round, they need to have prepared arguments that can match, and overcome their opponent. Preparing arguments as the negative is a much different feel than the affirmative. The negative often times must decide which strategy to deploy during the affirmative speech because the affirmative debater may not disclose their plan prior to the first constructive. Therefore, the negative must prepare several different strategies for the multitude of possible affirmative cases and be prepared to find these strategies quickly before the first negative's constructive. This requires that the negative have an efficient filing system for their evidence.

Regardless of the filing system, though, the negative has a somewhat greater degree of freedom in their preparation than the affirmative because they are not bound by codified requirements that must be in their constructive speech. Essentially there are two strategies that can be prepared, combined, and deployed in an infinite number of ways. The first strategy is direct refutation, or disputing an argument that the affirmative debater made in the first affirmative constructive. The other strategy is indirect refutation, or disputing the fundamental thesis of the affirmative's case through the creation of a detailed argument that was not discussed in the first affirmative constructive.

The negative debater need not choose one strategy at the disposal of the other, both direct and indirect refutation can occur in the first negative constructive. In fact, judges have generally come to expect that debaters utilize both strategies. Each strategy has a number of variations that can combined to create an overall story that can compel an audience to reject the affirmative proposal. This chapter first covers the variations of direct refutation in terms of stock issues, then explains the different types of indirect refutation, and finally describes some general ways that a negative debater could compose these arguments to form a complete negative strategy.

Direct Refutation

Direct refutation is the process of disputing an argument that the affirmative made in the first constructive. This is the typical method of off-case debating argumentation that most people picture when they think of debate. One person makes a claim, and the other person refutes it; but, there is an excellent structure that has developed through competitive debate which can assist any debater to employ direct refutation. This structure is called four point refutation. It is called four point refutation because, go figure, of the four points: the claim, the response, the reasoning, and the conclusion. Many remember the four points as "he/she said," "I say," "because," "therefore."

To better understand this let's take an example. If the affirmative made the argument that an individual argued that "private prisons are less expensive than public prisons." One could refute this following a simple four-point organization.

1. My opponent claims that private prisons are less expensive than public prisons.
2. I argue that the comparison is flawed
3. Because private prisons typically house medium and low security inmates, whereas public prisons need high security cells.
4. Therefore, my opponent has no grounds for their claim.

Refuting Harms

If one were to use direct refutation on the first of the stock issues there are a few different variations that could be utilized. Recall from the previous chapter that the harms stock issue argues that the status quo is problematic. This is essentially a categorical claim; meaning, that if given the choice of calling the present good or bad, one should call it as bad. The obvious ground for the negative, in terms of direct refutation, is to argue that one should categorize the present situation as good instead of bad. More simply, the negative could argue that there are no harms in the status quo. The negative should follow up this claim with the reasoning that the harms do not exist as a matter of fact, or as a matter of perspective.

1. **Refuting harms as a matter of fact**. Arguing that someone is factually wrong often makes people feel that they are accusing their opponent of being ignorant. The result is that debaters instinctually shy away from this type of direct refutation making it an underutilized strategy. This is unfortunate because establishing matters of fact should be one of the first orders of business in debates. Debaters should scrutinize what their opponents claim to be facts. For instance, a debater may argue that the United States economy is currently in a recession. She may then back such a claim with

economic statistics. The natural reaction is to assume that one cannot refute statistics because they are reporting "just the facts." This is far from true. First, it is impossible to determine if any economy is in recession, at best statistics tell you if an economy has been in recession. The United States may well have pulled out of recession since last measured. And second, economist do not universally agree to which statistics to look to in order to determine economic situation. Ultimately, debaters should question the accuracy of factual claims.

2. **Refuting harms as a matter of perspective**. A similar approach to directly refuting the harms stock issue is to argue that the affirmative's perspective of the status quo is biased. This response is also surprisingly difficult for beginning debaters to grasp. For instance, a debater might take a position during a debate about global warming that the rising temperature of the planet is bad. One response that many have made is that global temperature has fluctuated throughout history and we are simply experiencing one of these fluctuations. Notice that this response does not dispute the factual nature of the affirmative's claim that global warming is occurring, it simply reframes the debate. Global warming, therefore, is something that we must adapt to, not resist. Furthermore, one could cleverly argue that global warming is good because it would thaw the frozen tundra and give life to a host of new flora and fauna.

It is not enough to question the existence of harms in the status quo, debaters must explain why the lack of harms should result in a loss for the affirmative. The simplest reason for some types of debate are that the rules require each of the stock issue be met in order to award an affirmative victory. But debaters should not rest their laurels on rules, further explaining the reasoning behind these rules is an excellent way to display their skill. In the case of harms, there are at least a couple of reasons why this stock issue is a critical

Voting Rights Debate

There has been an increase in the amount of laws regulating who can, and cannot vote, in the last five years. On one side of the debate, the advocates of voting restrictions argue that they just want to prevent voter fraud. On the other side, one of the responses is that voter fraud is virtually nonexistent; therefore, any restriction will likely prevent legitimate voters from having a voice. This particular exchange shows how refuting harms (voter fraud) functions in real-world arguments.

part of any affirmative case. First, without harms there is no reason to act. Most people know the old adage "if it ain't broke, don't fix it." This saying is very persuasive, and might just persuade your judge. In terms of argumentation theory, when there are no harms to the status quo, one should presume to continue acting as normal. This concept is known as presumption, and was covered earlier. The second reason is related to the first: that meddling with status quo risks the creation of damages in the future. If you have ever been bugged by a loose thread dangling from an article of clothing then you are familiar with this concept. The loose thread was not really a problem until you started pulling on it. These arguments are not the final say when it comes to the role of harms in a case, but they are sufficient to force the affirmative to respond.

Refuting Inherency

Recall that inherency is the barrier that prevents the status quo from fixing itself. There are a few specific responses that arise in unique situations, but generally the two variations to refuting inherency are that the harms will fix themselves, or that the harms can fix themselves.

1. **Structural inherency takeout**. The former of the two requires evidence that there are steps being taken currently to reverse the harmful trends. One might expect the affirmative to be prepared well enough that such a response is infrequent, but you would be surprised how often the affirmative runs a case that is already in the process of occurring. In fact, the cases that tend to have the most literature are those that are widely supported; thereby, increasing the likelihood that policy makers have given the proposal a serious look, and maybe even begun implementation. The other response, that the status quo can solve the current harms without a change of policy, is similar to the previous response, but is more open to hypothetical scenarios. This is a very typical response given to the topic of raising the minimum wage, that the "invisible hand" of the market will push up wages without government intervention.

2. **Attitudinal inherency takeout**. The previous chapter outlined two different types of inherency: structural and attitudinal. The above section describes to answers to structural inherency, so this section with explain a general response to attitudinal inherency. Simply stated, the negative can argue that this type of inherency creates an impossible burden for the affirmative because no agent in the world can legislate an attitude. Attitudinal inherency is a type of catch-all concept that functions in a way to fulfill the inherency stock issue without the rigor of researching identifiable barriers to the status quo solving for the harms. Recall that it argues the

existence of a social attitude that causes the perpetuation of harms. Therefore, the affirmative must somehow guarantee a plan capable of making everyone agree with a certain argument. As student of argumentation, you should know how unfeasible this is. An excellent example of attitudinal inherency is the smoking debate. Picture an affirmative debater arguing that the illnesses resulting from smoking constitute an epidemic. After establishing these harms the affirmative would be obligated to explain the inherency, but since there is no law requiring people to smoke the debater would likely argue that the inherent barrier that must be overcome is the social attitude toward smoking. This argument should include evidence explaining how smoking is seen as rebellious and simultaneously glamorous. Regardless of what the affirmative policy is, the negative already has the option to argue that it is impossible to outlaw attitudes favoring rebelliousness and glamour, therefore smoking will continue to be a problem. The affirmative might argue that legislation can regulate behavior even if it cannot regulate attitude. The negative can respond that the ability to regulate behavior without removing the attitude proves that attitude is not an inherent barrier at all; therefore the affirmative has failed to prove this necessary stock issue. Additionally, an affirmative debater that relies on attitudinal inherency for his case risks argument of circumvention when it comes to solvency (covered later in this chapter).

3. **Alternative causality**. Another strategy that can be used when refuting inherency is to claim that the harms exist for a different reason than what the affirmative argues. This is known as alternate causality. A negative debater should argue alternate causality if the affirmative uses poor reasoning in the first constructive. It might seem that you are arguing for the affirmative side, but there are times when alternate causality is a valuable strategy. The most valuable part of this strategy is that the negative debater can demonstrate that he possesses superior skills of logic than his opponent. For instance, say an affirmative case argues that the United States is currently in a recession, and it is the lack of enforcement of immigration laws that prevents the country from pulling itself out of the economic downturn. The affirmative goes on to explain her immigration policy and how it will solve the economic problems. The negative can seize the opportunity to explain that our economic situation is not a result of immigration policy at all, but is instead a result of decades of deregulation which gave corporations far too much freedom. He could continue on by arguing that if one truly wishes to help the economic situation of the US then it is economic policy, not immigration policy, which needs to be altered.

All of this work arguing against inherency would go to waste if the negative does not explain why the lack of inherency should result in a loss for the affirmative. Aside from the rules of NFA-LD requiring this stock issue, inherency plays a vital role in any policy debate. This stock issue is essentially the spot where the affirmative explains what they feel is the cause of the harms; therefore, if the affirmative looses this stock issue, or simply fails to include it in the first affirmative speech, then the negative call them out.

One argument that the negative should make is similar to Senator Bidden's argument below, that without inherency there is no way of being certain of the cause of the harms. Without this certainty, it is quite possible that the policy of the case might not remove the harms from the status quo. The economic bailout plan at the end of 2008 is a prime example. US lawmakers were basically presented with a do-or-die situation: give $700 billion to collapsing banks and lenders, or face an economic collapse larger than the great depression. No time to consider how we got in this situation. There is a problem and we need to act. Lawmakers acquiesced, and many have now criticized that the money has been put into the hands of the very people that created the problem in the first place.

In addition to not solving the harms, the negative could argue that failing to isolate the cause of the harms actually increases the risk of compounding the problems in the status quo because of a rash policy decision. If the affirmative has identified a problem, but then described a false cause inherency, then the plan is now affecting something that may not have been a problem to begin with. Recall the immigration example above. The affirmative's policy alters the migration of people to and from the United States. This flow is what defines the workforce, and perhaps the stability on domestic business. The point is not that these scenarios are going to happen, but that one should not even take the risk. In short,

The 2008 VP Debate

The issue of global warming was debated between Joe Bidden and Sarah Palin. The question posed to both candidates was whether or not global warming was a result from human activity. Governor Palin explained that she was not interested in what is causing global warming, only what we should do about it now. Senator Bidden's response was that it is impossible to solve a problem without first knowing its cause. This exchange is at the heart of inherency.

inherency is necessary because of the principal that all policy decisions should be based on a sound understanding of the cause of a problem.

Refuting the Plan

The plan is technically not one of the stock issues, at least according to the NFA-LD rules. Regardless, this section details ways to directly refute the various parts of a plan. In fact, in competitive debate there are some arguments that are made against plan with such regularity that plans themselves could be said to have a set of stock issues. What follows is a fairly comprehensive list of what are often referred to as "spec" arguments (short for specification). For instance, and argument declaring the importance of agent specification is called "a spec," enforcement specification is "e spec," and so on.

1. **Agent specification**. The agent is the organization or entity that institutes the mandate of the plan. Some examples of agents are the United States Congress and the United Nations General Assembly. If the affirmative team fails to clarify the agent of the plan then the negative has the opportunity to point this out. First the negative should declare their intentions by saying something like, "my first response to the plan is agent specification." Next, the negative should explain that the plan is lacking an agent, or that the agent is unclear. For instance, if an affirmative were to declare that the plan's agent was the United States Federal Government, the negative might be confused whether this were an act of congress, or an executive (presidential) order. Then the negative should argue that any plan should have an agent specified within its description because without a specific agent it is unclear who is claiming jurisdiction over the policy. This is important because the agent drastically affects the nature of the policy. Legislation from congress is very different than executive orders. Finally, the negative should conclude that without a clear agent the affirmative is effectively missing a plan from their case. No judge should vote for an affirmative case that is missing a plan.

2. **Enforcement specification**. The argument about enforcement specification begins from a different area than agent specification, but concludes in a very similar fashion. Enforcement specification basically argues that there are no consequences to violating the plan specified. In other words, what happens if someone decides to ignore this new law? Are they jailed? Fined? Forced into community service? Exiled? Negative debaters should begin this refutation by first stating their intention to argue enforcement specification. Second, point out the lack of specification in the affirmative plan. Third, explain that this specification is necessary in order to

determine if the consequences are too harsh, too lenient, or just right. The entire debate would look very different depending on the severity of the enforcement. Fourth and finally, explain that it would be poor decision-making for a judge to for a plan without first knowing the consequences for violating that plan (notice how similar '"e spec" and "a spec" are in their conclusions).

3. **Funding specification**. By now you should be able to somewhat predict what funding specification should look like. This spec argument focuses on where one is to get the resources needed in order to pay for the proposed plan. Although the word "funding" likely brings to mind "money," debaters should also consider material resources to be a potential focus of a funding specification argument. Follow the structure from agent and enforcement specification arguments above. Begin by stating the upcoming argument is going to be funding specification, and then explain that the source of funding for the plan is unclear. Follow this with the argument that specifying funding is important because one should be aware of where the resources are coming in order to pay for any policy. Money is not infinite, and paying for one public policy often requires pulling money from other sources. For instance, congress was notorious for paying for federal projects by dipping into the Social Security trust fund. Conclude the refutation by explaining that a judge should consider any plan that lacks funding specification to be incomplete, and any case with an incomplete plan should be rejected.

4. **Time frame specification**. Explaining when the policy is to take affect, or over how long a policy will be active is time frame specification. This concept is rooted in real-world policy making. California has recently passed several laws regarding driving while using the cell phone. Each time a new law was passed there was a date that in the law that specified the first day the new cell phone law would start being enforced. Therefore obligating the affirmative to follow similar requirements is not at all unusual. A negative debater should first explain that they are running time-frame specification. Second, explain why the time frame for the policy is vague. Third, argue that a time frame is important in any plan

> **Plan specification power tags**
> Debaters like to use short-hand language to refer to common argument. Plan specification arguments are typically shortened using the following terms:
> - a-spec = agent specification
> - e-spec = enforcement specification
> - f-spec = funding specification
> - tf-spec = time-frame specification

because there may be events that one would want to not happen at the same time as the start of the plan. Fourth, close with the argument that without a time frame there is a gap where the plan should be and no good policy decision can be based upon a case without a complete plan.

Refuting Solvency

Good intentions are easy to come by, proposing an effective plan is more difficult. Solvency is a stock issue that is ripe for refutation. Often times, the reason that a plan has not yet been implemented to solve the harms articulated in the case is that the problem is really complicated, and finding the right solution is tricky. It does not matter how significant the harms are, if the plan cannot solve them then a judge should not vote for it. There are a couple of standard solvency arguments that can be applied to a multitude of affirmative cases.

1. **No solvency**. The first argument is a direct "no solvency" response. This argument is trickier than many think. Many debaters simply argue that the plan does not solve for the totality of the harms. For instance, an affirmative might make the argument that because people of color are disproportionately sentenced to death, that banning the death penalty would reduce the harms of racism. For the negative to argue that the plan doesn't solve for all racism isn't enough to form an offensive reason to vote for the negative. Therefore, a "no solvency" response needs to function to remove 100% of solvency. For example many debate topics argue the merits of colonizing the moon, or Mars. To refute solvency for cases like this, the negative could argue that it is impossible to build large extraterrestrial habitats with today's technology. Notice how this argument doesn't just mitigate solvency, it eliminates and chance of it.

2. **Circumvention**. Another predictable response to solvency is circumvention. This argument says that people will bypass the laws or rules that are supposed to solve the harms This response to solvency is typical when the affirmative has underestimated the enforcement needed to make a plan advantageous, of have neglected to explain the enforcement of the plan altogether. An example topic is any environmental regulation, such as limiting industrial emissions. A circumvention argument would be that companies will relocate manufacturing to countries with relaxed environmental regulations and just pollute elsewhere.

Remember, refuting solvency must be accompanied by an explanation about why an affirmative case that lacks solvency ought to be rejected. Remind your judge that any proposal has intrinsic costs, like time and money, that cannot be recouped.

Voting for a case that doesn't solve is effectively voting to continue the harms, plus the automatic costs of implementing the plan. This is worse than just allowing the harms to continue to exist. In fact, an affirmative team might have well-rehearsed harms and inherency, and still loose an entire debate to solvency "takeout."

Exercise: 4 Point Refutation

The purpose of this exercise is to help students identify different parts of a 4 point refutation and enable them to understand how the components are different. Reorganize the following sets of sentences in to the proper 4 point format.

Minimum Wage
1. But be assured, without more purchasing power from all people the economy will suffer.
2. My opponent claims raising the minimum wage will possibly hurt business, which is bad for the economy.
3. Therefore, the economy would be worse without raising the minimum wage.
4. This is because our consumer driven economy will not function if people can't buy products sold by businesses.

American Football
1. In fact, cheerleading is statistically the most dangerous sport having the most sever injuries most frequently.
2. Hence, physical risk should not be the reason any sport is banned.
3. But, all sports present the potential of bodily harm.
4. They state American football should be banned because of medical complications stemming from playing.

Gun Control
1. Our evidence shows there are currently over 300 million firearms currently legally owned by people in the United States alone, and these with illegal weapons will still be used in gun violence.
2. They clearly stated that they think increasing gun regulations will alleviate gun violence.
3. Therefore, Pandora's box has been opened and cannot be closed, the guns will remain in the hands of people whether or not the future regulations occur.
4. My response is that guns will still be available everywhere to those who want to do harm.

Disadvantages

Human beings have a long history with tragic stories. Many of our oldest surviving stories end in tragedy. Many of the fairy tales from across the world were tragedies, before they were remade by the movie industry to have a happy ending. Many of Shakespeare's most celebrated works are tragedies. Most religious texts are tragedies. This is in stark contrast to the many happy endings that contemporary movie-goers might experience today. There is something compelling about a sad story that draws people in. One of the most practiced strategies in debate makes use of a tragic story, and it is known as the disadvantage. In this section we are going to examine the parallels between telling a tragic story and the structure of a disadvantage. Then, we will look a few examples of popular disadvantages in debate.

Uniqueness

There are three fundamental stock issues of every disadvantage. The first of which is known as uniqueness. This stock issue is also the most difficult to understand for many beginning debaters. Uniqueness is any argument, or set of arguments, that identifies a particular area of life that would otherwise be unaffected by the proposition advanced by the affirmative. Debaters should explain the status quo in the uniqueness, but focus on an area they foresee experiencing negative outcomes. The hard part about uniqueness is not getting ahead of yourself. Don't jump to the conclusion of the tragic story. There are other stock issues that need explanation between the uniqueness and the end.

Links

The next stock issue is the link. A link is any argument or any set of arguments that explain why the proposal advanced by the affirmative triggers the disadvantage. It is more-often-than-not that a debater will explain multiple links in this section. One of those links should always be an explanation of the specific section of the proposal that is the specific offender. Sometimes the affirmative offers a proposal or plan that has several parts. A real-world example is the Affordable Care Act. This piece of legislation was hundreds of pages long, and there are several sections that both Republicans and Democrats agreed on, but it was those areas of disagreement that created so much contention. Representatives and senators focused only on those sections when arguing in public about the disadvantages of the act. In addition to this link argument, it is customary to include what debaters call and "internal link." Internal links explain the immediate affects of the proposal. They explain the "chain-reaction" that is set into motion once the proposal is implemented. Internal links stop short of explaining the tragic outcomes of this chain reaction. That is the function of the last stock issue of a disadvantage.

Impacts

An impact is any argument, or arguments that explain the tragic consequences of a proposal advanced by the affirmative. Arguing compelling impacts is deceptively difficult. Beginning debaters often offer impacts that are too vague, or vastly exaggerate the magnitude of the negative outcomes. It should be the goal of any debater to explain impacts that are of the highest probability, and only then explain the magnitude of that particular impact. It is fairly common for debaters to forego any explanation of how probable an impact is and only try to maximize the magnitude of the impact. Having a blind-spot for probable impacts results in many disadvantages ending in global thermal nuclear war. Debaters love finding some internal link story that allows them to argue the most dystopian of futures.

Overlooking any of these stock issues risks loosing your audience to the feeling that your disadvantage is "incomplete." Additionally, such an oversight leaves openings for your opponent to exploit. If it appears that you have not fully developed a disadvantage, you just might lose a major source of offense for your debate. Take your time and fully explain the uniqueness, links, and impacts of a single disadvantage before moving on to another part of your speech. Telling tragic stories takes time, and, if history is any indicator, a well-told tragedy will leave a lasting memory on your audience.

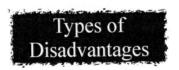
Types of Disadvantages

In any debate, if you are on the negative, then disadvantages are your bread and butter. You should never enter into a policy debate without some idea of a disadvantage you are going to run. But, beginning debaters often find themselves stuck when trying to compose a well-developed disadvantage. The first step is learning what are the stock issues for a disadvantage, and if you haven't learned what those stock issues are, then you should complete that lesson first. But that one lesson is not enough. People don't compose disadvantages every day, so the activity is foreign to them. Therefore, it is a good idea to get familiar with some generic disadvantages in order to see some tested disadvantages. Therefore, this section will go over three common disadvantages that occur regularly in debates. The following disadvantages occur so regularly because they are relevant, or link, to so many cases. Remember, the assumption is that you have already completed the disadvantages lesson earlier, so there will be jargon in this lesson that was covered in the previous lesson.

Federalism

The first common disadvantage is called federalism, and it is a very American argument. In fact, arguments about federalism began with the American Constitution and have not stopped since. The essential argument is that a free society requires a very careful balance government power and individual freedom, and that the affirmative team throws off that balance with their advocacy. Here's the break down.

1. **Uniqueness**. The first stock issue typically covers the 10th amendment to the Constitution. You see, the amendment says that "The powers not delegated to the United States by the Constitution, nor prohibited by it to the States, are reserved to the States respectively, or to the people." Basically, this means that if the Constitution doesn't explicitly say that the federal government has the power to do something, then it's the states that are in charge of the issue in question. You might also include some evidence about the success of states to solve important problems, especially if that evidence is relevant to the topic of debate. For instance, if the resolution is about education, then the uniqueness evidence should be related to education.

2. **The link**. The next issue is the link, and the federalism DA is most applicable when the affirmative is running a case for nationwide reform for education, health, and other welfare policies. It doesn't work so well for topics like national security or foreign relations. So a good rule of thumb is to only run federalism arguments on domestic topics.

3. **Internal link**. The next issue is the internal link, and this is where things can get tricky. At this point in the disadvantage, the goal is to set up your impacts. One of the most popular arguments is to explain why this violation of federalism will open the door for abuses of power. For instance, if the topic is "the USFG should substantially reform education in the United States," then the internal link argument could be that federal control over education could give the government the ability to select "appropriate" materials. Such a power is easily abused by any politician that happens to work his or her way into a position of power. For example, people recently accused a Texas school board of choosing history books for political reasons rather than choosing the highest quality.

Imagine one organization dictating what millions of students are forced to read.

4. **Impacts**. This leads to the impact, which is typically tyranny. The earliest of debates between federalists and anti-federalists were steeped in what was the best strategy to avoid tyranny, because the people who fought the revolutionary war were very skeptical of powerful governments. But you can also argue that federalism promotes public engagement because the governments are closer to the people, and that federalism promotes innovative solutions to problems because we get numerous "laboratories of democracy" developing a variety strategies.

The Federalism Debate

The United States form of government has never had a time where there was universal agreement. There was even disagreement about whether the Constitution ought to be signed and ratified, there were competing interpretations advanced by the founding fathers. On one side were the Federalists, who in favor of ratifying the new Constitution, and Anti-federalists, on the opposition. The arguments in favor of ratifying the Constitution were published over the course of several weeks, and proved to be instrumental to acceptance of the Constitution, and the form of government that we operate under today.

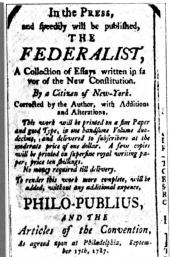

Politics

Similar to the federalism DA, is politics. The politics DA basically states that even the best of intentions will encounter political opposition, and might result in unintended consequences.

1. **Uniqueness**. The uniqueness point typically introduces a political situation: like there is an immigration bill that is soon to pass, or that there is an election cycle coming up. It might seem odd, because the political situation in the uniqueness often times doesn't seem to be relevant to the topic at all.

2. **The link**. The link isn't so much about what the plan is, as it is that passing any plan tends to upset one's political opponents. Notice that this link is very generic, making it applicable to a great many debate cases. This is appealing because debaters can use the same disadvantage in a number of different contexts.

3. **Internal links**. The internal link describes what these political opponents do in response to the passage of the plan. So in response to sweeping educational reform, the opponents to reform push hard to kill immigration reform. This might sound a little childish, and it is. But in debate terms many people like to explain that politics is a "zero sum game," or that for every winner, there is a loser. So the opponents will be be extra motivated to chalk up a win after a loss. This is supported by the trend that whichever party wins the presidential election tends to loose elections two years later during the midterms.

4. **Impacts**. The impacts that follow stem from whatever you selected in the internal link. So if the disadvantage focuses on immigration reform, then the impacts are all the families that continue to suffer. If the disadvantage focuses on the environment, then the impact might be that Alaskan National Wildlife Reserve will be exploited for resources. The options are nearly infinite, which makes the politics disadvantage exceptionally customizable, and really unpredictable.

Masking

The last generic disadvantage of this lesson is known as masking. Masking is a good disadvantage when you are struggling to develop a disadvantage because the fundamental argument is that the affirmative only appears to solve the problem, and that the appearance of solvency results in people being less diligent, and therefore makes the problem worse by pushing it underground.

1. **Uniqueness**. The uniqueness argument typically requires that the debater point out alternate causes to whatever the problem is. So for the education case, the problem might be the falling test scores of US students, and the plan could be to include public pre-kindergarden for all children. The negative has ample ability to argue that there are several things that influence education scores other than pre-K; things like teacher pay, class sizes, emphasis on the arts, just to name a few.

2. **The link**. For this plan, debaters could argue that it will be heralded as a good thing, and you might even see a difference in test scores, but it is the perception that education was fixed that is important.

3. **Internal link**. The perception that education was fixed that will lead to the internal link, which is people loosing focus on how to improve education in our country, and they will find comfort in believing that the affirmative has solved the

problem already. Specifically, people suffering from poverty will probably still continue to perform poorly on tests because their living conditions will be a bigger influence than one extra year of education.

4. **Impacts**. Debaters need skill when explaining the impact, because it still sounds like the plan has a net advantage to the status quo. The impact is that all of the suffering left in place after the plan is past is compounded year after year because society ignores the problems that remain. In other words, the plan condemns the poor to years of continued suffering just so we can marginally increase test scores.

If you find yourself regularly participating in debate tournaments then you are likely to run into theses disadvantages several times. They are common for a reason, they apply to a lot of topics and have a long history. Federalism is a signature American debate. Politics are an ever-present force in government. And some degree of masking happens with any plan. The goal should be to craft custom disadvantages depending on the topic you are given, but that is sometimes difficult. These disadvantages give a nice foundation for any beginning debater to experiment with. And even if you ultimately fall out of favor with any of the previous disadvantages, being familiar with them makes it easier to anticipate responses when you are on the receiving end.

Exercises: Disadvantages

It is very important you understand how disadvantages function because they are very common in debate. The purpose of this exercise is to further your understanding of the elements or parts of a DA. Follow the directions below.

1. Read the affirmative debate scenario.
2. Numbered elements of a DA are provided against the affirmative but out of order.
3. Reorganize the answers in DA format.

Debate scenario: the resolution is "The United States should substantially reform it's transportation infrastructure." You don't know what the affirmative is going to argue, but you have enough information to compose a disadvantage that applies to most cases. Place the disadvantage in the following order: 1. uniqueness, 2. link, 3. internal link, 4. impact.

1. There are two primary methods of mining coal in the United States today, surface mines currently in the United States. The most common way coal is obtained is from a method known as mountaintop removal/valley fill coal mining, or MTR, which has been referred to as strip mining on steroids.
2. Most of our energy comes from the burning of coal. The nation's fleet of over 100 coal plants is responsible for 57 percent of the electricity generated in the U.S., more than any other single electricity fuel source. Coal is typically burned to create steam, which is then piped at high pressure over a turbine, causing it to rotate and produce electricity.
3. After the coal companies blast apart the mountaintops, they dump the rubble into neighboring valleys, where lie the headwaters of streams and rivers, like the Kanawha, Clinch, and Big Sandy. The exposed rock leaches heavy metals and other toxics that pose enormous health threats to the region's plants and animals — and people.
4. Any plan to significantly substantially reform transportation infrastructure would likely require an equally substantial increase in electrical energy, and therefore an increase in coal mining. These plans may include, but are not limited to, electric cars, high speed rail, and traffic signal upgrades.

Exercise: Disadvantages

It is very important you understand how disadvantages function because they are very common in debate. The purpose of this exercise is to further your understanding of the elements or parts of a DA. Follow the directions below.

1. Read the affirmative debate scenario.
2. Numbered elements of a DA are provided against the affirmative but out of order.
3. Reorganize the answers in DA format.

Debate scenario: the affirmative is defending the construction of a high-speed rail system in California. You are the leader of opposition and want to argue that such a plan will result in a disadvantage of the California government kicking poor people off of their land to make room for the project. Place the disadvantage in the following order: 1. uniqueness, 2. link, 3. internal link, 4. impact

1. In order to accommodate the additional miles rail being proposed, the government will have to exercise the use of eminent domain—the exercise of the power of government or quasi-government agencies to take private property for public use.
2. Forcefully removing lower income individuals from their land hurts their ability build wealth and escape the cycle of poverty that traps too many Americans.
3. The decision regarding what land will be seized for public use has a history of targeting the poor. Like in Napa Valley California, in preparation for the high speed rail, all the poor winery workers are the people being ousted off their land, yet vineyards and the wealthy elite remain unscathed.
4. There is currently no single stretch of land in California that is available to accommodate a high-speed rail. California has some of the largest cities in the nation, and the resulting population density has left no corridor through which the rail could go.

Counterplans

We learned in the affirming chapter that stock issues are certain arguments that tend to recur from debate to debate. When people want to make a case, they often times advocate a plan (the affirmative uses plans to solve problems) to solve a problem. So it makes sense to devote a significant amount of time describing the harms, the inherent barrier, and the solvency. But there are often multiple ways to solve a single problem. (the negative can solve problems too) A Counter Plan is used by the Negative team to solve a problem in a different way than as proposed by the Affirmative. Whenever a policy debate round is ensuing and the affirmative presents a plan, the negative team has the opportunity to utilize a counter plan. So, for this lesson, we are going to explore the three stock issues of counterplans.

Plan Text

The first element of a Counter Plan is the Plan Text. A Plan Text is a sentence or two that explicitly dictates what your plan will do. For example, "The United States Federal Government will pull all troops out of the Middle East." Plan Texts should be very concise. They should be very explicit and should only do one thing. Do not use flowery off-the-cuff language during the reading of a Plan Text. It is one of the most important single sentences of the entire debate. There should be no confusion as to the Plan Text. Like Plans, you might want to specificity certain elements other than the text itself. Agency, Enforcement, Time frame and Funding are all specifics that might need to be acknowledged to have a good Counter Plan. Remember, Agency normally is the governing body that has the power to implement your plan. The Enforcement is the body that will actually see that the plan is carried out. Time frame is the window when the plan will begin and end. Finally the Funding is simply showing how the money will be gathered to accomplish the logistics of the plan. Luckily, you might be able to use the information from your opponent's plan to fill in one ore more of these details. You may be wondering why the plan is the first issue articulated in a counterplan and not, say, the harms. The reason is that, by definition, when you run a counterplan you are conceding that there are harms that need fixing. The whole point of the Counter Plan is that it is supposed to solve the same problems the affirmative solves for but in a different way.

Solvency

Since the goal of a counter plan is as an alternative solution to the harms, the next stock issue is solvency. This issue is extremely important because it levels the playing field between the affirmative and negative debaters. Too often do negative debaters find themselves in rebuttals arguing to oppose passage of a plan only to have the affirmative respond by saying "The only person in this round that has a plan to fix the problems we face is the affirmative." This appeals to many judges because many affirmative debaters quickly learn how to focus on significant human problems. In fact, this is the exact response that democrats use to respond to republican criticism of Obamacare; that even if there are disadvantages to Obamacare, the republicans have no alternative way of solving the healthcare problems that Obamacare solves. So far this argument seems to have gotten a lot of traction. Counter plans prevent these types of arguments in rebuttals and remove a powerful argument from the affirmative's arsenal. But, just like affirmative plans, you should not take solvency for granted. The way that your plan solves the problems is not always self evident. Use examples of similar counter plans that have worked in the past, expert testimony that explains why the counter plan should succeed, or some other evidence.

Competition

Counter plans first lay out a plan text, then goes over solvency, and finally addresses competition. What is competition? In debate we use the word competition to refer to the forced choice between plans and counterplans. This means that the counter plan is not just something that also solves the harms, but it is something that solves the harms better than the affirmative's original plan. In other words, the judge ought to vote against the plan because of the counter plan. Remember, the negative's first burden is to explain why the judge ought to vote against the affirmative, not just to be another affirmative voice on the resolution. Competition is a element of a counter plan and needs to be addressed in every single round a counter plan is used.

MINI GLOSSARY

Competition: In debates, it is the forced choice between plans and counterplans.

1. **Mutual exclusivity**. One way a debater can argue competition is that the two plans are Mutually Exclusive. Mutual Exclusivity is a concept, which simply illustrates the two things, cannot logically or physically be done at the same time. An example of mutually exclusive plans, the affirmative Plan is to pull all troops out of the Middle East, Neg Counter plan is to leave only special forces in the middle east, like navy seals or army rangers. These plans by basic fundamental concept and understanding cannot be done at the same time. The government cannot take out ALL the troops and Leave some troops. They are considered to be mutually exclusive.

2. **Comparative advantage**. Another strategy that is used in debate to show how a counter plan is better or more competitive then the plan is demonstrating flaws in the plan.

This is often referred to as comparative advantage. Affirmative plans may inadvertently cause problems. A good negative team will highlight pitfalls in the Affirmative plan. The easiest way to establish a comparative advantage, is to run a disadvantage. In fact, in most cases it makes sense to run the disadvantage first and the counterplan second. In our example with our affirmative team's plan to "Pull all troops out of Middle East," there may be disadvantages to that plan for example; one could argue that a power vacuum left by pulling out all American troops would be filled by the most ruthless and power hungry groups in the region. This may be enough to convince your judge to vote against the affirmative, but this disadvantage is exactly the type of argument the counter plan seeks to avoid. In other words, Counter plans must avoid all the disadvantages the Negative brings up against the plan. The two arguments work together to provide reasons why the counter plan should be preferred or is more competitive.

3. **Topicality**. A final way of demonstrating competition is the most controversial, and that is to argue that the counter plan is anti-topical, or that the counter plan disproves the resolution. So if the topic is to increase gun regulations, the counterplan would be to decrease gun regulations. If the topic is to increase sanctions on Russia, the counterplan would be to decrease sanctions on Russia. The reasons behind the controversy are beyond the scope of this lesson, but it is important to know that the dispute exists.

Counterplans are really one of the more intuitive debate positions there are. It is very typical to contemplate different ways to solve single problems. In debate, to outline a complete counterplan, one needs to explain the text, solvency, and competition. These stock issues give a sense of completeness to the counterplan, but also give a strategic advantage to the negative in a policy debate.

Types of Counterplans

The core strategy to any negative debater should focus around well-developed critical arguments, like disadvantages and other counter contentions. Unfortunately this is often not enough to persuade a judge to oppose the affirmative. Even if you are able to prove that the proposed plan comes with *some* disadvantages, it doesn't mean that the disadvantages *outweigh* the advantages. Under these circumstances it is good to offer an alternative, or counterplan. By now you should be familiar with what a counterplan is and the stock issues needed for a complete counterplan, so this lesson builds on that knowledge by offering some examples of typical counterplans that have regularly popped up in certain debates over time. If you are not familiar with counterplan structure, you should first review that lesson because there may be some terms in this lesson that you are unfamiliar with.

Alternate Agent

Let's jump in with the alternate agent counterplan. This type of counterplan does the exact same plan proposed by the affirmative, but has a different agent enact it. In particular, we are going look at what is known as the states counterplan. This counterplan is literally made to be accompanied by the federalism disadvantage. So you should also review the types of disadvantages lesson. Let's recall the scenario where the topic of the debate is that "The USFG should substantially reform education policy in the United States." The affirmative suggests the plan of public preschool for all, and the negative runs a federalism disadvantage. The only thing is that any affirmative worth their salt is going to have a good story about how poorly the education system is functioning in the United States currently, so they can easily argue "either we attempt to make the education system better, or we are stuck with the status quo."

1. **Plan text**. It's a difficult position to be on as the negative. So, offering a states counterplan is a way to solve for the harms, while avoiding the risks of the federalism disadvantage. The counterplan text would should sound something like "The 50 United States should independently adopt public preschool for all citizens."

2. **Solvency**. Notice that the solvency argument should be simple, because it would mirror the solvency argument from the first affirmative. They should have already explained why public preschool will boost the quality of education for Americans. You could literally review their evidence as you own solvency. This is important because it takes away the ability for the affirmative to argue that "only the affirmative is offering a solution to the education problem." A likely argument to emerge in the rebuttal, if not in the second affirmative.

3. **Competition**. The solvency argument also easily sets up the competition argument because the negative debater needs to only refer to the arguments made in the federalism disadvantage. Essentially, you argue that the states counterplan solves for the education harms, while simultaneously avoiding any risk of federal tyranny of corruption. You might also explain that the resolution either directly or indirectly requires the affirmative to defend federal action, thereby making non-federal actions (like state laws)

fair ground for the negative. Notice that this strategy makes the whole debate shift from whether or not we should have public preschool, to what the proper role of government ought to be. This does not mean that the negative automatically wins, just that they are able to draw on more arguments than before and increase their *chances* of winning. There are many ways to run alternate agent counterplans other than the states counterplan. On international topics you can suggest the UN rather than the US enact a certain foreign policy. You could argue that the African Union is better at solving African problems than the European Union.

Exclusionary Counterplan

The next type of counterplan is the exclusionary counterplan. This type of counterplan is far more conceptual than the states counterplan. This type of counterplan is when the negative excludes one section of the plan, but proposes enacting all of the rest. This strategy works best for plans that have multiple mandates, or parts. For instance, when the Affordable Care Act, or Obamacare, was being argued in the Congress, there was a disagreement about whether or not there should be a "public option" included in the law. So imagine a debate where the affirmative proposed healthcare reform with the option to purchase insurance from a publicly own company, and the negative counterplanned with healthcare reform without that option. This is a good example of an exclusionary counterplan. Another real-world example involves climate change. Often times international agreements exclude certain developing nations from the rules regarding carbon emissions.

1. **Plan text**. In a debate where the negative runs an exclusionary counterplan, the trick is to run a disadvantage that directly links to the part that you are excluding. For the healthcare debate, you run a disadvantage on the public option (like cost, or inefficiency), and then run the exclusionary counterplan. Or for the global warming plan, you run a disadvantage about how limiting carbon emissions will hurt developing nations, and then exclude those countries in the counterplan.

2. **Solvency**. Exclusionary counterplans have a weakness, and it is found in the solvency section. This is because excluding part of a plan necessarily means that it doesn't do as much. The solvency section of the exclusionary counterplan still grants partial solvency for the remaining parts in the counterplan.

3. **Competition**. The competition stock issue uses the disadvantage as the primary reason that there is a forced choice between plan and counterplan. If you pass the plan you

have solvency plus the disadvantage; if you pass the counterplan, you have some solvency but without the disadvantage. This can be devastating to an affirmative team because they may not have prepared for such a nuanced strategy. They may not have thought about making exceptions to the plan.

Consult Counterplan

The last type of counterplan that this lesson will cover is known as the consult counterplan. This type of counterplan is built on the idea that we ought to consult an important actor prior to passing the plan. Plan text. This type of counterplan is particularly useful in international topics, but is still useful for domestic issues. For instance, the public preschool case mentioned earlier could be counter planned with consulting the teachers unions prior to passing the bill. The trick is to run a disadvantage that argues the teachers union will react negatively to the plan if they are not consulted. For instance, public preschool might be seen as an increased workload without an equitable increase in pay, and the impact might be nationwide strikes. It is important to explain in the text of the counterplan that the consultation will be binding, or in other words: if the teacher's unions reject the plan, then the plan automatically fails. This is important because you can argue in the competition section that there is a forced choice between absolutely passing the plan outright, versus consulting teachers and maybe passing the plan but only if they agree to it. You should also explain how consultation avoids the disadvantage. So, for this example, you could say that consultation gives teacher's unions a chance to revise contracts to meet the increased workload. Therefore, consultation is a way to avoid workers strikes.

These counterplans are a very short list of the many different types that exists; furthermore, you might need to craft a custom counterplan depending on the affirmative you encounter. These are merely meant to give you a primer on the many ways that you can approach the counterplan. It is good to know these types because they are so common. You might even have to face them in a round, and if you do, what would you say. At any rate, being familiar with typical counterplans is a good way to broaden your knowledge base in this activity.

Exercise: Counterplans

The purpose of this exercise is to demonstrate how easy it is to form counterplans quickly and efficiently. There are millions of possibilities as to how you form your counterplan but the following are examples of very common types of counterplans to begin with. Remember counter plan texts should be concise and clear leaving no room for ambiguity or vagueness. Follow the directions below.

1. Read the Affirmative Plan Text provided.
2. Create one federalism disadvantage, with an accompanying states counterplan.
3. Create one consult counterplan using any agency provided.

Affirmative Plan Text
- United States federal government should substantially reform K-12 education.
- California should label Genetically Modified Organisms (GMO) in all food available for human consumption.
- The United States federal government should ban the death penalty.
- The United States should legalize the recreational use of marijuana.

Agencies

Center for Nutrition Advocacy
American Civil Liberties Union
American Teacher Association
American Legislative Exchange Council

Kritiks

The world of competitive debate is like any other hobby or activity that one can participate. It has a subculture, it has a history. It has gone through growth and conflict, and it has popular figures that have changed the activity itself. Bill Shanahan is a debate coach that is widely credited with introducing a type of argument to debates known as kritiks (for some unknown reason, debaters prefer the German spelling of the word, even referring to a kritik as a "K"). The debate community has never been the same. It has gotten to the point that you cannot be competitive at the highest levels of debate without a thorough understanding of how to run a kritik, or at least how to answer them when they are run against you and your arguments. In this section, we will introduce you to the fundamentals of kritiks. First, we will cover a brief overview of what kritiks are, then explain the structure of a kritik if you want to run it in rounds, and finally provide an example. A bit of advice before going forward. There are a few other lessons that you should familiarize yourself before learning about kritiks. Specifically, you definitely want to read the fiat section, but it would be helpful for you to understand some other oppositional strategies before moving forward with kritiks, considering it is a more advanced negative strategy.

What is a Kritik?

I don't want you to think of kritiks as some sort of foreign or different argument that you've never heard of before. More than likely, you have made an argument that could be classified as a kritik because it has a couple of key characteristics.

1. **Pre-fiat**. The first characteristic of a kritik is that it is typically argued to be a pre-fiat issue. This is why it's important for you to understand what fiat is before moving forward. As you can recall, fiat is the idea that you imagine a world in which things take place in order for you to argue whether or not benefits will come from a policy or disadvantages. Therefore, pre-fiat means to consider some issues before imagining a policy to take place. A pre-fiat issue is something that must be dealt with prior to getting into a policy debate. The disadvantages and advantages, the criteria, the stock issues, pre-fiat issues are things that take priority over all the other issues. You should be able to see why this is important because pre-fiat issues, if they are won or lost, could determine the outcome of a round regardless of any of the other arguments that happen regarding the policy.

2. **Challenging assumptions**. In essence, when you argue that any issue is a pre-fiat issue, you're putting it at the top of the list, the first thing that a judge must evaluate when they are

deciding who wins the round. But you can't just declare something to be a pre-fiat issue, there has to be a reason. And the reason why kritiks are considered pre-fiat issues is because of the fundamental characteristic that they are challenging assumptions from the opposing debaters. The logic here is that if your fundamental assumptions are flawed, then your conclusions cannot be sound. This is pretty basic logic. If your premises are flawed, then you can't have a sound conclusion. Very much the same in kritiks. If there is a fundamental assumption that creates the foundation of the arguments you are making on your case, and that fundamental assumption is flawed, then the entire case is flawed. It is this essential characteristic of kritiks, the challenging of fundamental assumptions, that make them very popular and actually fairly common argument. Take the real world example of the Affordable Care Act, also known as Obamacare. There were many arguments that were made about the details of the policy, about how premiums will work and how the subsidies are going to work. But by far the most popular argument that was made in the media by Congress members was that it was socialist in nature, and because socialism doesn't work, this can't work. Notice how they are focusing on the fundamental assumptions of the policy, rather than specific disadvantageous outcomes. Of course, there is a debate about whether or not Obamacare is even socialist, but the point is that arguing about the fundamental assumptions that create the foundation of the Affordable Care Act, those questions preempted any sort of policy discussion about the act itself. In other words, you could come to a conclusion about the value of the Affordable Care Act without looking at any of the policy details if you are going to evaluate it based on its socialist underpinnings alone. So you can see how a critic isn't all that foreign. In fact, it's a fairly common argument that people make all the time.

Using Kritiks

So how do you run it in a round? The best answer to that question is to outline the structure of a kritik, and for debaters to address each stock issue, in order, with a fully formed arguments. There are four parts.

1. **Framework**. The framework itself has a couple of things that are typically included. The first one is a discussion about fiat. A very popular phrase that people like to use at this point is that fiat is an illusion. In other words, that fiat is an imaginary game that we play and it isn't as important as the fundamental assumptions that we carry with us outside of this round. Basically, you're arguing that we really aren't lawmakers and this really isn't Congress. We're not actually passing anything. We're just having a debate. The second part

of framework that you want to include is a discussion about the theoretical or philosophical underpinnings that you want to challenge. This is where you lay out the fundamental assumptions of capitalism or socialism, but it could also include other sort of approaches like racism or sexism. Any other type of "ism" that you can think of would be well placed in the framework as a discussion point.

2. **Links**. The next stock issue of a kritik is the link. The link is where you attach the kritik to something that your opponent has said. You want to quote them directly. You want to point out the argument that they made in the prior speech that has given rise to this kritik. Make sure that the words that they have used somehow link to the kritik that you are making. Sometimes people actually use the resolution itself as a link, and that they are kritiking the resolution. This is a somewhat controversial approach, but still is something that needs to be debated out in the round.

3. **Impacts**. Impacts for kritiks are just like impacts in a disadvantage or in an advantage. The only difference is that you have to think about pre-fiat impacts. Remember, you are forgoing the imaginary world of a policymaker. We're not pretending that we are in Congress or passing laws. We're recognizing that we are just debaters in this round, and the words and rhetoric that we're using have impacts on the people in this round. So the impacts should be about the people in the round itself.

4. **Alternative**. The last stock issue of a kritik is a bit controversial, and it is the alternative. There are some people that argue that an alternative isn't necessarily required, but many people say that it is still a good idea to provide an alternative. What an alternative is, is basically you explaining what the other option other than the kritik is that we could use. What other type of rhetoric can we use? What are the other fundamental assumptions that we should live by other than what your opponents have presented?

Example Kritik

So let's take this structure and apply it to a specific scenario. Namely, let's take a look at the scenario that's unfolding in Syria. For the last several years, Syria has been embroiled in a civil war that has been drawing in more and more world powers. There has been an ongoing debate about what the role of the United States should be. So let's say that the resolution is that the United States should get engaged in the Syrian civil war, and the affirmative team argues for a greater military presence through the use of air strikes and ground troops. In a typical policy debate, the negative team would argue whether or not

127

there would be enough troops, whether or not they can fulfill their mission, whether or not that would solve the problems in Syria. But if the negative team decided to run a critique, it would be a different strategy. For instance, a kritik that might apply in this situation is known as a neo-colonialism kritik, and it sounds something like this.

1. **Subpoint a, fiat is illusionary**. It is an imaginary game that we play as debaters, and we don't actually have any influence over policy decisions. There isn't going to be an actual invasion into Syria at the end of this round. The only thing that's truly going to happen is our assumptions about how to engage the international community are going to be molded by our rhetoric. The second part of the framework argument is that neo-colonialism is an approach to international relations where military power is used to intervene into conflicts in order to solidify the United States' foothold and dominance in the world stage.

2. **Subpoint b, the link**. The affirmative team is using the United States military power to intervene in Syria and maintain its military might over others. These policy decisions are never neutral. For instance, take a look at the United States' position on Bashar al-Assad, the president of Syria. They want him out, whereas other international actors don't necessarily want to see him go. This is very much in line with US interests, but not necessarily global interests.

3. **Subpoint c, the impacts**. We as debaters and as critical thinkers don't ever question the United States' involvement in these areas. And we should be critically questioning whether or not we should be involved yet again in a Middle East conflict. In the past we have been dragged into quagmires that seemed to have no end. Why would this be any different? All it does is create a cycle of violence that the United States gets involved in the Middle East and that creates backlash, and that backlash manifests itself in violence against people all over the globe, including Americans. It is time that we stop this cycle, right now, and reject this idea of neo-colonialism.

4. **Subpoint d, the alternative**. Reject intervention in Syria. Support the people that are most affected by the civil war in Syria, namely the refugees. In essence, don't militarily intervene, but instead react on a humanitarian level. Don't send guns, but accept people that are being displaced from their own homes.

Realize that in an actual round you would be citing evidence, and it would be a much more detailed and sophisticated argument that took up more time than is taken in this particular lesson. But essentially that is the flow of this argument and the transitions from stock issue to stock issue within the kritik.

We have just scratched the surface of kritiks by first looking at what a kritik generally is. How to structure a kritik, and looking over an example. There are dozens of examples of kritiks available on the Internet with just a little bit of research. They have all the evidence compiled and are structured out for you. You really should check them out. Even though kritiks are a relatively new development in the world of competitive debate, they have become an essential part of a debater's approach to any type of topic. It increases the amount of tools that they have to respond to affirmative cases. You really should explore the possibilities that kritiks have to offer.

Topicality

What do you call 10,000 lawyers at the bottom of the ocean? A good start. What do you call 25 lawyers buried up to their neck in cement? Not enough cement. How many lawyer jokes are there? Three, the rest are true stories. Lawyers get a bad rap. There are hundreds of lawyer jokes that circulate, and recirculate through the United States, and they usually involve a negative view of the profession. My guess is that people don't really have the patience to argue about things they think are self evident, like the definition of words. One famous example is when then President, Bill Clinton, was being questioned about his alleged infidelity with a woman and said "there's nothing going on between us." It turned out there was a prior relationship, and when people accused of lying he responded, "It depends on what the definition of 'is' is." Many people said that this was a lawyer's answer. Debaters also get a bad rap, and for much the same reason. It is all too often that debates focus on the definition of terms, thereby making any arguments about the substance of topic impossible. Unfortunately, language isn't a perfect medium for communicating ideas. Words have a way of being interpreted in very different ways. Arguments reflect this reality, so debaters have developed a position that addresses the conflict that arises over definitions, and it is called topicality. The focus of this lesson is to explain the stock issues of a topicality position. There are four: counter-definition, violation, standards, and impacts.

MINI GLOSSARY

Topicality: a standard argument in debate rounds whose central issue is whether or not the affirmative advocated a case that support the resolution.

1. **Counter-definition**. If you are going to have a debate about definitions, it makes sense to explicitly lay two definitions side-by-side and compare the benefits of each. This leads to the first stock issue of topicality: counter-definition. This issue is just as it sounds, you supply a counter-definition for one or more words from the resolution or topic from the debate. In fact, it is common practice to name the entire topicality position after the word that you are counter-defining. Let's work with one example resolution throughout the lesson, "The United States should increase it's constructive engagement with Cuba." This was an actual resolution in the past, and some people complained about the vagueness of the term "constructive engagement" at the time, so I think it makes for a good example. If I were on the opposition I would look up the term's history in order to get a better understanding, and discover that this term was used to describe using economic incentives, rather than sanctions, to influence the policies of foreign governments. So instead of withholding trade as a punishment for oppression, we would increase trade to encourage reducing oppression. So the first point on the "constructive engagement" topicality position would be that the "The definition of constructive engagement is the relaxing of trade restrictions for the expressed purpose improving human rights." This definition is still vague, but there is one detail that it introduces, that of trade. Basically, the negative is trying to find a predictable definition in order aid in opposition research. This definition helps because now research can be limited to the effects of trade, rather than just any and all types of "engagement." Notice that it not required that you define things word-for-word. In this case, I treat "constructive engagement" as a single term and offer one definition. Defining them separate, I might have a completely different interpretation, creating a completely different debate.

2. **Violation**. Defining terms in a resolution is virtually a necessity regardless of whether or not there is a debate about definitions, but it is especially important to have definitions prepared if the affirmative team interprets the resolution in a way you didn't anticipate. This leads to the second stock issue of topicality, the violation. This point argues that the affirmative's interpretation "violates" the counter-definition; in other words, the affirmative's interpretation and the negative's interpretation are incompatible. To support this argument, negative debaters need to quote from the first affirmative constructive. There needs to be things that were said in that speech that prove the violation. Let's work with our previous example. The resolution is "the US should increase constructive engagement with Cuba." The affirmative approaches the podium, thanks the audience and the judges, and begins to explain that they interpret the resolution to mean

that they need to engage Cuba in order construct a democratic nation; therefore, they conclude that the affirmative will defend the invasion of Cuba. It is easy to see how this interpretation is incompatible with the counter-definition discussed earlier. All of the supposed advantages that the affirmative would argue are based on military action rather than economic action. Notice that the dispute isn't that the affirmative has presented a case that isn't debatable, there is ample reason to conclude that invading Cuba is a bad idea. Topicality, merely argues that their interpretation violates the meaning of the term from the resolution. This point of the topicality position is hard to prepare, because it only exists once the affirmative has spoken. Therefore, listening is very important. Furthermore, thinking of questions that clarify the affirmative's position might be helpful. For our example, "how is this invasion going to affect our economic trade with Cuba?" or even more direct "is economic trade with Cuba part of this invasion?" The answers to these questions are the evidence that you can use in the second point of you topicality position. "The affirmative violates the definition of constructive engagement when they answer my question by saying the invasion halts all trade with Cuba."

3. **Standards**. It is tempting to conclude that you have won the debate once you are able to show that the affirmative's interpretation violates your counter-definition, but that is really just the beginning. Now you have to explain why the judge should conclude that the negative definition is superior to the affirmative definition. This brings up the stock issue of standards. Standards are reasons why the negative's interpretation is the best interpretation of the terms in the resolution. Simply saying "that's just what the words mean" is not enough to win topicality. Words have several interpretations, and the only thing that the violation proves is that the interpretations are different, not that either is better. Essentially, this means that if you began a sentence with "our definition is better than theirs because...", then anything that logically finished that sentence would be a standard for topicality. There are some common standards. Perhaps the most helpful standard for the constructive engagement topicality is that of field contextuality. Field context means that the term in question has particular meaning when used in a particular field of study. In other words, in the context of foreign relations, constructive engagement has consistently been used to

MINI GLOSSARY

Field contextual definition: the idea that a word of phrase has particular meaning, and ought to be defined, by referencing the field of study which it is used.

describe liberal economic policies, and has stood in stark contrast to military options. Another common standard is grammar, that grammatically the negative has a more accurate interpretation than the affirmative. For the Cuba topic, the negative might identify "constructive engagement" as a compound term, kind of like "attorney general" refers to a specific job title in the government, and not "a generic lawyer." Grammatically, the word constructive modifies the word engagement to create a very specific meaning. There are many other common standards that debaters use in competition: the standard of ground argues that the negative's definition better preserves debatable ground for both sides, framer's intent argues that the negative's definition is in line with what the writers of the resolution intended the debate to be about, predictability argues that the negative's interpretation is a more predictable interpretation and results in higher quality research and preparation. But, you can create standards if you are able to articulate any reason why one definition is better than the other. It is typically best if there is an easy, one or two word title in order to reference the standard throughout the topicality position. It increases how memorable the standard is, so in rebuttals the judges is able to recall your reasoning.

4. **Impacts**. The final stock issue that of impacts. This point includes and explanation about what the consequences ought to be for an affirmative that provides a faulty interpretation. One common argument is that the topicality is an "a priori" issue. This simply means that determining whether or not the affirmative presented a topical must be decided prior to evaluating the pros and cons of their case. The reason is that if the judge determines the affirmative presented a case that doesn't support the resolution, then he or she can't reasonably conclude that the affirmative won the debate. The one and only responsibility of the affirmative is to prove the resolution true. It doesn't matter if they can research the advantages of a different topic, they must successfully argue in favor of the topic that both teams were assigned. So the affirmative might have great reasons for military engagement with Cuba, but they haven't presented reasons for constructive engagement. In short, the a priori impact says that if the affirmative looses the topicality argument, the judge doesn't even need to look at the case to render a verdict. Another common impact is simply that topicality is a voter. This means that the affirmative cannot ignore this issue, if they do then it is an automatic win for the negative. Some of the justification for this argument are the same as the a priori impact that I just explained, that the affirmative has one job…support the resolution. One last common impact is that of the prima facie burden. This means that the affirmative must be topical "on face," or in the first

speech. This argument prevents the second affirmative coming up in the following speech and offering topical arguments and just saying "our bad, ignore that first speech." While I don't think that would be a persuasive strategy in the long run, technically one could make logical arguments why that is permissible. The prima facie impact is the negative nipping that argument in the bud and forcing the affirmative to rely on, and only on arguments articulated in the first affirmative to prove that they are topical. All of these impacts point to one thing, that is the affirmative loses topicality they loose everything. At this point I think you see why topicality has become such a prevalent argument in competitive debate, it is extremely potent. The negative might have no good arguments against the affirmative's case, but have one well structured topicality position and theoretically still win.

After learning the four stock issues of topicality—the counter-definition, violation, standards and impacts—perhaps you see why some people look at topicality in much the same way they perceive lawyers: as people who bicker about definitions rather than the issues. But hopefully you also see why topicality is useful. Sometimes the affirmative team presents a case that doesn't directly support the topic, and expecting the negative to be prepared for every debate in the world seems unfair. Topicality is a structured way to articulate that point. But, sometimes people abuse this position by always arguing about definitions and avoiding the substance. If you happen to become this type of debater, don't be surprised if people joke that 10,000 topicality debaters at the bottom of the ocean sounds like a good start.

Exercise: Topicality

Debate scenario: The resolution is that the United States should outlaw the death penalty. Your opponents get up and spend the entire first affirmative constructive laying out a case in favor of legalizing marijuana. Write a topicality response that is appropriate for this situation. Make sure you use all four elements in your topicality position.

Exercise: Topicality

Debate scenario: the resolution is "The United States should substantially reform its transportation infrastructure." Your opponent lays out a 1AC which makes the case for privatizing interstate highways. In essence, changing highways into toll roads. You think there are several disadvantages to this proposal, but you also think that this case isn't topical because of an argument you prepared. Unfortunately, the stock issues are out of order.

1. Changing the administration or ownership (e.g. privitizing roads or the post office) may lead to infrastructural changes, but it is not itself a reform of a physical, permanent structure. In other words, the affirmative is arguing for a reform of domestic transportation administration, not domestic transportation infrastructure.
2. This issue is important because the affirmative must prove infrastructure reform is a good idea, but has only argued that administrative reform is a good idea. Without a case that is on topic, the affirmative can never hope to win this debate, and you should vote for the opposition.
3. My definition of infrastructure is preferable because it keeps the debate focused on the essence of the resolution, namely the fiscal and environment impacts of large public works projects. The alternative definition avoids this debate entirely and instead chooses to focus on tired economic theories.
4. The opposition considers the definition of transportation infrastructure to be the physical, permanent structures that create the underlying foundation for our national transportation system. This includes, but is not limited to roads, rail, air and sea ports, bridges, and even sewage.

Chapter 7
Rejoinder

Answers to Disadvantages
- -Uniqueness Responses
- -Link responses
- -Impact responses

Answers to Counterplans
- -Solvency Deficit
- -Disadvantages
- -Permutations

Answers to Topicality
- -Meeting the Definition
- -Counter Standards
- -Impact Responses

Rebuttals
- -Offense/Defense
- -Decision Calculus

When we use the term "resolution" in argumentation, it references the topic of any particular debate. When musicians use the term "resolution," they are generally talking about how to finish songs so they sound "complete." It is a difficult to explain, but musical resolution means the movement from a dissonant chord to a consonant chord. When this happens, it is common for listeners to experience a sense of closure and finality to the song.

Debates also progress through stages of consonance and dissonance. Two opposing teams advance two competing cases, and support those cases with as much evidence as is possible. It can get a bit overwhelming as an audience member, or as a judge. I is important that debaters know how to resolve a debate, just like musician resolve a song. In chapter 4, we covered the concepts of burden of proof, and burden of rejoinder. In this chapter, we are going elaborate on rejoinder by explaining how to respond to disadvantages, counterplans, topicality, and finally how to approach rebuttals.

Answers to Disadvantages

You need to be able to answer the arguments of you opponent directly, and if your opponent constructed a well-developed disadvantage, then coming up with quick answers might be a bit intimidating. Fortunately, just like in chess, there are predictable patterns to that allow competitors to develop quick and effective responses to their opponents. In this seminar we will focus on common answers to disadvantages. Each stock issue in a disadvantages has common answers, so we will follow the structure of a disadvantage and explore the responses that debaters can make on the uniqueness level, link level, and impact level. We know that a disadvantage is more likely in a policy round than in a value round, but you will see that these responses are applicable for all types of debate. Additionally, some of the examples used in this section might strike you as odd. We get it. But remember, these examples are simply illustrations of potential arguments, you ought to pick and choose which you think are best and practice them.

Non-unique

By now you should understand the importance of establishing uniqueness for any disadvantage. An opponent can target your uniqueness and dismantle an entire disadvantage. Such a tactic is known as the non-unique response. There are essentially two ways to argue a disadvantage is non-unique: by saying the disadvantage is going to occur regardless of the advocacy, and by saying that if the disadvantage were true that the impacts should have happened already. Let's consider a hypothetical example. The affirmative advocates investing in natural gas as an alternative energy source, with the advantage of reducing the dependence on foreign oil and lessening the chance for international war. The negative develops a complete disadvantage which essentially argues that natural gas contributes to global warming and they have some pretty good uniqueness evidence to support that claim. They also have some pretty well-researched impacts to global warming. This is a pretty intimidating scenario for the next affirmative speaker, but a response to the uniqueness for this disadvantage yields some unorthodox arguments.

1. The first type of non-unique is to argue that the disadvantage will occur regardless of the plan, in this case global warming is going to happen regardless of whether or not we invest in natural gas. For some debaters, this seems like a bad response because your plan does nothing to solve a major problem, but the logic is that global warming is neither a reason to for the plan, nor against the plan. Global warming is something that is going to happen no matter what, but war for oil is preventable so we should do the plan.

2. The other type of non-unique is to say that the impacts should have occurred already. If the argument is that natural gas is going to make global warming worse, then we should have seen a spike in greenhouse gases since the 1980's, when hydraulic fracturing (the newest way to extract natural gas) was first developed. But we don't see that spike, just the same steady increase in greenhouse gases that was happening well before fracking. In short, there is reason to believe that there is no unique correlation between global warming and natural gas.

You might be unimpressed with either of these responses and that is understandable. Non-unique is inherently defensive. You aren't scoring points, you are preventing your opponent from scoring points. Offense is flashier. But you should realize that if your opponent fails to address either of these arguments, they can't access their impacts. In other words, the disadvantage goes away. It has no bearing on the plan. Which means, in a judges eyes, the debate is no longer a choice between war for oil, and global warming. The debate is only about whether or not we should do something to avoid war, and that is an easy decision for the affirmative.

Responding to Links

So non-unique alone is sufficient to defeat a disadvantage, but it isn't absolutely necessary. There are some devastating arguments that the affirmative can make in response to the link-level of a disadvantage.

1. **No link**. The first is 'no link.' This is simple. In a debate, a link is the explanation of the causal relationship between your advocacy and some really bad impacts. It links your advocacy to those impacts. So a no link argument simply dispels the causal relationship between the advocacy and the impacts. Another hypothetical. The affirmative advocates using electronic tablets for teaching. The negative argues a disadvantage which starts with noticing that tablets are made with rare earth minerals, and ends with research about how a lot of money in the rare earth minerals market funds some pretty horrible human rights abuses. The no link response might be for the affirmative to point out that Apple recently announced that it checked it's suppliers and can verify that none of the commodities come from these areas. So as long as the plan specifies Apple tablets, then there is no link between tablets for students and conflict minerals. The no link response works equally well for internal links. In fact, the previous example was actually a response to an internal link on a conflict minerals disadvantage.

2. **No brink**. The next link-level response is the no brink. This is a creative argument that essentially says that there is no definitive moment where the actions of the plan necessarily trigger the impacts. Some smokers use the no brink response when told they should quit because they might get cancer. They say, "yeah, but now is a bad time." If they were a debater, they might say "no brink, while cigarettes increase the likelihood of contracting cancer this one cigarette is not enough to trigger that impact," which would be very confusing to the average person. But that is the essence, "yes there are risks, but the plan is not enough to trigger the impacts." This argument is hard for some debaters to handle when arguing a global warming DA. The no-brink response is that even if the plan generates greenhouse gases, it is not significant enough to affect global warming one way or the other.

3. **Turn**. The final link-level response we will cover is called the turn. This is fundamentally different from all of the arguments we have gone over in this lesson so far, in that it is offense where everything else has been defense. What used to be called a turnaround in debate has been shortened to turn, and it means that what at first seemed to be a reason for one side, has now become a reason to vote for the other. Recall the

global warming disadvantage from before; a link turn would be to explain that natural gas electrical power plants emit only half as much as a coal fired power plant. Therefore, more natural gas would (arguably) reduce greenhouse gas emissions. In short, what was a global warming disadvantage is now a global warming advantage; thereby, creating two reasons to vote for the affirmative (avert war and reduce global warming).

Responding to Impacts

A lot of debate about disadvantages happens at the link level, but debaters should be aware of impact level responses as well because they can be powerful. There are two fundamental impact-level responses: no impact and impact turn.

1. **No impact**. No impact is the "so what" of argumentation. Basically, the argument is that even if the impact of the disadvantage occurs, it is not significant enough to vote against the advocacy. For a global warming argument there are many significant impacts that a team can choose: rising sea levels, extreme weather, drought, famine, resource wars, etc. But there are also relatively insignificant impacts. Imagine that an opponent runs a global warming DA and the only articulated impact is that global warming will shorten skiing season. This is a very real impact that might result from climate change, but if the case is about war for oil, then a shorter ski season comes nowhere near the level of significance for a judge to vote. The affirmative should say "there is no impact to a shortened ski season." Which means, "who cares if people ski less as a result of averting war?" But debaters get creative with no impact arguments, using it in ways that real policy analysts never would. Think about this, how would you respond to the following argument about global warming leading to rising sea levels. "There is no impact to rising sea levels because mainly rich people live on the beach and they can afford to move." This may sound ridiculous, and it is, but it is still an argument that requires a response, and that response may suck up enough time from a debater to mess up their time allocation. And because it is a defensive argument, there is little risk if your opponent successfully responds to it.

2. **Impact turn**. The other impact level argument is the turn, and the concept is the same as the link level turn, but an impact turn argues that the impact that the opposition declared to be bad is actually good. This is far less common than the link turn, but if done successfully can confound your opponents. For instance, if the impact to global warming is melting ice caps, the impact turn is that less ice would open up trade routes north of Canada and Russia that would be a

massive boon to the world economy. There is even literature that exists you could cite to support this argument. This unconventional argument is just one of the many "global warming good" arguments that have been written about. You may personally disagree with it, at least I hope you do, but it does pose an obstacle that your opponents must overcome if they want to win the disadvantage. Plus, because of it unconventionality, it might throw your opponents for a loop. In fact, impact turns typically confuse debaters because many of them never question their fundamental assumption of what they think is good and bad.

As you can see, there are general tactics for answering disadvantages that can be applied to any and all topics. It is helpful during prep time to go through this list of generic responses and test out responses for how they sound. You will not like them all, but the point is to generate enough responses for you to choose the best one, rather than feeling like you are only allowed to make one response to a disadvantage. Understanding uniqueness, link, and impact level responses is vital to having a successful "middle game" in debate. Because, after all, once the constructives are over, the debate is just beginning.

Exercise: Answering disadvantages

Answering arguments is just as important as making your own. The purpose of this exercise is to better comprehend the different ways to answer various arguments.

Read the negative disadvantage against your affirmative plan to raise minimum wage:

Uniqueness: Employers can't afford to pay employees more.
Link: Affirmative Plan increases employer costs by increasing minimum wage.
Internal Link: Cost increase will devastate small business.
Impact: Economy will suffer irreversible catastrophic failures.

Answer this DA by attacking the uniqueness argument in two ways.

1. Articulate how the impacts would have already happened when similar actions were taken in the past.
2. Articulate how the impacts will happen regardless of your plan.

Exercise: Answering arguments Exercise

Read the negative disadvantage against your affirmative plan to invest in nuclear energy.

Uniqueness: Power plants emit CO2 which contribute to global warming
Link: The affirmative plan creates nuclear power plants.
Internal Link: Prolonged emissions will cause global warming.
Impact: Increased temperatures can devastate farming and lead to famine.

Answer this DA by attacking the link level.

1. NO LINK- Does their DA link to your plan if nuclear power plants do not emit CO2? Write or discuss how there is **no link** using this information.
2. LINK TURN- If power can be made with no emissions does that help the problem they brought up? Write or discuss that you solve for their impacts turning their DA into your offense.

Read the DA against your affirmative plan to subsidize electric cars.

Uniqueness: Electric cars require power plants which emit CO2.
Link: Affirmative plan increases demand for power and more power plants.
Internal Link: Increase in power plants will speed up global warming.
Impact: Arctic ice will melt.

Answer this DA by attacking the impact level.

1. NO IMPACT- despite ridiculousness, give a reason why its not bad if Arctic ice melts.
2. IMPACT TURN- Articulate how opening northern ship routes helps trade.

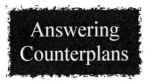

Answering Counterplans

In a debate, it customary for the affirmative to propose a plan, and for the negative to simply oppose the plan. But, as we learned in the counterplan lesson, the negative can propose their own plan as a way of creating a forced choice between whether or not to do the affirmative plan. This sometimes confuses debaters, and they are at a loss when it comes to refuting the counterplan. The knee jerk response might be to simply argue the disadvantages to the counterplan, but there are several nuanced, and clever responses to counterplans that are often overlooked in debates. That is why in this lesson, we will explore some of those responses. We will first explore how a typical disadvantage can take out a counterplan, then discuss solvency take outs, and finally discuss the controversial issue of topicality.

Disadvantages

There are some pretty standard responses to counter plans. This means once the negative team has put forth their disadvantages and counter plan, the Affirmative will normally attack it in a couple different ways. The first response a negative team should expect is a disadvantage presented by the affirmative to the counter plan. In the same way the negative is expected to show how the plan has flaws by using a disadvantage, an affirmative team can use them to show pitfalls in the counterplan. Sometimes this results in gruesome arguments about which plan is "less bad." If I can show the disadvantages of plan will equate to 1000 people dead and the disadvantages of counter plan is 100 people dead, by numbers alone the counterplan is more preferable. Normally there will not be a concrete statistic that can simply win the debate, but numbers are very important and being aware of numbers and statistics relevant to the resolution will benefit a debater. Let's apply this to a real life debate. There is a debate in the court of public opinion regarding vaccines. In a debate, it would be reasonable for the affirmative to propose that vaccines should be mandatory for all public school students. The negative could counterplan with the "personal belief exemption" that would allow for parents to opt out of vaccinating their child because of the belief that vaccines are dangerous. The affirmative could argue an "outbreak" disadvantage to the counterplan outweighs "adverse reactions" disadvantage to the plan. Of course, it probably makes sense to phrase your arguments in terms of how many people are saved, rather than how many people aren't killed as a result of rejecting the counterplan.

Solvency Deficit

The next response is too often overlooked in the debates. The affirmative team can attack

142

the solvency of the counterplan. Remember back to our lesson on stock issues. Essentially an attack on solvency is simply saying the counter plan does not solve for the problems presented in affirmative problem or harms. This situation happens more often than you might expect. A recent topic called on affirmatives to defend developing the moon for water. Literally, to go to the moon and mine the ice for water. While you may be thinking why we would go through the trouble of going all the way to the moon just for water, many of the affirmative debaters cleverly argued that developing the ability to survive off of planet earth is essential to surviving extinction scenarios like killer asteroids. They also argued that additional water supplies could help against droughts on Earth. A common counterplan was for the negative to argue in favor of desalinization of water. While there are disadvantages to run against desalinization, there is a gaping hole in the solvency story. Namely, desalinization doesn't protect us against killer asteroids. This is what is known as a solvency deficit. Affirmative teams will always say the Plan solves better, its up to the negative team to illustrate how the Counter plan solves the exact same problems, all of the problems, in ways that don't have flaws as the affirmative plan.

Topical Counterplans

Finally, is the issue of topicality. This answer to counterplans is a bit more controversial than the others because it gets technical and procedural. Topicality is an argument normally brought up by the Negative team that claims the Affirmative is not arguing a case that supports the Resolution. When the affirmative argues against a counterplan sing topicality, it sounds like this. "The negative team has the responsibility to disprove the resolution, and therefore must only advance counterplans that are non-topical." Perhaps an example would help. Let's say the topic is the regulation of guns. The affirmative argues that we should ban the sale of assault rifles. The negative says that it would be better to mandate smart gun technology for assault rifles. As you can see, there is a forced choice between the plan and counterplan, because one requires a ban on assault rifles, but the other still allows their sale. But both plans are a form of gun regulation. Some affirmative debaters argue that regardless of which plan you vote for, you are voting in favor of gun regulation, and should therefore cast your ballot for the affirmative team. This theory is not universally accepted, but it is at least an option that you may want to explore.

These are three simple generic ways to answer counterplans: the disadvantage, the solvency deficit, and topicality. If these tactics still seem inadequate, I urge you to watch the permutation lesson for another devastating strategy against the counterplan. Counterplans, in general, risk complicating and confusing debates that would otherwise be straight-forward, but you don't need to succumb to that pitfall. Keep your answers simple, reasonable, and intuitive and you will begin to see all types of ways to refute counterplans.

Permutations

There is another strategy that has been developed to answer counterplans, and it requires its own section. Imagine a debate where the affirmative proposes a plan, and the negative proposes a counterplan. One expects the second affirmative to make typical responses, like a disadvantage to the counterplan, or a solvency takeout. But, this particular debater argues that the judge can vote for passing the plan, *and* counterplan. This approach comes up in debate frequently and there is a theoretical argument called a "permutation," or sometimes shortened to "perm," that helps clarify exactly what the obligations of both the affirmative and the negative team are to prove. Therefore, in this section we'll be discussing stock issues and competition, then we will talk about protecting ground, and finally some examples and applications.

Competition

Let's contextualize competition and stock issues to better understand the perm: Competition is an argument that tests whether or not there is a forced choice between the plan and the counterplan. To understand an idea like "competition," it's helpful to look to some other theoretical arguments to provide some context. This takes us back to a fundamental part of debate theory, stock issues. And, specifically what the affirmative team is obligated to address to win a debate. Generally speaking, if the affirmative teams meets their stock issue burdens, then they win the round. A negative team might decide to run a disadvantage explaining why the affirmative advocacy would cause more harm than good. If the DA in fact outweighs the solvency of the affirmative team, then this is considered a good test of competition. But the idea of competition also applies to counterplans. For instance, what would happen if the affirmative team gave $1 million to help feed the poor, and in response the negative team states that $1 million isn't enough money so they offer a counterplan that feeds the poor with $2 million dollars. Is this a competitive strategy? In other words, are you forced to choose between these two strategies? The answer is no. You could approve of the $1 million plan, as well as the additional $1 million plan. The point is, you are not forced to choose the plans. Ultimately, if you vote for both plans, one of them was the original affirmative plan, and they deserve to win the debate.

This is why the permutation is an important concept. It protects the affirmative's ground by exposing that there is no forced choice between the affirmative and negative advocacies. An affirmative could essentially argue that we can first give the homeless $1 million, and then give them another million. The point is, giving more does not prove that the plan is an inherently bad idea. In fact, it is a good idea and we should do more of it. It might be helpful to think about stock issues here: does the affirmative still have solvency? Without a specific DA or critique explaining why the affirmative team doesn't have the solvency, most would consider the "offer more money" counterplan to be non-competitive.

This is really important because theoretically every negative team would win every round because they could simply do more than the affirmative does. Negative teams would simply offer more money, support, and resources in order to claim more solvency. All without explaining why the affirmative strategy creates some risk. Can you see how this protects the Affirmative's ground? The 2nd affirmative speaker needs to recognize the possible use of a perm and be ready to execute the perm in their speech. This is because a perm is usually applied in direct refutation to the negative team's strategy outlined in 1st negative speech. Remember there are so few opportunities to defend your positions in a debate round, force the debate to focus competition in the 2nd affirmative and be prepared to continue this discussion throughout the rebuttals.

Arguing Permutations

You should be thinking: Ok, that's all pretty cool. But, how do I actually execute a perm in a debate round? There are differing opinions, but the following three approaches will you get acquainted with them.

1. **Testing competition**. Some will say the perm is "simply a test of competition" meaning that they're not actually asking to do both the plan and the counterplan or critique. They're instead asking "if" you could and maybe should do both, but NOT actually advocating both. They hope to convince their judge that this infraction is enough to punish the negative team for stealing affirmative ground. The emphasis here is that the perm is just a theoretical argument.

2. **Advocating the perm**. The other option is the perm as advocacy, where the 2nd affirmative speaker is willing defend all or part of both the affirmative and negative strategies. An important note: be creative with your perms. There are many common questions people have about perms. Do you need to advocate all of what your opponents were defending? Not

always. Be creative in finding ways to combine both strategies together and find ways how the two strategies actually complement each other.

3. **Net-benefit to the perm**. Just because you can perm, should you always do so? This depends on who you ask. Generally speaking, the 2nd affirmative speaker will want to identify a "net benefit to the perm," or some additional good thing that happens with the permutation. Being able to articulate a net benefit to the perm is the strongest position for the affirmative to be in. Many in the debate community would suggest if there's no net-benefit to the perm, what's the point advocating the perm.

Example Permutation

For our first example let's say you and your partner research an awesome plan idea for cleaning-up beaches. You do rigorous research and know all of the good things that come from beach cleanups, and you develop an awesome case. Instead of arguing against beach cleanup, your opponents instead suggest that the real problem globally is war. The first negative speaker suggests a counter plan, which is to fiat world peace. The first negative speaker goes on to articulate that the impacts of world peace are clearly better than any impacts of clean beaches, therefore the negative team should win. Can you perm this counterplan? Does it test the competition of the affirmative strategy? This might sound intimidating at first because the counter plan seems very strong, but rest assured the permutation offers solace here. You might be strategic and how you run a perm in this example and defend two simultaneous arguments.

1. Suggest a perm as a test of competition. Articulate that the perm merely asks can you both do beach cleanups and advocate world peace? I hope so! There doesn't seem to be any reason why clean beaches and world peace conflict with each other. So the test of competition is an argument about ground and fundamental questions about stock issues, asking the judge to consider the affirmative ground as intact.
2. Defend the perm as advocacy. The second affirmative speaker should stand up and confidently perm the plan and the counter plan simultaneously. And additionally claim a net benefit to the perm, which is that clean beaches and a world free of war is the best possible option, and there are no reasons why clean beaches and ending war conflict with each other. The perm is net beneficial because it has benefits from both the plan and the counterplan, in total the perm is a stronger position than solely the counterplan.

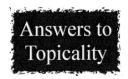
Answers to Topicality

I have heard innumerable judges of debate. Talk about how much they hate when the argument of topicality is brought up in a round. Yet, the argument is brought up so often that you have to conclude that there are plenty of competitors that are winning with it. It is just good strategy to prepare responses for such a common argument. Regardless of whether or not you consider topicality to be a generally good argument. We are going to cover some of the most basic responses to topicality by first, going over the argument known as we meet. Then counter standards and finally how to respond to impacts. It is important that you are familiar with the topicality lesson before going any further Because many of the references made in this lesson come from that video.

Meeting the Counter-definition

The first general response is known as we meet. It can also be considered I meet if this is a one on one debate. We meet is typically what you say in team debates. This is a direct response to the violation stock issue of topicality. If you remember, the violation of topicality essentially argues that the affirmative isn't supporting the resolution as is their burden. This argument is predicated on the negative offering up a counter definition. So when the negative offers up a counter-definition and the affirmative says we can work with that, you can make the we meet our argument. Essentially saying, hey, no harm, no foul. This argument is considered defense rather than offense. But, it is 100% defense. If you meet the counter-definition and there is no violation Then there are no standards that you need to evaluate and there are no impacts too with the topicality position in and of itself. Topicality goes away in its entirety and it is not a voting issue.

Counter Standards

The second common response to topicality are counter standards. Recall that standards are reasons why you would prefer the negatives interpretation over the affirmatives. So a counter standard is a reason to prefer the affirmative's interpretation over the negative. Two of the most common counter standards are debatability and fairness. Debatability is the argument that whatever the case is that the affirmative has decided to talk about is being debated in pop culture, in politics, or just right now. Whereas fairness is basically just the affirmative asking the judge to determine whether or not it is a fair interpretation. This is an answer back to a standard in which the best interpretation is the one that should be fair. There are many ways to interpret a resolution, and as long as the affirmative team has fairly defined it and defined it in a way that it is debatable, then there should be no other reason to vote them down on topicality.

Impact Responses

Next, let's talk about how to respond to impacts on topicality. The most common impact that the negative gives is that topicality is a voter, and many people don't know how to respond to this, but there are ways to respond on the impact level.

1. **Don't vote on potential abuse**. The first is, don't vote on potential abuse. Basically saying that the only reason topicality is a voter is if the affirmative has taken ground away from the negative team. As long as the negative team still is able to run disadvantages without the affirmative delinking from them, or other counter-warrants to these arguments, then there is no reason to vote against the affirmative team. They have a disadvantage on the negative one way or the other.

2. **The reverse voting issue**. Another common response to the impact level of topicality is a bit more controversial. And it is known as the reverse voting issue. Basically this states that if the negative team loses topicality, then you should vote against them and for the affirmative. There are some reasons that people give for it. For instance, the claim that topicality is at its core a time suck or a way of making the affirmative waste time on one argument In order to undercover other arguments. So basically, the sit dates that if the negative team kicks topicality or if they drop it in their next speech, then it becomes a reverse voting Voting issue. Another common warrant people give for a reversed voting issue, is the standard of fairness that if topicality is an all or nothing position for the affirmative to win or lose on, then it should be an all or nothing position for the negative team to lose on.

When the affirmative challenges the negative with a reverse voting issue, sometimes it results in the negative team collapsing down to just topicality, making that argument the one and only thing that is going to be determining the winner of the round. This is what's known as suicide T. It's called this because the only thing that is going to win the ballot is the topicality argument. You live or you die by this one position. The topicality argument is ubiquitous within competitive debate, but that means you should be able to predict responses fairly easily, Some of those most common responses are the we meet, counter standards, and impact responses.

These are solid, predictable answers, that debaters can make on any topicality argument. These are some of the fundamental arguments. You will find that there are more nuanced arguments that you can make depending on the topic of debate. Perhaps understanding and practicing these responses will finally satisfy all those judges that talk about how much they dislike topicality. In debate rounds and they'll start voting against it.

The Opposition Block

When teams debate, as opposed to one-on-one debate, there is very often a moment where all of the debaters, from both teams, have each been given the opportunity to construct argument and they transition into rebuttals. The only thing is that very often it is the negative, or opposition that is given the first rebuttal. This phenomenon is commonly called the "opposition block." Debaters should be aware of this transition, and plan accordingly. There strategies that the negative, and affirmative ought to prepare in advance in order to best adapt to the opposition block.

The negative debaters can coordinate which arguments each are going to cover. Since the negative is given two back-to-back speeches, they can deliver it effectively like one long speech. The benefits of this approach are, first, that it overwhelms the affirmative debater that follows the block. This is very simple arithmetic: it is very difficult to respond to a twelve minute speech with only four minutes. And second, it avoids a redundant rebuttal. It is too easy to fall into pattern of repeating the arguments from the last negative constructive, in the first negative rebuttal. Instead of maintaining the attention of the audience, it might lead them to boredom. It is also much easier for your opponent to rebut arguments if they are repeated several times, because the time it takes to repeat the argument is essentially wasted.

As the affirmative, it might be fairly intimidating being in a debate against a team that understands how to use the opposition block to their advantage. Still there are a few strategies that help to even the playing field. First, focus energy on their offense. Remember, not all arguments are equally potent, some are critical to the round, and dropping them are automatic losses. Many people put topicality in this category, but any off-case argument that is well-formed is potentially dangerous. Make sure you have at least one response for each. Second, group as many arguments together, and offer a single response. If you have done you job in the constructives, then this could be very efficient if you cross-apply some of your

Opposition block: a phenomenon common in team debate where the last negative constructive is immediately followed by the first negative rebuttal, effectively giving the negative team back-to-back speeches.

previous arguments to theirs. Third, leave time for your voters. There might be very few. There may only be one. Don't think that is inadequate. If you have handled all of your opponent's arguments, then having a single, solid voter could be seen as a sign of confidence.

The opposition block is a phenomenon that doesn't appear in every type of debate, but if you find yourself facing an opposition block there are things that you can do to best prepare. On the negative, use the block to your advantage as much as possible to overwhelm your opponent and maximize the credibility of the whole team. On the affirmative, take out your opponent's offense, be efficient, and don't ignore the offense on your side.

Rebuttals

In the game of chess there are different stages that have been studied and even been given names. Now, these names aren't very creative, but still there are distinguishable stages in the game. For instance, at the very beginning of the game it's known as the opening, and many chess players memorize the moves that they're going to make for a good ten to twelve moves. Once they get out of the opening they are in what's called the mid game, and they use tactics to respond to the movements of their opponent. But, by the end, they enter in what's known as the end-game, and in debate there are similar stages. For instance, the first couple of speeches by the leaders when they're giving their constructives, you could consider those the openings in which both teams are laying out their strategy and their fundamental arguments. And when the members come up and give their speeches that would be the mid game. But when you enter into the rebuttals; that's the end game. That's when you need to seal the deal. That's when you need to convince the judge to vote for your side or against the other. Ultimately rebuttals are incredibly important speeches in the game of debate, and we're going to study them right now by first, looking at the difference between offense and defense. Secondly we're going to cover an idea known as impact calculus. And finally talk about how to organize rebuttal speeches.

Offense Versus Defense

The first important thing to understand about rebuttals is the difference between offense and defense. Many people are familiar with these two terms when it comes to a sports analogy, so I'm going to roll with that. Let's think about basketball, that's one of the easiest analogies. You can have offense, which is actually putting the ball through the basket and scoring points. But you can prevent your opponents from scoring points themselves, and both of them are required in order to have a successful team and the winning outcome. The same thing is true in debate. You're scoring points for yourself you're gaining favor with the judge, and they are going to be more likely to vote for you when you have offense. But you also want to prevent your opponents from gaining favor with the judge, and that's where defense comes in. Let's say you are on the affirmative. When you are giving your stock issues—making arguments—that is your offense. When you are answering disadvantages, for instance no link, non-unique, answers like that, then that is your defense. So you want to have both of these elements present within your debate. But my advice in rebuttals is for you to highlight the offense. Highlight it at the beginning, and at the end. Just like in your constructive speeches, you want to have somewhat of a thesis. Something that is the focus of your debate, of your rebuttal. And you want that focus to be the offense. But do not neglect the defense. You want to remind the judge that you have answered your opponent's arguments that you have taken out there offense, and so those defensive arguments still need to be included. But do not highlight them as your thesis, because that is not how you're going to gain, that's not how you're going to win the round. You need to focus on the offense. So when you're on the affirmative, point out how you were winning all of your stock issues. When you are on the negative you want to point out how you had successfully argued topicality or disadvantages or counter plans. But you also want to include somewhere in the middle, the meat of your rebuttal, explanations about how your defense is preventing your opponents from gaining the ballot in this round.

Impact Calculus

Aside from offense and defense, the next important thing that people need to know about rebuttals is a concept known as impact calculus. Now this sounds like a really fancy term but it's pretty simple. Basically, what you're doing is trying to convince the judge that you have secured the most impacts in the round; that your arguments are heavier, they are weightier, than your opponents. There are a couple of easy ways to do this and they are broken down into probability and magnitude. These concepts should not be foreign to you.

1. **Probability**. Probability means that there is a high likelihood that the impacts are going to happen now. Remember impacts could be good or bad. In the affirmative case, the impacts that you have are on your solvency that you are explaining how many people are saved, or how much suffering you reduce due to the plan that you are proposing, or just to the advocacy that you are in favor of. Even in a value round there are still impacts, and the probability of those impacts happening are one way for you to convince the judge that they ought to vote on your side. The inverse of that is magnitude.

Closing arguments in the Amistad case.

In 1839, dozens of people were kidnapped from Africa and imprisoned on the Spanish slave ship, La Amistad. The prisoners revolted and killed some of their captors. They were then captured by the US navy and imprisoned in Connecticut, where slavery was still legal at the time. Abolitionists hired lawyers to to defend the Africans, and the case went all the way to the supreme court, where John Quincy Adams gave an impassioned closing argument that was published to a wide audience, and eventually represented in a feature film. These closing arguments were key to the Supreme Court's decision to rule in favor of the mutineers.

2.**Magnitude**. Magnitude is just how large the impacts are how important they are. This is why many debate rounds devolve into discussions about nuclear war, because nuclear war has a high magnitude impact. Lots of people are going to suffer. There's going to be massive amounts of death. The thing is, though, that nuclear war has a low probability, so you have to balance these two out. One reason why people don't vote in favor of the nuclear war scenario is specifically because of how low the probability is. Especially considering what the topic is that you might be debating. Let's say the case was about increasing technology in schools, and somehow your opponent draws some link to be between including iPads for students and nuclear proliferation. That's a tenuous link and a very low probability, yet high magnitude impact. So in rebuttals you might not be able to outweigh on the magnitude level, but you point out how incredibly low probability the disadvantage is. And that's a way for you to win in the rebuttals, for you to argue that your impacts about education outweigh nuclear war, not on magnitude, but on probability. You still want to argue the magnitude of your arguments even if somebody is making a ridiculous claim to nuclear war. Regardless these are two of the most stable ways to argue a rebuttal.

Organization

The last thing, and perhaps the most difficult when it comes to rebuttals, is how do you organize this speech. The reason this is difficult is because you have been in a debate for half an hour, forty five minutes discussing issues over and over again in a particular order, and often times debaters follow that order all the way through, even through rebuttals. I'm here to tell you that you might want to switch up the organization when it comes to rebuttals. It's a bad idea just to repeat the arguments in the order that everyone has been hearing them. The best thing for you do is to prioritize these arguments. So what you ought to do is create a list of voters. Voters are critical elements within the debate that ought to result in a ballot one way or the other. Typical voters include topicality, a high magnitude disadvantage, fulfilling stock issues. These things are typical voting issues, and you can explain why you are winning those on a multitude of different levels. Even if you are on the affirmative perhaps you have argued successfully to turn a disadvantage. That turn, in and of itself can be a voter, and you can make that into its own issue. You could prioritize that as the most important issue in the round.

I urge you not to just follow the organization that you have been following throughout the round. It is impossible. You can't cover everything. Not only that, if you try to, you're more than likely going to lose the judge's attention. So divide up the entire debate into three or four voters and divide up the time that you spend on each in the rebuttal equally. Prioritize those voters into a hierarchy. Start with the most important one. Your best argument should be the one that begins the rebuttal, and the rebuttal should sound like this. "If you don't vote for the first voter. Then you can vote for the second, and even if you don't vote for the second then you can vote for the third." This "even if" a pattern that you develop is kind of like setting up a gauntlet that the opposition has to go through in order to successfully win this round. It sets it up as sounding as if there is a lot of work that the judge has to do in order to vote for your opponent. Make it sound as though there are multiple reasons to vote for you by organizing your rebuttal into voters, not just regurgitating the round thus far.

So there you have it, three basic strategies on how to approach rebuttals; offense versus defense, impact calculus, and organization based on voters. Debate and chess hold a lot of similarities, and one of those similarities is how each of those go through different stages. The rebuttals are just like the endgame in chess. Incredibly important if you want to win the game in chess, and if you want to win in debate, you've got to know how to close. And rebuttals are your chance to shine. Make sure that you make these memorable. That you focus on the critical issues. You can't cover everything. Rebuttal speeches are very short, and the debate to this point was very long. Don't even try to cover all the arguments, just the most important ones. Make sure you balance your offense and defense. Make sure that you have probability. And magnitude and make sure that your voters shine.

Chapter 8
Video Setup

Introduction

Early attempts at using a file-sharing approach to asynchronous debate proved inefficient. In theory, waiting for video downloads and managing storage space don't sound like insurmountable obstacles, but in practice each recorded speech compounds the frustration that comes with using video as a medium for asynchronous debate. This is especially true when one considers the myriad of free applications that exist to facilitate video sharing in today's information age. As of yet, there is no online service that is specifically tailored for the needs of asynchronous debate; fortunately, there are free applications that, with a little bit of management, make it possible. This chapter is going to go through the simple steps you need to take to setup an online video debate.

Video Sharing Applications

There are several video sharing sites that exist, but by far, the most popular is YouTube. This website has seemingly unlimited space for users to upload videos, simple privacy settings, and several other features like the ability to make playlists and simple video editing tools. We are going to focus on this particular video sharing application, as well as other Google applications, in this textbook because of how accessible it is to the public at large.

Getting an account is easy and free. Because YouTube is owned by Google, you will need to create a Google account. If you already have gmail, then you already have an account. If not, go to google.com.

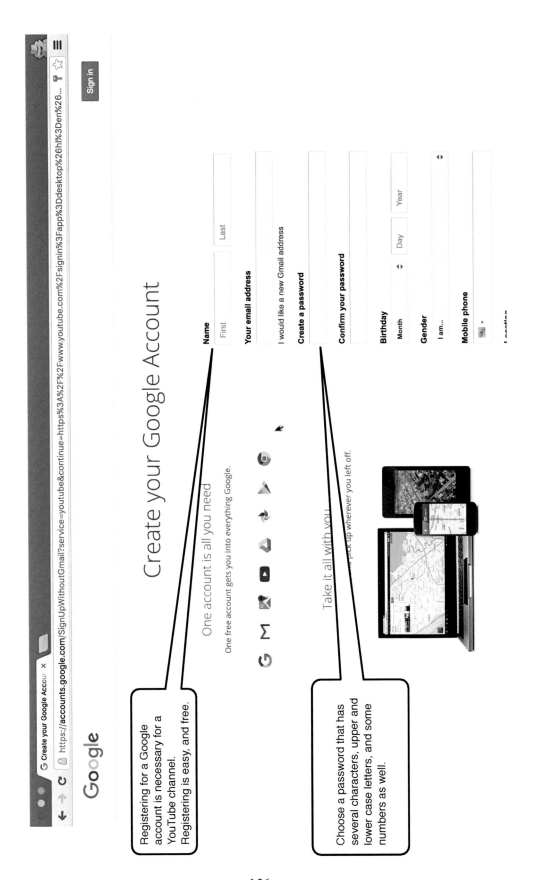

← → C 🔒 https://accounts.google.com/SignUpWithoutGmail?service=youtube&continue=https%3A%2F%2Fwww.youtube.com%2Fsignin%3Fapp%3Ddesktop%26hl%3Den%26...

Sign in

Google

Create your Google Account

Registering for a Google account is necessary for a YouTube channel.
Registering is easy, and free.

One account is all you need

One free account gets you into everything Google.

Take it all with you

Pick up wherever you left off.

Choose a password that has several characters, upper and lower case letters, and some numbers as well.

Name

First   Last

Your email address

I would like a new Gmail address

Create a password

Confirm your password

Birthday

Month   Day   Year

Gender

I am...

Mobile phone

Once you have an account, and have accessed the YouTube application, you should take the time to change a few default settings. In particular, it is highly suggested that you change the security settings for the videos you will upload. To do this you will need to access your creator studio by clicking on the picture in the upper right hand corner of the screen. This will bring up the creator studio button.

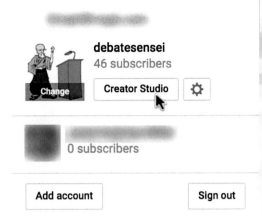

debatesensei
46 subscribers

Change   Creator Studio   ⚙

0 subscribers

Add account   Sign out

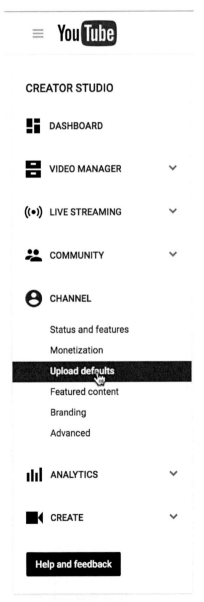

≡ You Tube

CREATOR STUDIO

▪▪ DASHBOARD

▤ VIDEO MANAGER   ⌄

((•)) LIVE STREAMING   ⌄

👥 COMMUNITY   ⌄

👤 CHANNEL

    Status and features
    Monetization
    Upload defaults
    Featured content
    Branding
    Advanced

▮▮▮ ANALYTICS   ⌄

🎥 CREATE   ⌄

Help and feedback

Once you are in your creator studio, look at the menu on the left and select 'CHANNEL.' This will bring up another menu, and select 'Upload defaults.' The very first option on the resulting page is the privacy setting. There are three options. Public means that anyone can view the videos that you post, and they are searchable in YouTube. Unlisted means that your videos are not searchable in YouTube, so viewers much have the URL to the video if they want to watch it. Private means that videos are not searchable in YouTube, and viewers must be given special permission to watch the video by the account holder. We strongly urge you to select 'Unlisted' for your default setting to maintain privacy, but also to avoid the hassle of approving every viewer that wants to see your debate.

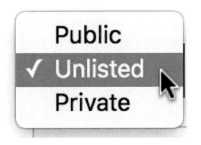

Public
✓ Unlisted
Private

 **Lighting**

Even for amateur producers of video content, lighting is a critical element for making good images. If you have the ability to shoot in natural outdoor light, that is ideal, and it's free! But for many people, shooting outdoors is inconvenient because they do not have availability during the day for recording debates, or there is too much noise outside for clear audio. If you find yourself in this situation, then you will need to think about how to setup lighting for the best shot possible.

Be sure to avoid the mistake of having too much backlighting. This is when the source of light come primarily from behind the subject. The result is that the person on camera looks like a talking silhouette. Instead, follow a standard three-point lighting configuration. The purpose of the three lights is to avoid distracting shadows on the object. Focused light is the best, but if all you have are lamps that you can arrange, then something is better than nothing. Be careful about using fluorescent light, because the camera will accentuate any flickering during recording.

Standard Three-Point Lighting

#3 Back Light

Object

#1 Key Light

#2 Fill Light

Cameras
The ubiquity of cameras is rapidly changing our society. Asynchronous debate wouldn't be possible if not for the widespread access to video recording. The result is a wide selection of options than you have when deciding to record, each with benefits and drawbacks.

Traditional video recorders have several settings and features that allow you to customize the look of your recording, so they should be considered an option. Some of the benefits include the ability to attach the camera to a stable tripod, the ability to zoom in and out to frame your shot, and the ability to add devices like remotes and microphones to add even greater quality to the recording. The biggest drawback to using a video camera is undoubtedly the cost, but if you have access to one, then you should seriously consider using it for your debates.

It is much more likely that you have access to a smartphone with video recording capabilities. This is sufficient for the purposes of asynchronous debate, but it is good to be aware of the shortcomings of recording with your phone. One drawback is that you need to think about how to place you phone while recording. There are specialty stands that are made for recording with you phone, but most people don't have one, and settle on propping up their phone on a flat surface. The most common outcome is an "upshot" of the speaker, which is rarely flattering. The alternative is to hold the phone while speaking, which gives the appearance of a selfie, but also occupies your hand while speaking. This is not necessarily a bad thing, but requires coordination, especially if you are using notes during your speech.

The third most common option is to simply use the camera built into a computer, or webcam. These cameras have become standard on laptops, and are fairly inexpensive to purchase for a desktop. The benefit is that they are easy to stabilize, and you also have a computer screen nearby for any evidence or notes that you want to reference during the speech. The computer screen, though, is also a drawback because it is easy to read your information off the screen. Speakers should practice spending most of the recording time looking directly into the camera.

Audio Sound is easily the most overlooked factor in producing a quality video, but there is a reason why some of the most famous YouTubers in the world are always on screen talking into a large microphone, or are wearing a headset with a built-in mic. Take the time to not only consider what audio equipment you are going to use, but also to test out your equipment before hand. There are a few options to consider when thinking about how to record the audio for your videos.

Practically all recording devices, whether they are laptops, smartphones, or video camera, have a built-in audio recorder that synchs with you video when recording. While this is convenient, there are some common draw backs. One is that the built-in device isn't always of the highest quality, so you have to place the microphone fairly close to the object, which then affects the framing of your shot. Another is that   if you are recording outside, any wind that might occur could be recorded, resulting in a loud static-like sound. Still, if you find that you built-in device is adequate for the purposes of asynchronous debate, consider yourself lucky as use it.

If your built-in device proves inadequate, a fairly inexpensive solution is to use a headset with microphone combination. These have become increasingly popular with gamers, as well as YouTube commentators. The benefits are that the microphone can be placed close to the speaker's mouth to pick up every word, as well as avoid a lot of the ambient noise in the room, or other echoes. These headset are somewhat limited because they don't necessarily plug into video cameras or phones, but work well with computers that have cameras installed. Additionally, you have to deal with the visual of speaking the apparatus on your head.

A third option is to purchase a traditional microphone that plugs directly into your video recorder. This might get costly if you are not careful, but the quality is unparalleled. These microphones still need to be place close to the speaker's mouth, so it is likely that it will be in the shot while you are speaking. Be careful about breathing into the microphone, as it will cause distracting pops in the recording.

Chapter 9
Video Debate

Citing Sources
- In-text
- Description Section
- Annotations

Visual Aids
- Best Practices

Cross-examination
- Hangouts On Air

Video sharing has had a dramatic affect on the daily lives of Americans, but one of the more intriguing uses has been amongst musicians, who used to have to live in close proximity to each other to practice performances, and record tracks. Now, musicians can live thousands of miles apart and send recording back and forth. Artists can listen to a single musician, and contribute their own additions to a song until it forms into a complex and sophisticated piece. Applications and websites have been developed to aid in the collaboration process. For instance, the actor Joseph Gordon-Levitt started HitRecord, and online collaboration website that allows musicians, and other artists, to work together on projects, even if they never met each other.

Joseph Gordon-Levitt

We are just now beginning to see the affects of video sharing on debate as an art-form. While this is an exciting time for debaters, there are remarkably few resources that help beginners to participate in video asynchronous debates. The purpose of this chapter builds off the last and introduces some best practices for this nascent activity. Some of the possibilities that video asynchronous debate creates, that do not exist in traditional debate, include source citations, visual aids, transition options, and remote cross-examination.

Citing Sources in Asynchronous Debate

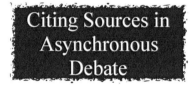

Up to this point, the preparation for recording asynchronous debate is not much different than preparing to record anything, but there are unique expectations for these recordings that you don't find in other areas. One of those expectations is the citation of sources that you cite in your speech. In traditional debates, it is easy to meet this expectation by verbally stating the source, but when video is medium, there are more options, and debaters must know which method they are going to use before they start recording.

1. **Verbal citations.** The easiest way to cite sources is to simply provide a verbal citation during the course of your speech. There are obvious benefits to taking this approach. It is easy to incorporate verbal source citations. It is also good practice for live debates, where verbal source citation is the only option to introduce your evidence. There are drawbacks, though. Verbal source citation takes up valuable speaking time, and if there is

a strict time-limit, this can impede on the number, or detail of the arguments you want to introduce. Additionally, verbal source citation might cause even the best of speakers to stumble as they speak, resulting in several "retakes" of the recording, or just a less-than-professional appearance of delivery.

2. **In the description section.** Video asynchronous debate allows debaters new methods for introducing source citations that are modern and dynamic. One method is to simply add the source citations into the description section of the video. There are several benefits; one being that viewers can easily locate your sources while listening to your speech, rather than trying to parse out your source citations from the recorded speech. Another being that there are already several standards for source citations, like MLA and APA formatting, that can be borrowed and incorporated into the description section to offer a uniform look to all entries. In fact, it is great practice for students that have to produce a works cited, or bibliography for their assignments anyway. The drawback to including citations in the description is that there is likely a character limit (for YouTube, it is 5,000 characters). Source citations require a lot of characters, so a debater might reach this limit with relatively few sources.

3. **Annotations**. Another method of source citation that video asynchronous debate affords is the ability to add annotations to your video. YouTube makes this easy with simple editing tools. There are several types of annotations that are offered, each with a different look and function. You can access the annotation options through the video manager, and select to edit any particular video. Be sure to choose which type of annotation you want to include, because some are more appropriate than others. For instance, the 'Title' option will place the words you enter in the center of the screen in large block letter, whereas the 'Note' option uses smaller lettering and can be moved around the screen. Based on these features, a 'Note' would be more appropriate than a 'Title.'

It is uncommon in traditional debate for speakers to plan on incorporating visual aids into their speeches. The amount of planning that it would require to anticipate which visual aids might be useful in a debate make it an unattractive option. But, because asynchronous debate allows for greater preparation time between speeches, and the rapidity at which graphs, charts and other visual aids can be produced electronically, the possibility for the integration of visual aids into debates is now a reality. There are many different types of visual aids for you to choose from.

1. **Charts and graphs.** One category of visual aids is the use of graphs, tables and charts. While these types of visual aids can be very effective when communicating numerical information, they're not often considered a favorite type of visual aid because they don't add much attention or excitement to the speech itself. That does not mean to avoid the use of these particular visual aids, just be very considerate about when you use them. For instance, if you want to show how something has increased or decreased over time, then a line graph might be a very appropriate choice for that information. If, on the other hand, you want to compare different quantities of things then a bar chart might be the most appropriate.

2. **Pictures**. Another type of visual aid is to simply use photographs. You need to make sure that your picture is large enough for your audience to see. Be critical about the quality of the image that you're using. Enlarging some images will just make them pixellated and people won't be able to identify detail. Make sure that you mount a printed photograph on sturdy board like foam core.

3. **Audio and video.** While watching or listening to a clip can be fun additions to your speech, you need to be careful that they are not replacing you as a speaker. Even a 30 second clip in a 5 minute speech is a significant amount of time. So make sure you consider how long your clip is that you're going to include. Additionally, you need to make sure that you have the right technology to deploy the audio or video aid that you're going to use. This is not as simple as it sounds. Just pulling up a video from YouTube sometimes means that there is a commercial that is added onto the beginning. This can skew your entire time allocation, so make sure that you know that it is queued up to the exact moment that you need.

Regardless of which type of aid that you choose, you will need to take the time and plan how you are going to incorporate it. Keep visual aids simple. They should make what you are discussing easier to understand, not more complicated. This should require little or no explanations. Do not go overboard on labelling parts of your visual aide. Do not incorporate too many numbers or words. If your visual aide is too busy, people are going to get caught up in the image and stop listening to your arguments.

Make sure visual aids are large enough for viewers to see. Is it a caption that takes up a small section, or will it take up the entire screen? Whichever one you choose will determine what visual aids are appropriate. If your visual aid includes words, make sure that you don't use too many fonts. Many fonts will just distract people, sometimes making the words themselves illegible. Also, the font that you choose says a lot about your professionalism. It's best to choose a font that does not draw people's attention away from your central message.

Make sure that you use color effectively. Make sure that you're focusing on the goals of the speech. Too many distracting colors means that people stop listening to you and start looking at the color scheme that you chose for your visual aid. And most of all, don't fall silent when your visual aid is revealed. It doesn't speak for itself, you speak with it. Visual aids do add complexity to your speech, but they also add a level of sophistication that helps people understand your information.

 In traditional debates, nothing can bore an audience more than a long rambling monolog with no organization. While that is still true for asynchronous debates, there are a number of options that are available to create organization and structure to your videos, and entire debates.

Within the Video

The first type of transitions to consider are the ones that happen within a single video. Even simple video editing software invariably offers standard transitions that you can drop between segments of video. It is strongly suggested that you choose very simple traditions, like 'fade to black' where the image steadily darkens until the entire screen is black, then lightens to reveal the next section of the video. You might also choose a 'cross-fade' where one segment slowly gives way to the next. The potential problem with this selection is that you might experience an overlap between the audio as well, resulting in incoherent double-talk for a short while.

If you shot your entire video in one take, then you will need to find appropriate moments to split the file so that transitions can be inserted. If you do not want to, or are unable to split your raw video file, then using the annotations mentioned earlier is an option. This time, the most appropriate option might be to include a 'Title' to indicate that you are moving on to another section of your speech.

Between Videos

The other type of transition that is important to create is the transitions between speeches. This is where playlists become useful. A playlist is a series of videos that are grouped together in a particular order, and are played automatically without stop. Think of it as listening to a music album. You could listen to one song and stop, or you can just play all of the songs in the album in the order that the artist put them. Luckily, creating playlists is easy.

To create a playlist using YouTube, you first need to go to your Video Manager. Instead of opening your videos, though, select the Playlist option from the menu, and then select 'New Playlist.' You will be prompted to give your new playlist a name. Make sure that it is simple, yet descriptive. You will also be given the choice of privacy setting. It is suggested that you make the playlist unlisted.

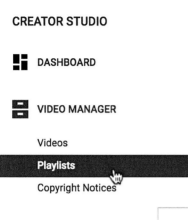

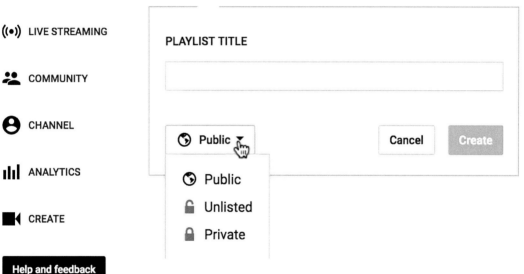

Once you have the playlist created, you can add videos. Under every YouTube video there is a button that says 'Add to.' Clicking this button allows you to add the video to the playlist that you created. You should see the title of the playlist upon clicking the button, or you can type in the title in the search bar that appears. Once you have found the playlist to which you want to add the video, then check the box to the left of the title and the video in question will be added to the end of the list of videos.

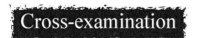
Cross-examination

One of the most difficult features of traditional debate to recreate asynchronistically is that of cross-examination. As we learned in Chapter 4, cross-examination is the question-and-answer period that happens during the course of certain debate formats. It is a popular moment in debate because there is direct interaction between the two opposing sides, and there is an art-form to asking difficult questions. Needless to say, synchronistic debate does not easily facilitate this feature, but there are some great applications that are free to use, and create an atmosphere that allows for cross-examination. Again, we turn to a Google application, but this time the application is called 'Hangouts On Air.'

Hangouts On Air allows two, or more people with a Google account to record a conversation, and then automatically upload the recording to YouTube. Additionally, the application detects who is talking based on microphone output, and instantly activates the camera for the speaker. The result is a video that is easy to follow, and does well to capture the natural rhythm of cross-examination. There are a few steps that you need to follow to set one up.

1. **Know who your opponent is.** This should be intuitive, but make sure that you have the contact information for your opponent. If, for some reason, you want to hold a Hangouts On Air with more than one person, it would be a good idea to create a 'circle' with your G+ account (which is automatic with any google account) to put all of the people and easily send an invitation.

2. **Go to the Hangouts On Air homepage.** You can navigate to this page through your G+ profile. There is a menu on the left, and one of the options says 'Hangouts.' When you click that menu item, at the top of the next page there is a link for Hangouts On Air. Alternatively, you can go here https:// plus.google.com/hangouts/onair.

3. **Create a Hangout On Air.** The click the button on the homepage and a form appears. You need to give the hangout a name, and add an audience. The audience should include the person who you are going to cross-examine, or the circle that you created with the people you want to include. You can start the broadcast immediately, or schedule it at a later time.

4. **Record the Hangout.** You will be redirected to your G+ event page. From there you must click the start button. The recording will not start immediately, so you can have your audience check in before you start. Once you are ready, click the 'Start broadcast' button, and after a short countdown, you will be live. When you are done, make sure to hang up, and the recording will automatically be sent to YouTube.

Chapter 10
Debategraph Basics

Account Setup
- Registration
- Virtual Classrooms
- Making New Maps

Features
- Settings
- Map Tabs

Creating Ideas
- Nodes
- Adding Media

Cross Links
- Adding
- Viewing

Home Page

The home page for debategraph has four primary sections: the View Window, the Map Buttons, the Settings Menu, and the Map Tabs. Each section offers a limited amount of options that together create the capability to graph an unlimited amount of arguments

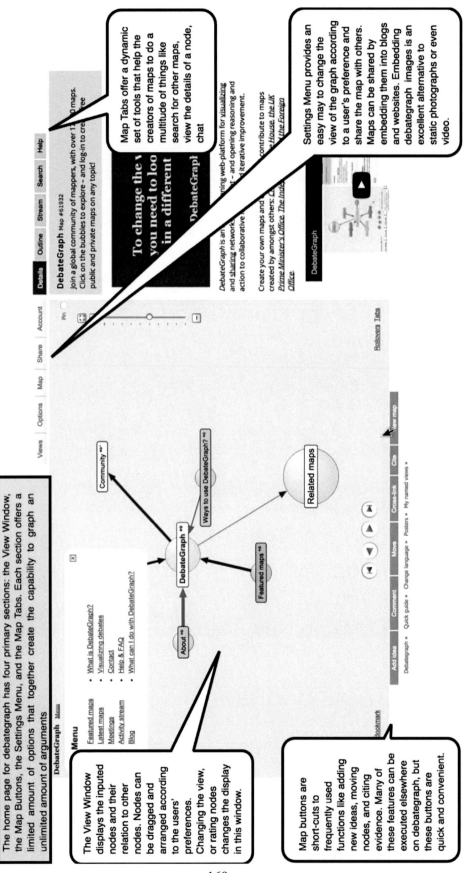

The View Window displays the inputed nodes and their relation to other nodes. Nodes can be dragged and arranged according to the users' preferences. Changing the view, or rating nodes changes the display in this window.

Map buttons are short-cuts to frequently used functions like adding new ideas, moving nodes, and citing evidence. Many of these features can be executed elsewhere on debategraph, but these buttons are quick and convenient.

Map Tabs offer a dynamic set of tools that help the creators of maps to do a multitude of things like search for other maps, view the details of a node, chat

Settings Menu provides an easy way may to change the view of the graph according to a user's preference and share the map with others. Maps can be shared by embedding them into blogs and websites. Embedding debategraph images is an excellent alternative to static photographs or even video.

Setting up Virtual Classrooms

Class management page

Class retrieved - click here for the class map

Your current classes   Argumentation and Debate COM-111-89934 ◇   New class

Name Argumentation and Debate COM-111-89934

Description

Welcome to Argumentation and Debate!! Students learn to construct, analyze, and deliver arguments in a structured format. Debate techniques are practiced during the course. This class is not a course in how to verbally fight. This class

Current students - to delete use ctrl/click   (Tick indicates confirmed)

Student, A (address@email.com) ✓
Student, A (address@email.com) ✓
Student, A (address@email.com) ✓
Student, A (address@email.com) ✓
Student, A (address@email.com) ✓
Student, A (address@email.com) ✓
Student, A (address@email.com) ✓

Enter additional students in format [email],[firstname],[lastname]

Update student list

Instructors can take advantage of the Classroom Management page to create virtual classrooms. This feature is ideal for online and hybrid courses, but is also a good way to manage discussions for classes scheduled in computer labs. These classrooms simultaneously maintain privacy of the students, while also allowing instructors to access their student's maps easily through a central organization

Debategraph keeps track of the courses you teach. Instructors need to have formatted rosters, with a course number, students' first name, last name, and email address. That information can be uploaded automatically, and will send out an invitation to all students whenever an assignment is created.

Students can be deleted if they are no longer in the class. New students can also be added manually.

170

Creating Assignments for Students

Class assignments

Select an assignment or create a new one

Current class assignments   Select assignment   ◇

New assignment name

Assignment description

Private assignment maps ▢   Select map grammar ◇   Create assignment

Select map grammar ◇

✓ Select map grammar

     Standard
     College debate
     Story
     Decision trees
     Hypothesis

Instructors will need to create assignments for each class of students. Every time an assignment is created, an invitation is sent to every email in the class with a link to the map.

The options that are selected at the time the assignment is created will apply to every student map at the time. Both student and instructor are designated as moderators to the map.

Navigating Classrooms

Classes are better suited to handle the information that students submit for their assignments, rather than having all students contribute ideas to a single map. If an instructor chooses to make all maps private, then only that instructor can see the student's map. Otherwise, students can navigate to the assignment node and view the maps of their classmates.

All maps are connected to a central node. Once you have created an assignment, you can follow the link to this node and easily observe the progress of each student.

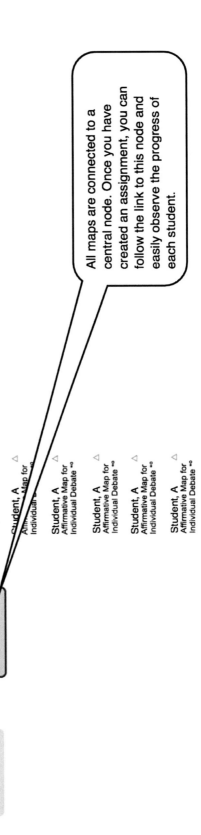

Student, A
Affirmative Map for
Individual Debate *°

Student, A
Affirmative Map for
Individual Debate *°

Student, A
Affirmative Map for
Individual Debate *°

Student, A
Affirmative Map for
Individual Debate *°

Student, A
Affirmative Map for
Individual Debate *°

Student, A
Affirmative Map for
Individual Debate *°

Student, A
Affirmative Map for
Individual *°

Student, A
Affirmative Map for
Individual Debate *°

Student, A
Affirmative Map for
Individual Debate *°

Student, A
Affirmative Map for
Individual Debate *°

Student, A
Affirmative Map for
Individual Debate *°

Affirmative Map for
Individual Debate *

Argumentation and
Debate COM-111-
89934 *

Registering for Debategraph

With the new Class Manager feature, registration for students is automatic. But if you find the need to register manually, the process is exceedingly simple.

Register

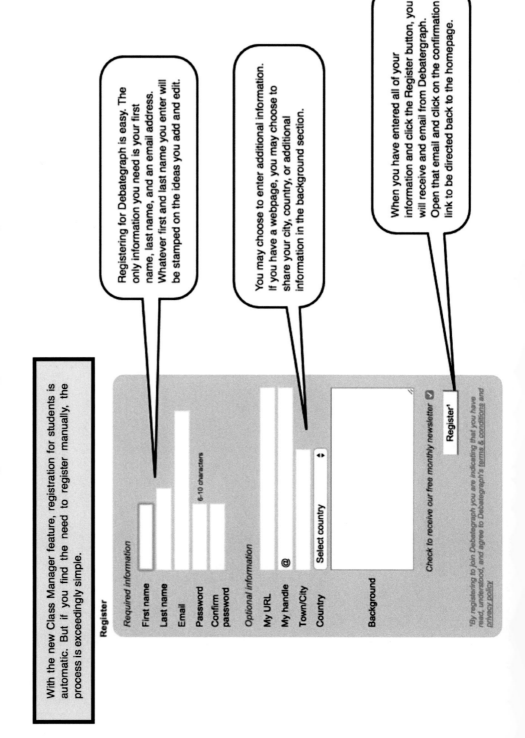

Registering for Debategraph is easy. The only information you need is your first name, last name, and an email address. Whatever first and last name you enter will be stamped on the ideas you add and edit.

You may choose to enter additional information. If you have a webpage, you may choose to share your city, country, or additional information in the background section.

When you have entered all of your information and click the Register button, you will receive and email from Debatergraph. Open that email and click on the confirmation link to be directed back to the homepage.

Creating Your Own Maps

There may be times that you will want to create your own maps. You can choose any title for your new map, but for this illustration we chose the title My First Map. New maps are useful to keep your work organized. Sometimes larger projects require several interrelated maps, each fulfilling their own function.

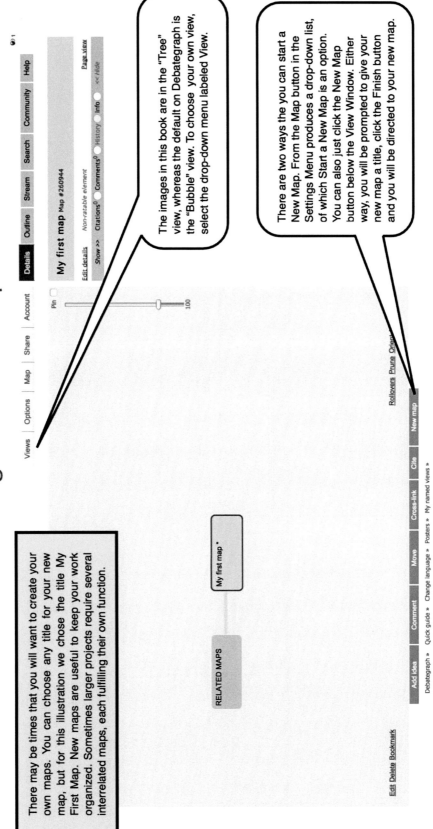

The images in this book are in the "Tree" view, whereas the default on Debategraph is the "Bubble" view. To choose your own view, select the drop-down menu labeled View.

There are two ways the you can start a New Map. From the Map button in the Settings Menu produces a drop-down list, of which Start a New Map is an option. You can also just click the New Map button below the View Window. Either way, you will be prompted to give your new map a title, click the Finish button and you will be directed to your new map.

Map Tabs

Details | Outline | Stream | Search | Community | Help

My first map Map #260944

Edit details   Non-ratable element   Page view
Show >>   Citations0 Comments0 History Info   << Hide

The Details tab lets you see all text, images, videos, widgets, and files associated with the idea selected on the map.

Details | Outline | Stream | Search | Community | Help

Find maps and ideas – via search or list

(A) Search for ideas & maps – or check box to Search citations

Search: All maps This map Affiliated maps
Search for: Any word All words Exact phrase
                                              Search

(B) Alternatively, display a list of:

All the ideas on this map   All my maps & bookmarks
All the ideas I have created on any map

The Search options let you find, move to, and cross-relate to any other idea on the current map, or the entire set of public maps.

Details | Outline | Stream | Search | Community | Help

14-15 NFA-LD: Develop the moon *
  Develop the moon. *
  1. Resolutional Analysis *
    D. Net benefits
    C. Build habitats on the moon. *

You can use the Outline tab in combination with the View Window to see the wider context and breadcrumb trail to the to of the map from your current location.

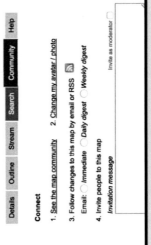

Details | Outline | Stream | Search | Community | Help

Connect

1. See the map community   2. Change my avatar / photo

3. Follow changes to this map by email or RSS
   Email: Immediate Daily digest Weekly digest

4. Invite people to this map
   Invitation message   Invite as moderator

The community tab has a number of settings and is divided into two sections: Community options is available to all members of the community, and Moderator options is only shown when you are the creator/moderator of the current map.

Details | Outline | Stream | Search | Community | Help

added a cross-relation to Warrant
#276775
Reducing the amount of waste in landfills is good for the environment
on Wednesday, June 26, 2013 12:06:00 AM
added a cross-relation to Warrant

The Stream tab provides a way for groups to collaborate in real-time for thinking through complex issues.

Details | Outline | Stream | Search | Community | Help

Click to open and close the Help articles

▶ Overview
▶ How do I explore the map?
▶ What do the different colors and arrows mean?
▶ The Different types of Views
▶ Add, Discuss, Move, Cross-link, Cite & New map buttons?
▶ The Details, Outline, Stream, Search & Community tabs?
▶ Contributing to an existing map?
▶ How do I edit the Detailed text?
▶ Heading, Summary & Detailed texts?

The Help tab has instructions and descriptions for Debategraph features

Settings for your new map

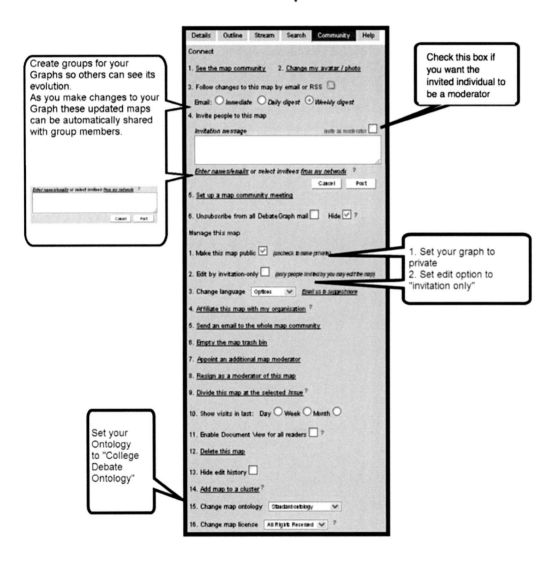

Create groups for your Graphs so others can see its evolution.
As you make changes to your Graph these updated maps can be automatically shared with group members.

Check this box if you want the invited individual to be a moderator

1. Set your graph to private
2. Set edit option to "invitation only"

Set your Ontology to "College Debate Ontology"

Adding an Idea

Views | Options | Map | Share | Account

In order to add an idea, click on Add Idea from the Map Buttons. This action will bring up the Entry Window, where you may enter in relevant information that helps to define your new node

Debategraph offers help and instructions throughout the website. In this case, a set of instructions and reminders appear above the Entry Window

You must enter a heading in order to save the node. A heading must be 70 characters or less, but should still represent one complete thought. This constraint is sometimes a challenge to work with, but it exists in order to maintain a level of legibility in the maps. You also have the option of adding a longer summary, which is up to 500 characters. When reading maps, the heading and summary are the most visible parts of a node, so you should choose the wording of each very carefully. A good technique is to think of the heading as the thesis to a short paragraph, and the short paragraph is the summary. You can also choose to have only a heading and no summary, which is useful if you wish to do line-by-line analysis of arguments

You will first need to choose what type of node this is going to be. There will always be a small selection of nodes from which to choose. These are suggested nodes, and you must select one of the options, but once saved, you can always change the node to any other type whenever you want. Because we are adding our first node to the map, our options are Resolution, Issue, and Protagonist. For a complete explanation of each type, see the next page

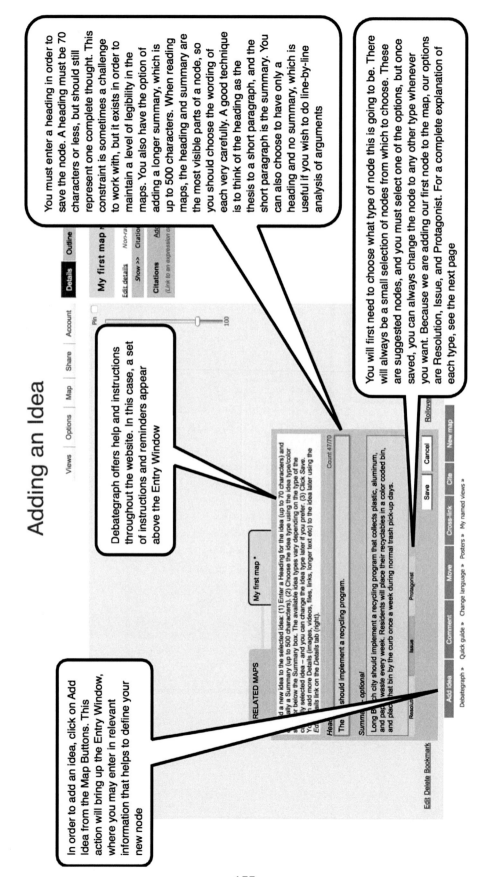

177

Basic Nodes

Nodes are the building blocks of maps in Debategraph, and there is a wide array to chose from. The nodes on this page represent the options available under the Competitive Debate Ontology. When adding new ideas, there are a selection of recommended nodes offered to help create your map. The suggestions are based upon relationships that commonly occur in competitive debate. You should not feel constrained to follow only these recommendations. They exist mainly to make mapping more efficient. The descriptions of each node can be found in Debategraph.

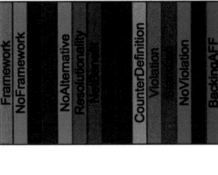

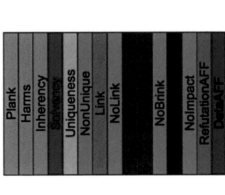

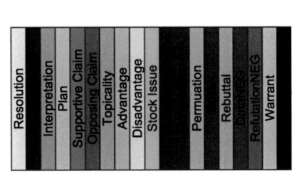

Editing Headings and Summaries

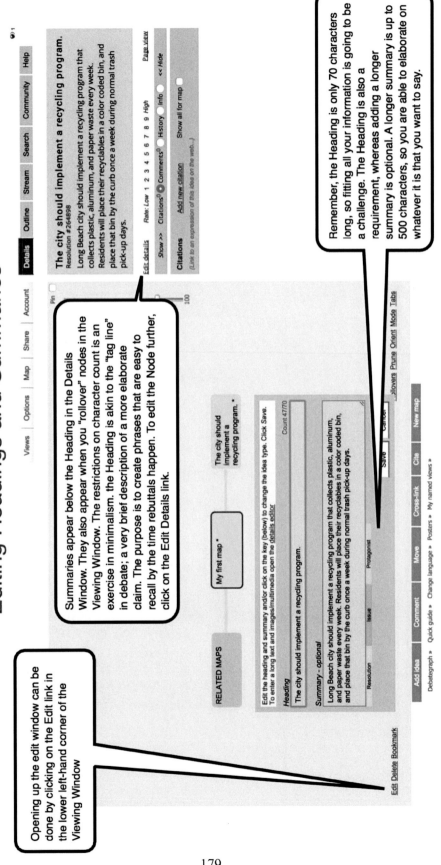

Views | Options | Map | Share | Account

Details | Outline | Stream | Search | Community | Help

The city should implement a recycling program.
Resolution #264898

Long Beach city should implement a recycling program that collects plastic, aluminum, and paper waste every week. Residents will place their recyclables in a color coded bin, and place that bin by the curb once a week during normal trash pick-up days.

Edit details   Rate: Low 1 2 3 4 5 6 7 8 9 High   Page view

Show >>   Citations⁰ ○ Comments⁰ ○ History ○ Info ○   << Hide

Citations   Add new citation   Show all for map
(Link to an expression of this idea on the web...)

Summaries appear below the Heading in the Details Window. They also appear when you "rollover" nodes in the Viewing Window. The restrictions on character count is an exercise in minimalism. the Heading is akin to the "tag line" in debate; a very brief description of a more elaborate claim. The purpose is to create phrases that are easy to recall by the time rebuttals happen. To edit the Node further, click on the Edit Details link.

Remember, the Heading is only 70 characters long, so fitting all your information is going to be a challenge. The Heading is also a requirement, whereas adding a longer summary is optional. A longer summary is up to 500 characters, so you are able to elaborate on whatever it is that you want to say.

Opening up the edit window can be done by clicking on the Edit link in the lower left-hand corner of the Viewing Window

RELATED MAPS

My first map *

The city should implement a recycling program. *

Edit the heading and summary and/or click on the key (below) to change the idea type. Click Save.
To enter a long text and images/multimedia open the details editor

Heading

The city should implement a recycling program.

Count 47/70

Summary - optional

Long Beach city should implement a recycling program that collects plastic, aluminum, and paper waste every week. Residents will place their recyclables in a color coded bin, and place that bin by the curb once a week during normal trash pick-up days.

Resolution   Issue   Protagonist

Save   Cancel   New map

Add idea   Comment   Move   Cross-link   Cite

...llovers Prune Orient Mode Tabs

Debategraph » Quick guide » Change language » Posters » My named views »

Edit Delete Bookmark

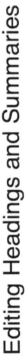

Edit Details Window

The Edit Details page is your opportunity to add more detailed information to support your argument. Here you have lots of space to construct your argument and/or layout your research and evidence. Debategraph supports all types of media, opening opportunities for students to construct their own diverse arguments in a visually appealing wway

Encourage students to use diverse forms of multimedia in the Details Window. Try to avoid using this section for long textual explanations. The whole map should provide all the necessary information. The details window is best suited for the inclusion of media to act as a visual aid to the specific Node

The Lock checkbox is helpful because you can prevent edits to your details, or leave the box unchecked to allow collaboration

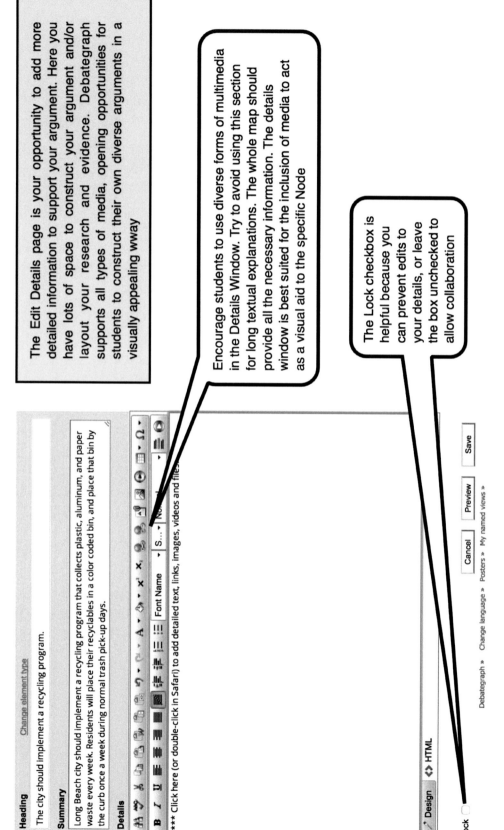

Heading Change element type

The city should implement a recycling program.

Summary

Long Beach city should implement a recycling program that collects plastic, aluminum, and paper waste every week. Residents will place their recyclables in a color coded bin, and place that bin by the curb once a week during normal trash pick-up days.

Details

Font Name   ▾ S.... ▾ No...

*** Click here (or double-click in Safari) to add detailed text, links, images, videos and files

Design   ◇▸ HTML

Lock

Debategraph » Change language » Posters » My named views »

Cancel   Preview   Save

Adding a Claim

If you select Add Idea from a Resolution node, one of the recommendations is that you add a Supportive Claim. Debategraph offers a great visual representation of arguments, but you must still enter your own claims Your claim is what you are willing or able to defend. The claim also begins to separate the ground in the debate between affirmative and negative. Compose your Claims carefully, aware that savvy debaters will carefully evaluate how strongly your Data and Warrant support your Claim.

Pro tip: Add a Qualifier to the Claim to specify your argument. For example, if the Claim is "Recycling solves environmental problems," the qualified Claim would be "Recycling *can help solve many* environmental problems." Qualifiers help to signal to your audience that you are aware of the exceptions to your Claim, and might enhance your credibility

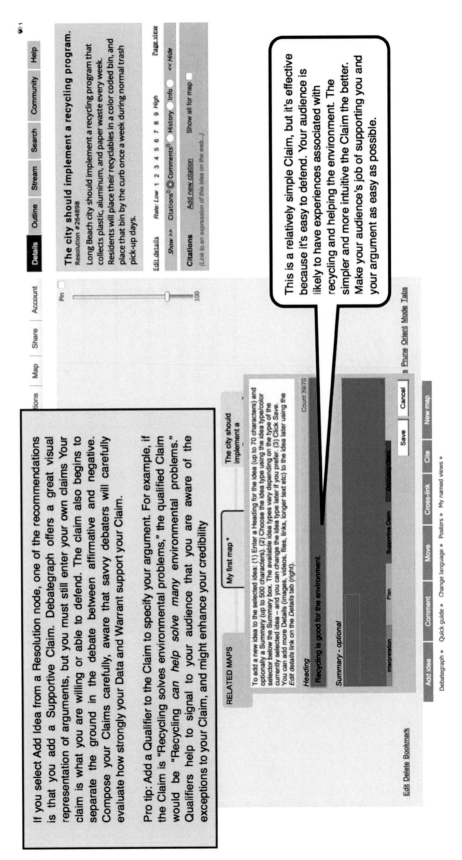

This is a relatively simple Claim, but it's effective because it's easy to defend. Your audience is likely to have experiences associated with recycling and helping the environment. The simpler and more intuitive the Claim the better. Make your audience's job of supporting you and your argument as easy as possible.

Adding Data

Data/evidence is important stuff. Not all data/information should be evaluated in the same way. It is important that your Data directly supports your Claim and that your evidence comes from a credible source. Always consider the credentials and credibility of the author/source. Credibility is usually established with credentialing, training, or experience. An experienced debater will use an author's biases or conflicts of interest to highlight problems or deficiencies in an opponent's evidence to their advantage.

Just like adding a Claim, you simply click on the Add Idea button. The difference is that there are a different set of options that emerge. The first option is Data. The reason for different options is that you are adding an idea to a Supportive Claim rather than a resolution. In fact, each node has a different set of recommendations when you choose to add an idea. This means you must be very aware to which Nodes you are adding ideas.

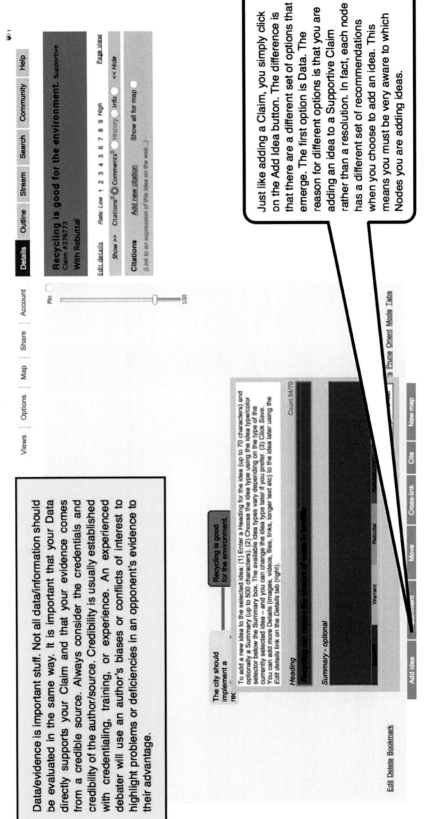

Editing the Details

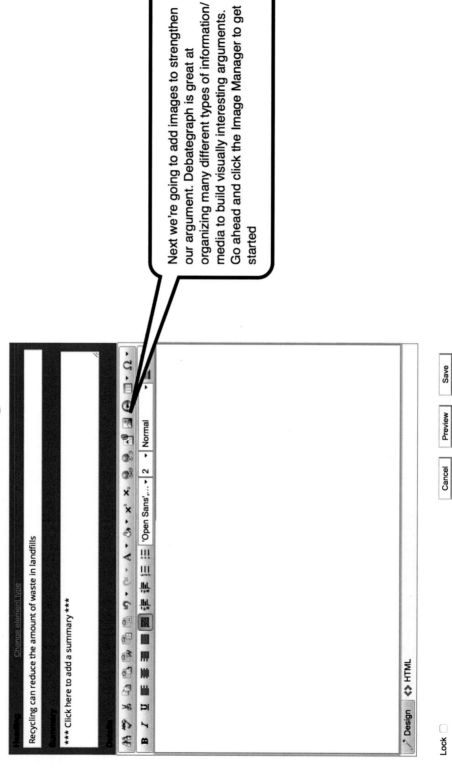

Heading — Change element type

Recycling can reduce the amount of waste in landfills

Summary

*** Click here to add a summary ***

Details

'Open Sans',... ▾ | 2 ▾ | Normal ▾

Design ◇ HTML

Cancel | Preview | Save

Lock

Next we're going to add images to strengthen our argument. Debategraph is great at organizing many different types of information/ media to build visually interesting arguments. Go ahead and click the Image Manager to get started

Adding Images

A picture is worth a 1000 words. Adding visual media is a great way to provide context for your argument and encourages your audience to relate to your argument in additional and complimentary ways. Just as well-constructed sentences and paragraphs read as poetry, there is a certain aesthetic value to simple, well constructed and relevant visual media

Here we are working to support the Heading/Claim by providing a graphic demonstrating the primary destination spots for our garbage. The largest part of the graph (54.2%) directly supports the Heading/Claim because it shows a significant amount of our garbage is being used as landfill instead of being recycled or composted. Use graphics to reinforce the textual parts of your argument and to show the relationship between the dominant elements of your argument.

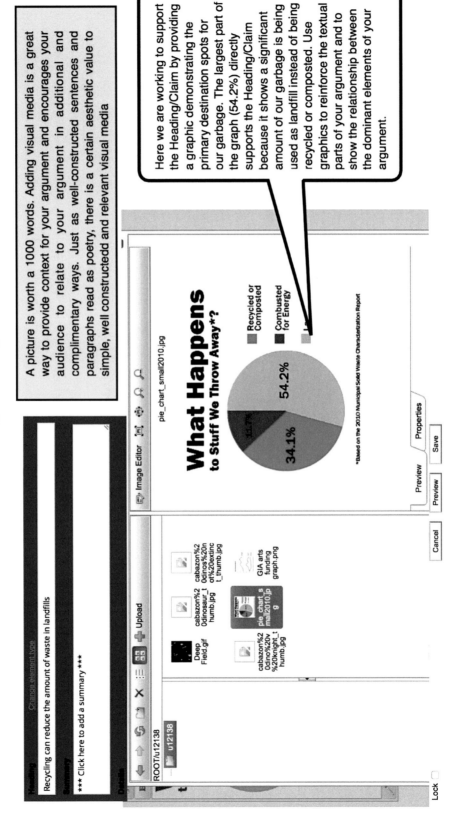

Adding Citations

Effectively citing your work allows others to follow up and examine the evidence that you are using. Don't be fooled by poor research or discredited sources. Always carefully examine the credibility of whoever is offering the evidence. Debategraph allows you to cite diverse digital sources and provides a framework for organizing your web-based research efforts.

Views | Options | Map | Share | Account

Details | Outline | Stream | Search | Community | Help

Pin

100

What Happens
to Stuff We Throw Away*?

Recycling can reduce the amount of waste in landfills through recycling.

54.2%

34.1%

■ Recycled or Composted

■ Combusted for Energy

*Based on the 2010 Municipal Solid Waste Characterization

Edit details   Rate: Low 1 2 3 4 5 6
Show >>   Citations[1] Comments[0]

Add new citation

Citations

[1] Recycling Basics

Author: The United States Environmental
mission of EPA is to protect human h
Publication date and info: Last updat
Cited by: Jared Kubicka-Miller 6:31 F
Also cited at: 276756, 276764
URL: http://www.epa.gov/recycle/rec

Recycling is good for the environment.

Rollovers Prune Orient Mode Tabs

Move | Cross-link | Cite | New map

Edit citation

Title
Recycling Basics

URL
http://www.epa.gov/recycle/recycle.html

Author or speaker (separated by commas)
The United States Environmental Protection Agency

Author background (optional)
The mission of EPA is to protect human health and the environment.

Publication date and info (optional)
Last updated on 12/28/2012

Excerpt / Summary (optional)

Notice that this citation has the EPA as the author. Sometimes, not all the information you need for the citation will be available. You should be critical of sources that do not cite an author. Typically, sources that lack an author's credentials lack quality.

185

Adding A Warrant With Summary

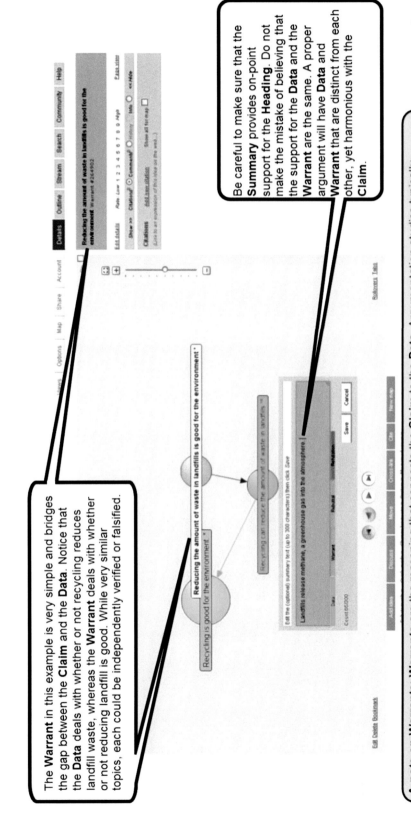

The **Warrant** in this example is very simple and bridges the gap between the **Claim** and the **Data**. Notice that the **Data** deals with whether or not recycling reduces landfill waste, whereas the **Warrant** deals with whether or not reducing landfill is good. While very similar topics, each could be independently verified or falsified.

Be careful to make sure that the **Summary** provides on-point support for the **Heading**. Do not make the mistake of believing that the support for the **Data** and the **Warrant** are the same. A proper argument will have **Data** and **Warrant** that are distinct from each other, yet harmonious with the **Claim**.

A note on Warrants: **Warrants** are the reasoning that connects the **Claim** to the **Data**. Argumentation studies typically focus on inductive reasoning, so understanding the different types of inductive reasoning is a great way to understand a **Warrant**. **Warrants** are the trickiest of the elements of an argument because they are often implied by an author. Furthermore, there may be several **Warrants** that are appropriate for any particular argument. Still, understanding the strengths and weaknesses of different types of logic is an invaluable tool for debaters to possess.

How To Add Video To A Map.

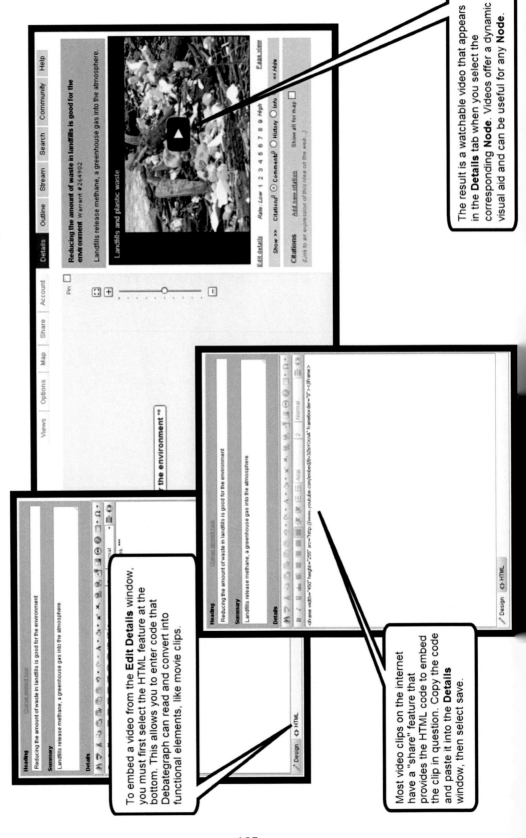

The result is a watchable video that appears in the **Details** tab when you select the corresponding **Node**. Videos offer a dynamic visual aid and can be useful for any **Node**.

To embed a video from the **Edit Details** window, you must first select the HTML feature at the bottom. This allows you to enter code that Debategraph can read and convert into functional elements, like movie clips.

Most video clips on the internet have a "share" feature that provides the HTML code to embed the clip in question. Copy the code and paste it into the **Details** window, then select save.

Adding Cross-Links

Cross-links offer another level of information to your maps, and can be used in a multitude of contexts. In this example, we are linking the Warrant and the Data. To create a Cross-link, you first need to select the Outline tab.

The next step to cross-linking is to select the Cross-link button below the View Window. This will bring an instructional pop-up.

Once the Outline tab is open, and the Cross-link has been selected, then you can select the Node to which you want to Cross-link. Be sure not to select your current Node, outlined in red, because that will result in an error message. When you click on a Node, a color-coded list of options emerges from which you can choose. In this case, we are going to choose Pointer as our Cross-link.

Views | Options | Map | Share | Account

Details Outline Stream Search Community Help

My first map *

The city should implement a recycling program. *

Recycling is good for the environment. *

landfills is good for the er

Reducing   landfills is good for the er

Deleted *

Select relation type…

| Equivalence |
| Relevance |
| Consistency |
| Inconsistency |
| Pointer |
| Improves |
| Also supports |
| Also opposes |
| Why |
| How |
| What |
| Who |
| Where |
| Exemplifies |
| Exacerbates |
| When. |
| Informs |
| Flow |
| Part |
| Influences |
| Increases |
| Determines |
| Decreases |
| Variation |
| Cancel |

Pin

100

Recycling can reduce the amount of waste in landfills

Reducing the amount of waste in landfills is good for

cycling is good the environment.

The city should implement a recycling program. *

To cross-link the selected idea (abov... another idea: (1) display the other idea [Cancel] on the *Search* or *Outline* tabs on the r... (2) click on the other idea, and (3) choose the link type from the selector ...pens Alternatively, you can drag the source idea on the *Outline* onto the target idea ...e *Outline*.

(These kinds of links are called *cross-relati*... and they allow you to make direct, meaningful connections between ideas in di...ent parts of the map. For more information about these links, click on the *H...*tab).

Rollovers Prune Orient Mode Tabs

Add idea | Comment | Move | Cross-link | Cite | New map

Edit Delete Bookmark

« Show outline on left Expand

Viewing Cross-links

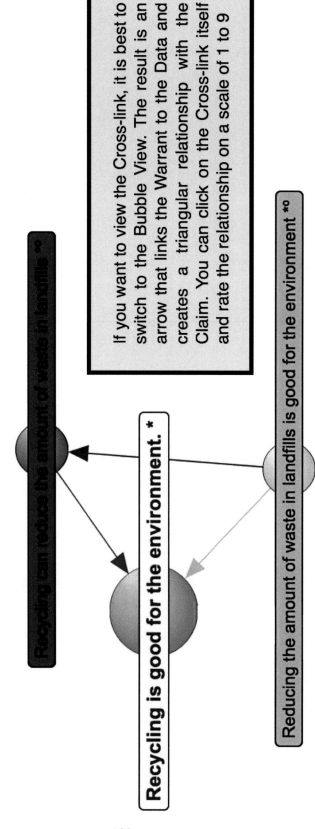

Recycling can reduce the amount of waste in landfills *o

If you want to view the Cross-link, it is best to switch to the Bubble View. The result is an arrow that links the Warrant to the Data and creates a triangular relationship with the Claim. You can click on the Cross-link itself and rate the relationship on a scale of 1 to 9

Recycling is good for the environment. *

Reducing the amount of waste in landfills is good for the environment *o

Chapter 11
Creating Arguments

Simple Arguments

- Claim - Data - Warrant

Adding Optional Elements

- Refutation - Rebuttal - Backing

Compound Arguments

- Keystone warrant

- Keystone data

Simple Argument

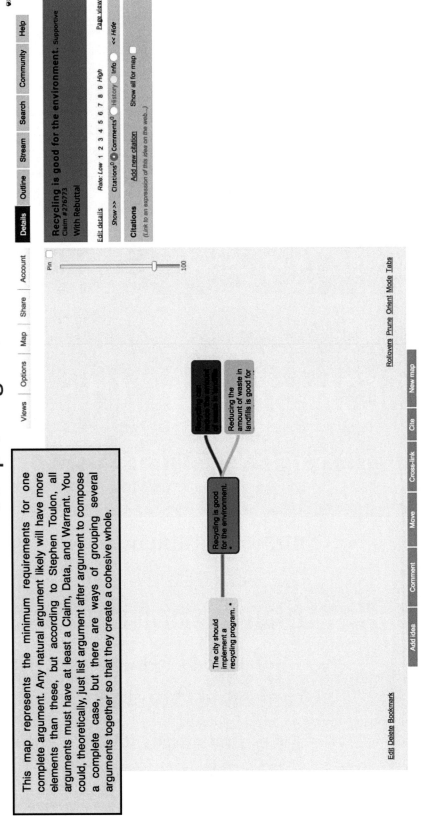

Adding Refutation

A note on Refutation: any Node may make an assertion that an opposing debater could refute. It is important to remember when adding Refutation that the Heading is written so that it directly responds to the Node in question. A Refutation Node acts as a Claim for the opposition; therefore, it ought to be supported with its own Data and Warrant.

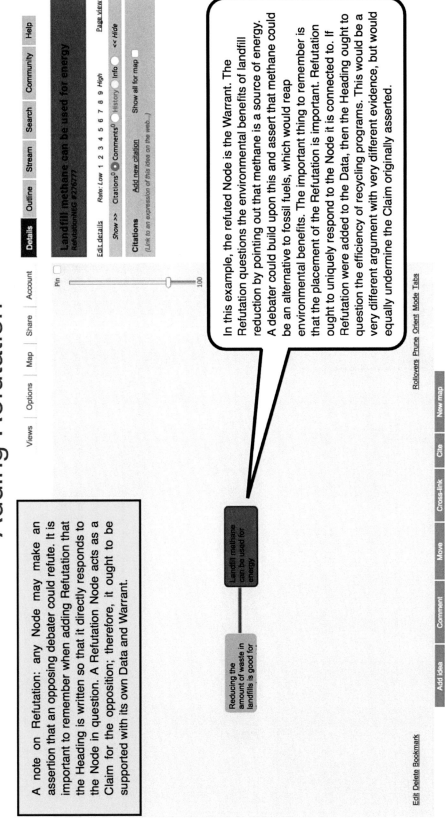

Views | Options | Map | Share | Account

Details | Outline | Stream | Search | Community | Help

Pin ☐

100

Landfill methane can be used for energy
RefutationNEG #276777

Edit details   *Rate: Low* 1 2 3 4 5 6 7 8 9 *High*   Page view

Show >>   Citations[0] ● Comments[0] ○ History ○ Info ●   << *Hide*

Citations   Add new citation   Show all for map ☐
(Link to an expression of this idea on the web...)

In this example, the refuted Node is the Warrant. The Refutation questions the environmental benefits of landfill reduction by pointing out that methane is a source of energy. A debater could build upon this and assert that methane could be an alternative to fossil fuels, which would reap environmental benefits. The important thing to remember is that the placement of the Refutation is important. Refutation ought to uniquely respond to the Node it is connected to. If Refutation were added to the Data, then the Heading ought to question the efficiency of recycling programs. This would be a very different argument with very different evidence, but would equally undermine the Claim originally asserted.

Rollovers Prune Orient Mode Tabs

Landfill methane can be used for energy

Reducing the amount of waste in landfills is good for ...

Add idea | Comment | Move | Cross-link | Cite | New map

Edit Delete Bookmark

Backing

Backing provides additional support for the Data or Warrant. Backing is helpful when any part of your argument isn't self-explanatory, but also helps to add credibility to your argument. Another benefit to adding Backing to a Warrant or Data is that you can preemptively address issues that an opponent might bring up. Realize that backing, while advised, is not necessary to have a complete argument.

Methane is an even worse greenhouse gas than carbon dioxide

Methane is 21 times more efficient at trapping heat than carbon dioxide. Relatively minor fluctuations in methane emmissions would have drastic affects on the earth's climate. Reducing the amount of methane in the atmosphere is of paramount importance.

Methane is an even worse green... e gas than carbon...

Landfill methane can be used for energy

Recyc... can r... e the amount ... aste in landfills

Reducing the amount of waste in landfills is good for

Recycling is good for the environment. *

When adding ideas, pay special attention to the information you put in the Heading versus the Summary. In this example, you can see that the information that you put into the summary is available when you "rollover" a node with your mouse cursor

193

Rebuttal

Rebuttal and Refutation are often treated as synonyms in common language, but in argumentation theory a Rebuttal is a way to support an argument in the face of actual or anticipated opposition. In fact, most debate formats refer to the speeches at the end of the debate as 'rebuttals.' Notice that this is different from Refutation, which is a response to a preexisting argument. The difference is subtle, but important. Debaters are sometimes hesitant to include Rebuttal in their argument because they fear it weakens their argument, but a Rebuttal is a great way to acknowledge the exceptions to an argument while still supporting the Claim as a whole. Strategically, a Rebuttal can preempt an opponent's Refutation, effectively answering an opponent before they even have a chance to voice an argument.

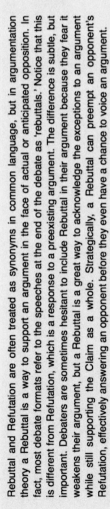

The Refutation makes a concession, that recycling centers tend to create pollution. This could be further supported with Data that would be attached to the Refutation by adding an idea. This concession might be a strategically good idea to deflate an opponent's argument, and to keep the focus on the holistic benefits of recycling, rather than assessing each stage of the recycling process.

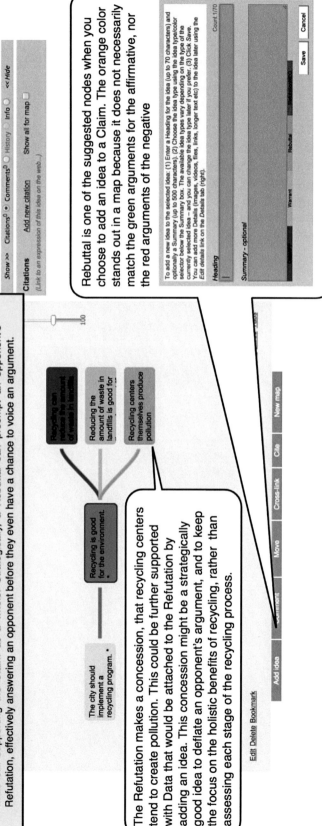

Rebuttal is one of the suggested nodes when you choose to add an idea to a Claim. The orange color stands out in a map because it does not necessarily match the green arguments for the affirmative, nor the red arguments of the negative

Compound Argument

Debategraph offer a new way of visualizing arguments, and through that visualization you can gain unique insight into the structure of arguments that is easily lost through verbal or textual communication. One insight is that arguments come in a variety of structures, each with their own strengths and weaknesses. One variation we call the Compound Argument. This is when multiple Data and Warrants support the same Claim. The benefits of using this approach is that you solidify the Claim that you are trying to advance. The drawback is that compound arguments easily become large and unwieldy.

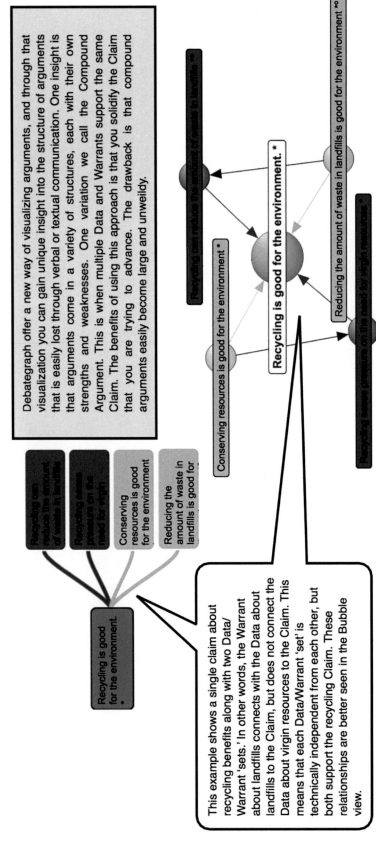

Recycling is good for the environment.

This example shows a single claim about recycling benefits along with two Data/Warrant 'sets.' In other words, the Warrant about landfills connects with the Data about landfills to the Claim, but does not connect the Data about virgin resources to the Claim. This means that each Data/Warrant 'set' is technically independent from each other, but both support the recycling Claim. These relationships are better seen in the Bubble view.

Keystone Warrant

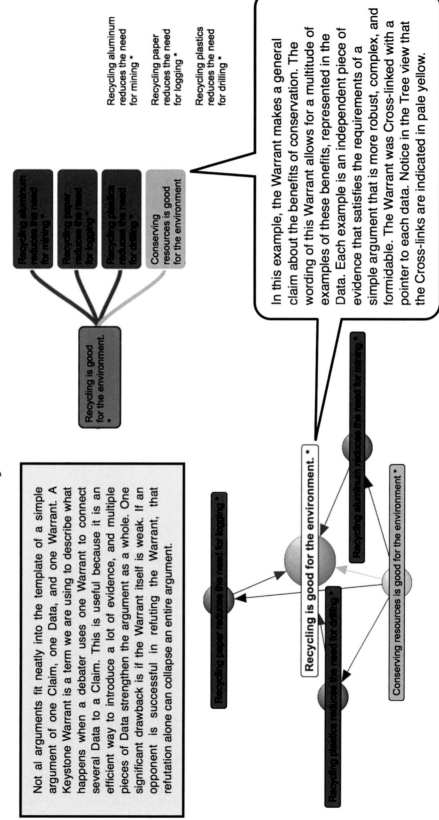

Not all arguments fit neatly into the template of a simple argument of one Claim, one Data, and one Warrant. A Keystone Warrant is a term we are using to describe what happens when a debater uses one Warrant to connect several Data to a Claim. This is useful because it is an efficient way to introduce a lot of evidence, and multiple pieces of Data strengthen the argument as a whole. One significant drawback is if the Warrant itself is weak. If an opponent is successful in refuting the Warrant, that refutation alone can collapse an entire argument.

Recycling aluminum reduces the need for mining *

Recycling paper reduces the need for logging *

Recycling plastics reduces the need for drilling *

Recycling aluminum reduces the need for mining *

Recycling paper reduces the need for logging *

Recycling plastics reduces the need for drilling *

Conserving resources is good for the environment

Recycling is good for the environment.
*

In this example, the Warrant makes a general claim about the benefits of conservation. The wording of this Warrant allows for a multitude of examples of these benefits, represented in the Data. Each example is an independent piece of evidence that satisfies the requirements of a simple argument that is more robust, complex, and formidable. The Warrant was Cross-linked with a pointer to each data. Notice in the Tree view that the Cross-links are indicated in pale yellow.

Recycling paper reduces the need for logging *

Recycling is good for the environment. *

Recycling aluminum reduces the need for mining *

Recycling plastics reduces the need for drilling *

Conserving resources is good for the environment *

Keystone Data

Another misconception that some people have when learning about argumentation is that one Warrant connects with one Data to one Claim. But there may be several reasons why a piece of Data is relevant to a Claim. Furthermore, each additional Warrants strengthen the relationship between the Claim and Data. On the other hand, too many Warrants might hurt the legibility of a map, and make a verbal explanation of the argument difficult or necessarily lengthy.

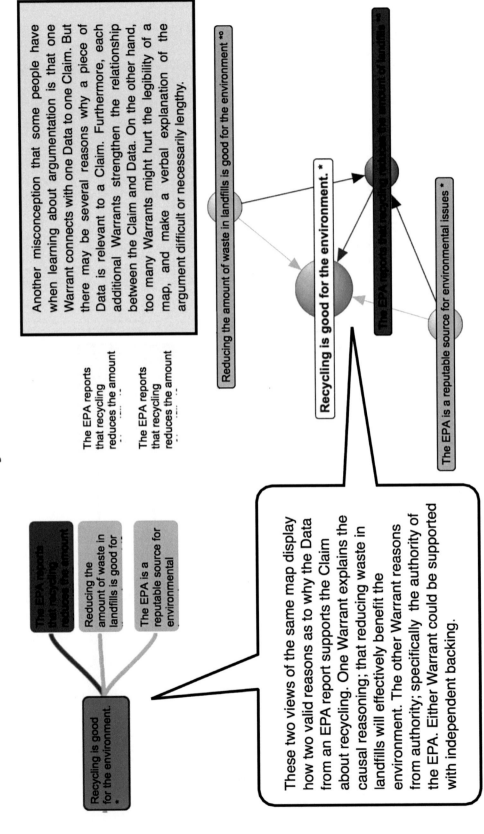

Reducing the amount of waste in landfills is good for the environment *o

Recycling is good for the environment. *

The EPA reports that recycling reduces the amount of landfills *

The EPA is a reputable source for environmental issues *

The EPA reports that recycling reduces the amount

Reducing the amount of waste in landfills is good for

The EPA is a reputable source for environmental

Recycling is good for the environment. *

These two views of the same map display how two valid reasons as to why the Data from an EPA report supports the Claim about recycling. One Warrant explains the causal reasoning; that reducing waste in landfills will effectively benefit the environment. The other Warrant reasons from authority; specifically the authority of the EPA. Either Warrant could be supported with independent backing.

Chapter 12
Mapping a Complete Debate

One of the most helpful ways to use Debategraph is to map actual verbal debates. Successful debaters typically learn a method of note-taking, called flowing, that helps them to keep track of the many lines of argument that occur during a formal debate. Flowing is useful during a debate, but also afterwards in order to learn from the arguments that occurred, and develop answers for future debates on the same, or similar topic. In this section, we map out a debate on the 2014-2015 National Forensics Association's Lincoln Douglas topic. That topic is "Be it Resolved: The United States Federal Government should increase its development of the earth's moon in one or more of the following areas: energy, minerals, and/or water."

You can watch the entire debate on YouTube if you want to compare the maps in this section to what was actually said. The title of the first affirmative constructive is shown here. We compiled a playlist of all the speeches and cross- examinations, and called it "Develop the Moon Matt v Jared." You can find it on the debatesensei YouTube channel. This debate kept to basic stock issues, advantages and disadvantages. There are many more strategies in debate that vary in complexity that we did not include. We present the following maps, again, in the Tree view. All debates should start with a resolution node.

Interpreting a Resolution

A. Development requires infrastructure

B. Resolution is about developing the moon

C. Build habitats on the moon. *

E. Should happen now

1. Resolutional Analysis *

Policy resolutions call for a Plan node. This Plan is stated in simple terms and includes all the information needed for the negative debater to understand the goal.

Including a criteria for the debate is also a simple clarification that can pay dividends in later speeches.

Numbering, or lettering your arguments is a good way to help your audience follow you train of thought. It is also easy to reference arguments later on in the debate. In this debate, the terms are not defined on a "word by word" level, but the resolution is interpreted as a whole

As the first speaker in any debate, the affirmative has both the right and responsibility to offer clarification to the resolution for the round. This includes offering definitions for the words and phrases found in the resolution itself, the burdens of the affirmative and negative for the round, and any proposed action that would provide context so that the debaters can have more specific, detailed arguments. When defining terms, the goal is not to "define your opponent out of the round." In other words, do not interpret the resolution in a way that there is a bias in favor of the affirmative, and that the negative has no ground from which to argue.

Plan Specifications

Plan specifications are represented through the Plank nodes, which are a slightly darker shade of brown. Omitting detail from your plan is one of the more common errors that beginning debaters make. Avoid this mistake and explain the logistics about your plan: who is in charge of enforcement, what are the mandates, what are the approximate costs, as well as other relevant details.

1. Paraterraforming

2. Terraforming

Funding through normal means

C. Build habitats on the moon. *

Explaining that funding will come from "normal means" is a very common explanation in debate. Some dispute that without explaining the funding source for a plan, that the affirmative is being unfairly vague. Others argue that it should be the burden of the negative to suggest what is the most likely funding source in the form of a disadvantage.

Complete Resolutional Analysis

1. Paraterraforming

2. Terraforming

Funding through normal means

C. Build habitats on the moon. *

A. Development requires infrastucture

B. Resolution is about developing the moon

E. Should happen now

1. Resolutional Analysis *

Background

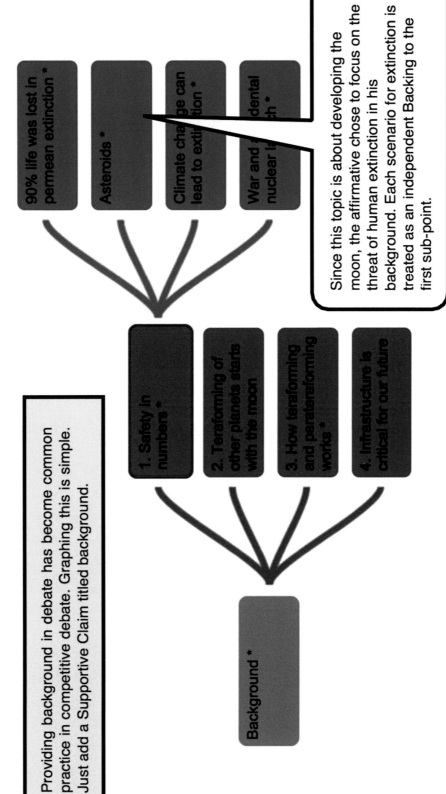

90% life was lost in permean extinction *

Asteroids *

Climate change can lead to extinction *

War and accidental nuclear launch *

Since this topic is about developing the moon, the affirmative chose to focus on the threat of human extinction in his background. Each scenario for extinction is treated as an independent Backing to the first sub-point.

1. Safety in numbers *

2. Teraforming of other planets starts with the moon

3. How teraforming and paraterraforming works *

4. Infrastucture is critical for our future

Providing background in debate has become common practice in competitive debate. Graphing this is simple. Just add a Supportive Claim titled background.

Background *

A Stock Issues Advantage

Once you have fully graphed the background information, you can move on to the supporting advantages. In this debate, the affirmative follows a stock issues format for their arguments. Review Chapter 3 for an explanation of the fundamentals of stock issues.

Notice the different shades of green denoting the different stock issues for the advantage. The harms focuses on survival of the human species, but the graph makes sure to stay true to the wording of the debater. The inherency argues that only learning how to survive on the moon can we go to planets beyond. And the solvency explains how habitats on other planets is an insurance policy for human survival.

Advantage 1: Escape hatch *

A. Bad things happen *

B. Go to the moon now, then to Mars in the future.

C. Insurance policy

C. Build habitats on the moon. *

Cross-links in the tree view appear pale yellow, regardless of node type. This cross-link points to the plan text as a reminder that the plan must be considered when deciding whether or not to vote for the advantage.

Advantages

Permean extinction killed 90% of life

Another recurring pattern for the affirmative is the listing of examples to support particular claims. This is a pattern also seen in the first sub-point of the background argument.

China H3

Fight over diamonds

Fight over uranium

We fight over oil

A. Fighting over resources *

B. We can harvest asteroids

C. Future is expansion

Advantage 2: Space solves Earth's problems *

A. Bad things happen *

B. Go to the moon now, then to Mars in the future.

C. Insurance policy

Advantage 1: Escape hatch *

Graphing arguments exposes certain patterns in arguments. Often times, these patterns are indications of a debaters style. The affirmative has two very similarly structured advantages, with the Harms node receiving additional support.

Complete Affirmative

The image to the right is a good example of the amount of nodes in a typical affirmative 6 minute speech. The four sections of the speech are clearly identifiable when the 'view all' option is selected under the Tree view. Debaters must make choices about what information they are going to include.

Topicality

Topicality is a popular position in debate. It essentially argues that the affirmative team interpreted the resolution incorrectly; therefore, the case does not properly support the resolution. There are four parts: a Counter Definition, Violation, Standard, and Impact.

The "ground" Standard is an important part of any Topicality. It essentially argues that the affirmative has interpreted the resolution that unfairly restricts what the negative should be allowed to argue.

a. Choice between residential, commercial, and

b. Teraforming and parateraforming is residential, not

Development *

1. Resolutional Analysis *

This particular Topicality argument focuses on the word "development" from the resolution. The counter-definition draws from land management literature. There are 2 standards, and 2 impacts, which explains why this particular position has a total of 6 supporting nodes.

Topicality and Resolutional Analysis

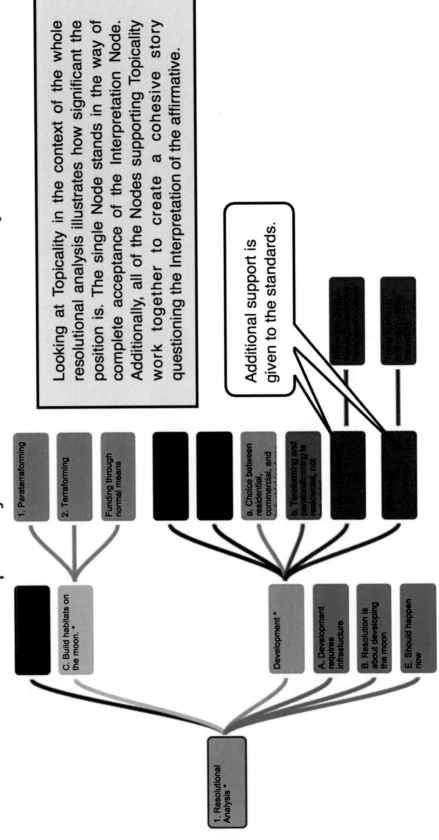

Looking at Topicality in the context of the whole resolutional analysis illustrates how significant the position is. The single Node stands in the way of complete acceptance of the Interpretation Node. Additionally, all of the Nodes supporting Topicality work together to create a cohesive story questioning the Interpretation of the affirmative.

Additional support is given to the standards.

1. Parateraforming

2. Terraforming

Funding through normal means

a. Choice between residential, commercial, and

b. Terraforming and parateraforming is residential, not

C. Build habitats on the moon. *

Development *

A. Development requires infrastucture

B. Resolution is about developing the moon

E. Should happen now

1. Resolutional Analysis *

Direct Refutation: Harms

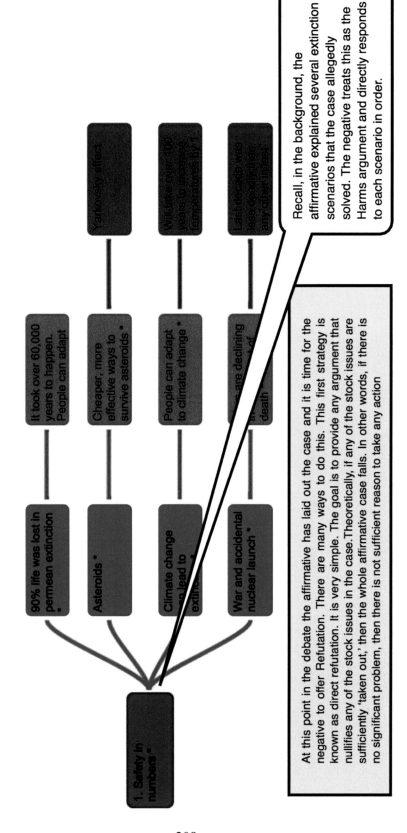

Yarkovsky effect

Will take over 100 years to increase temperatures by 1

Last decade was less deadly than any other in last

It took over 60,000 years to happen. People can adapt

Cheaper, more effective ways to survive asteroids *

People can adapt to climate change *

are declining
cause of
death *

90% life was lost in permean extinction *

Asteroids *

Climate change can lead to extinc

War and accidental nuclear launch *

1. Safety in numbers *

Recall, in the background, the affirmative explained several extinction scenarios that the case allegedly solved. The negative treats this as the Harms argument and directly responds to each scenario in order.

At this point in the debate the affirmative has laid out the case and it is time for the negative to offer Refutation. There are many ways to do this. This first strategy is known as direct refutation. It is very simple. The goal is to provide any argument that nullifies any of the stock issues in the case. Theoretically, if any of the stock issues are sufficiently 'taken out,' then the whole affirmative case falls. In other words, if there is no significant problem, then there is not sufficient reason to take any action

Direct Refutation: Solvency

Answering each stock issue is not always necessary. Debaters can refute all stock issues, or focus their efforts on just one. Remember, if any of the stock issues are sufficiently taken out then the whole affirmative falls. Solvency is often the easiest stock issue to refute because creating workable and effective plans to solve significant problems is complex.

The Solvency Refutation is much simpler than the Harms Refutation. A single argument about the feasibility of bio-domes effectively undermines all advantages because all the advantages depend on bio-domes being a realistic thing.

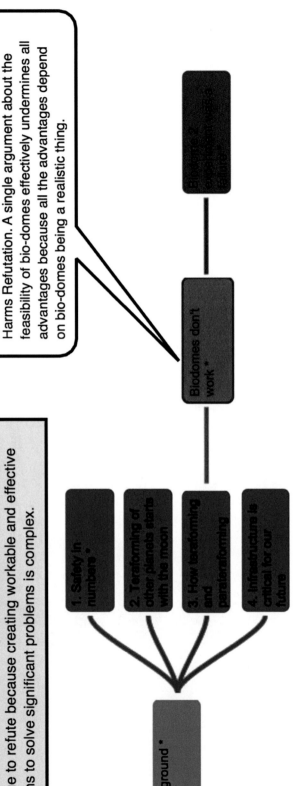

Biodomes don't work *

Biodome 2 experiment was a failure

1. Safety in numbers *

2. Terraforming of other planets starts with the moon

3. How terraforming and parraterraforming

4. Infrastructure is critical for our future

Background *

On-case Refutation

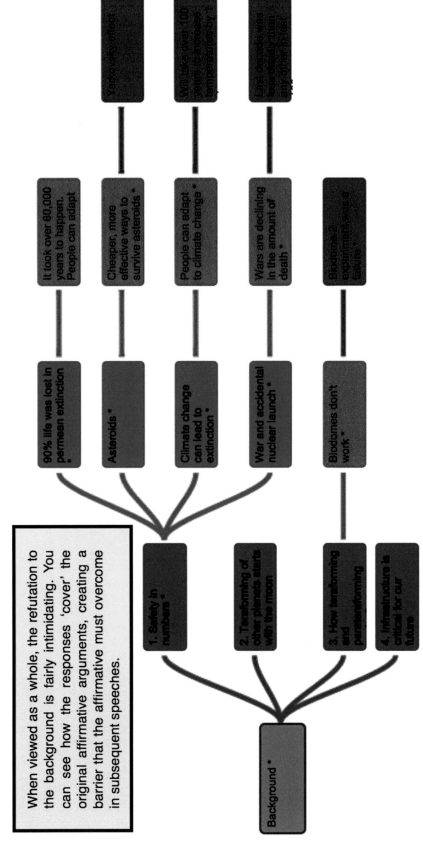

When viewed as a whole, the refutation to the background is fairly intimidating. You can see how the responses 'cover' the original affirmative arguments, creating a barrier that the affirmative must overcome in subsequent speeches.

90% life was lost in permean extinction *

It took over 60,000 years to happen. People can adapt

Yarlovsky effect

Asteroids *

Cheaper, more effective ways to survive asteroids *

Will take over 100 years to increase temperatures by 1

Climate change can lead to extinction *

People can adapt to climate change *

Last decade was less deadly than any other 16 last

War and accidental nuclear launch *

Wars are declining in the amount of death *

Biodomes don't work *

Biodome 2 experiment was a failure

1. Safety in numbers *

2. Terraforming of other planets starts with the moon

3. How terraforming and paraterraforming

4. Infrastructure is critical for our future

Background *

210

The Disadvantage

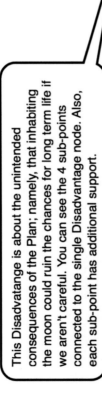

a. Life is unpredictable *

b. Microbes will be introduced to biodomes, *

Unintended Consequences *

Having a significant impact is important. This impact argues that microbes could make the moon uninhabitable, and that could be irreversable.

This Disadvatange is about the unintended consequences of the Plan; namely, that inhabiting the moon could ruin the chances for long term life if we aren't careful. You can see the 4 sub-points connected to the single Disadvantage node. Also, each sub-point has additional support.

Yet another tactic is the disadvantage. This is a structured argument about the negative consequences of the proposed plan. Basically, when you commit to running a disadvantage then you are committing to making several arguments that, when taken together, create a logical story about why the affirmative plan is bad. Disadvantages need: Uniqueness-or an explanation about a part of the status quo that is particularly affected by the plan. A Link-an explanation about what the plan does to the status quo. Set of Internal Links-these explain the immediate causal affects of the plan. And an Impact-the ultimate negative consequences of the plan.

Answering Topicality

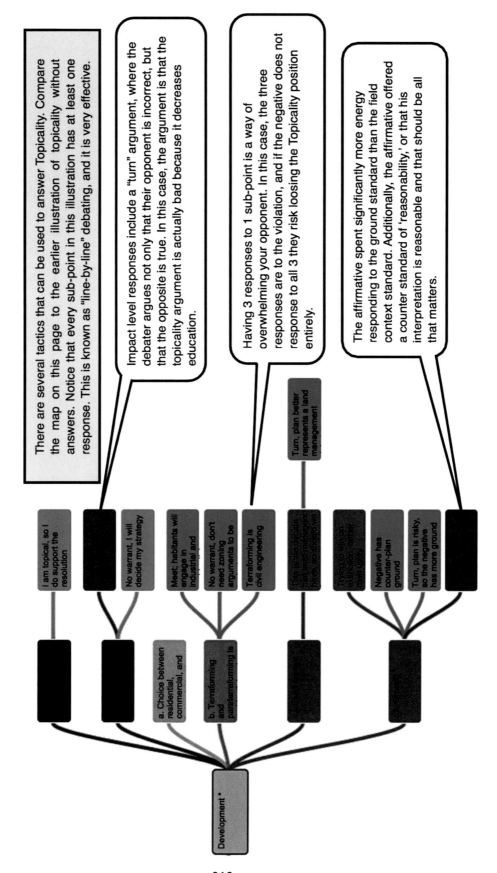

There are several tactics that can be used to answer Topicality. Compare the map on this page to the earlier illustration of topicality without answers. Notice that every sub-point in this illustration has at least one response. This is known as "line-by-line" debating, and it is very effective.

Impact level responses include a "turn" argument, where the debater argues not only that their opponent is incorrect, but that the opposite is true. In this case, the argument is that the topicality argument is actually bad because it decreases education.

Having 3 responses to 1 sub-point is a way of overwhelming your opponent. In this case, the three responses are to the violation, and if the negative does not response to all 3 they risk loosing the Topicality position entirely.

The affirmative spent significantly more energy responding to the ground standard than the field context standard. Additionally, the affirmative offered a counter standard of 'reasonability,' or that his interpretation is reasonable and that should be all that matters.

I am topical, so I do support the resolution

No warrant, I will decide my strategy

Meet; habitants will engage in industrial and

No warrant, don't need zoning arguments to be

Terraforming is civil engineering

Turn, plan better represents a land management

a. Choice between residential, commercial, and

b. Terraforming and paraterraforming is

Negative has counter-plan ground

Turn, plan is risky, so the negative has more ground

Development *

Answering the Disadvantage

There are more ways to answer a disadvantage than can fit on one page, but some of the most popular answers are as follows: No Link arguments claim that there is nothing connecting the disadvantage to the plan. Non-unique arguments claim that the disadvantage will occur regardless of whether of not the plan passes. No impact arguments claim that your opponent did not articulate a significant negative consequence to plan. And then there are turn arguments, which have already been discussed.

The affirmative has one turn argument in response to the Link.

The third response is a No brink response, which argues that an authority disagrees with the negative's analysis.

Mars rover already is going to spread microbes

Panspermia, Carl Sagan sides with the affirmative

a. Life is unpredictable *

Here the Non-unique argument attempts to dismantle a key part of the disadvantage.

b. Microbes will be introduced to biodomes. *

Unintended Consequences *

Rebuilding the Harms

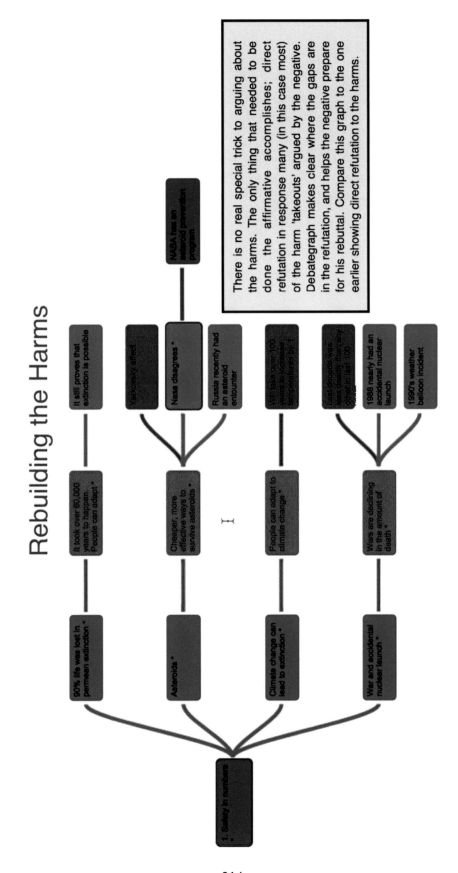

There is no real special trick to arguing about the harms. The only thing that needed to be done the affirmative accomplishes; direct refutation in response many (in this case most) of the harm 'takeouts' argued by the negative. Debategraph makes clear where the gaps are in the refutation, and helps the negative prepare for his rebuttal. Compare this graph to the one earlier showing direct refutation to the harms.

NASA has an asteroid prevention program

It still proves that extinction is possible

Yarkovsky effect

Nasa disagrees *

Russia recently had an asteroid encounter

Will take over 100 years to increase temperatures by 1

Last decade was less deadly than any other in last 100 years

1988 nearly had an accidental nuclear launch

1990's weather balloon incident

It took over 60,000 years to happen. People can adapt *

Cheaper, more effective ways to survive asteroids *

People can adapt to climate change *

Wars are declining in the amount of death *

90% life was lost in permean extinction *

Asteroids *

Climate change can lead to extinction *

War and accidental nuclear launch *

1. Safety in numbers
•

Rebuilding Solvency

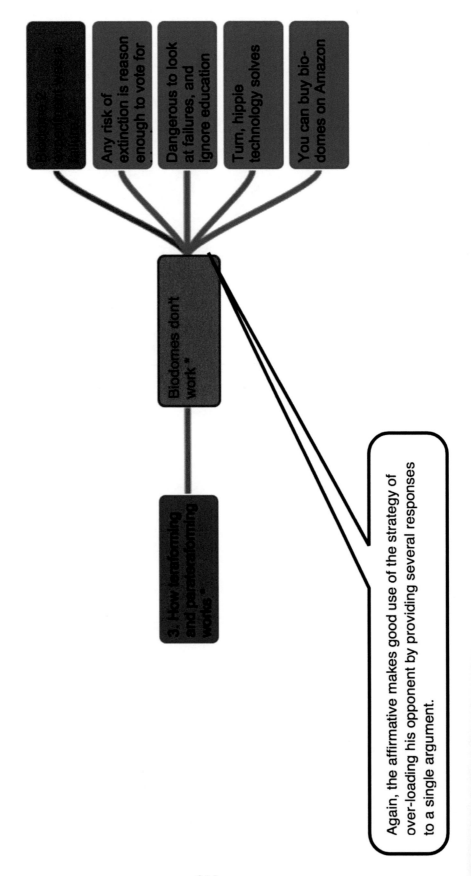

Biodomes?
development
failure

Any risk of
extinction is reason
enough to vote for

Dangerous to look
at failures, and
ignore education

Turn, hipple
technology solves

You can buy bio-
domes on Amazon

Biodomes don't
work "

3. How terraforming
and paraterraforming
works "

Again, the affirmative makes good use of the strategy of
over-loading his opponent by providing several responses
to a single argument.

Negative Rebuttal to Solvency

Compare this graph to the previous page and notice how all of the arguments made in the affirmative rebuttal each have at least one response made by the negative. The fact that the debater chose this issue first, and provided so much coverage is an indication that he considers it an important issue.

The resulting graph visually looks like the negative is literally "surrounding" the affirmative. There is no argument left unanswered in the solvency responses provided by the affirmative.

Hypothetical example

This is fear mongering *

Turn, bio-domes are dangerous, only the negative is being without

no evidence

no it doesn't

Why not use hippie tech to solve the world's problems?

Amazon doesn't sell bio-domes, only greenhouses *

Proves fear mongering *

Green houses would fail *

Proposing a plan that won't work

Biodome 2 greenhouse/overall failure

Any risk of extinction is reason enough to vote for bio-domes *

Dangerous to look at failures, and ignore education *

Turn, hippie technology solves *

You can buy bio-domes on Amazon *

Biodomes don't work *

3. How terraforming and geoterraforming works *

Negative Rebuttal for the Disadvantage

Therefore, Plan causes extinction. Turns case

The negative arguments "surrounding" the affirmative is even more pronounced in this graph. This is the rebuttal responses to the disadvantage. The negative is careful to respond to each of the affirmative's arguments from the previous rebuttal.

Building bio-domes on the moon is the opposite of planning

Non responsive to the methane argument

We should not consciously cause planetary

Have billions of single cell microorganisms

Mars rover already is going to spread microbes *

On our skin

Venting air

Might evolve unpredictably

Panspermia, Carl Sagan sides with the affirmative *

Irreversible

a. Life is unpredictable *

b. Microbes will be introduced to biodomes. *

Unintended Consequences *

217

Negative Rebuttal to Harms

The negative used this opportunity to point out a "dropped" argument. Pointing out dropped arguments is very popular in debate because debaters get to claim an automatic win when there there is no refutation.

Still can adapt in time

It still proves that extinction is possible *

It took over 60,000 years to happen. People can adapt *

90% life was lost in permean extinction *

Yarkovsky effect

Nasa disagrees *

Russia recently had an asteroid encounter

Cheaper, more effective ways to survive asteroids *

Asteroids *

Will take over 100 years to increase temperatures by 1

People can adapt to climate change *

Climate change can lead to extinction *

Last decade was less deadly than any other in last

1988 nearly had an accidental nuclear launch

1990's weather balloon incident

Wars are declining in the amount of death *

War and accidental nuclear launch *

1. Safety in numbers *

Extending Disadvantage Responses

The affirmative also does well by extending the Link Turn. He explains that learning how to construct a bio-dome cannot happen until we actually commit to going there and trying.

The affirmative invests significant effort into responding to the disadvantage. In particular the Nonunique argument is reinforced.

Unrealistic

Need a head start

We cannot study without going to the moon

unrealistic

Microbes are going to spread no matter what

Therefore, Plan causes extinction. Turns case *

Building bio-domes on the moon is the opposite of

Supports the nonuniqueness

Non responsive to the methane argument

We should not consciously cause planetary

Mars rover already is going to spread microbes *

Panspermia, Carl Sagan sides with the affirmative *

a. Life is unpredictable *

b. Microbes will be introduced to biodomes. *

Unintended Consequences *

Extending Dropped Arguments

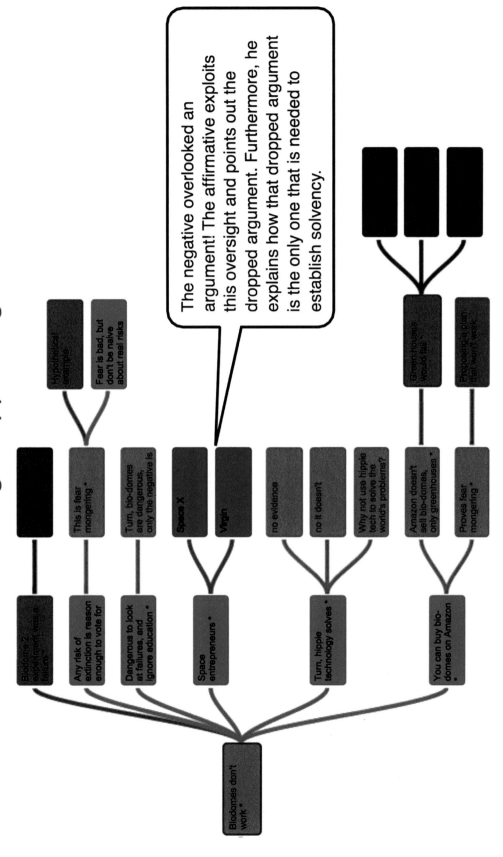

The negative overlooked an argument! The affirmative exploits this oversight and points out the dropped argument. Furthermore, he explains how that dropped argument is the only one that is needed to establish solvency.

Hypothetical example

Fear is bad, but don't be naïve about real risks

This is fear mongering *

Turn, bio-domes are dangerous, only the negative is

Space X

Virgin

no evidence

no it doesn't

Why not use hippie tech to solve the world's problems?

Green houses would fail *

Proposing a plan that won't work

Biodomes*2 experiment versus failure

Any risk of extinction is reason enough to vote for

Dangerous to look at failures, and ignore education *

Space entrepreneurs *

Turn, hippie technology solves *

Amazon doesn't sell bio-domes, only greenhouses *

Proves fear mongering *

You can buy bio-domes on Amazon .

Biodomes don't work *

A Complete Debate

Here is a complete map of a NFA LD debate flipped on its side. The arguments are illegible, but the structure is still apparent.

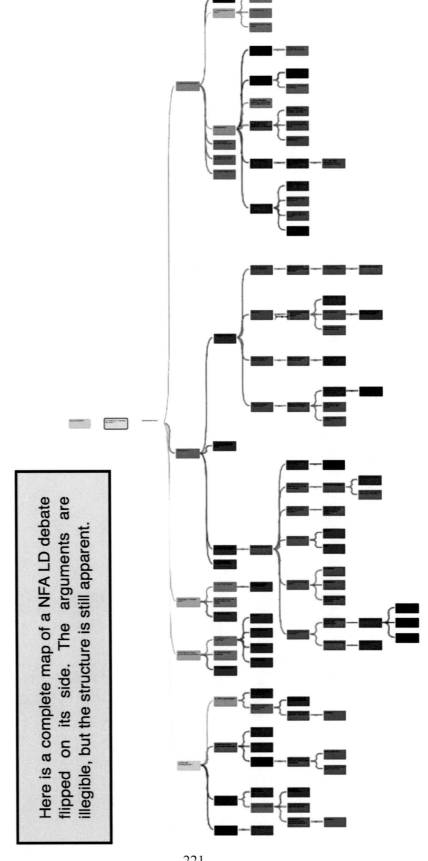

Chapter 13
The Legislative Bill

Topics

- Finding Topics - Selecting Topics

Using Stock Issues

- Harms - Inherency - Solvency

Alternative Views

- Radial - Expanded

Legislative Bill Assignment

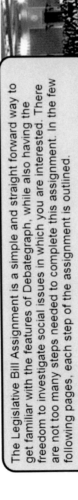

The Legislative Bill Assignment is a simple and straight forward way to get familiar with the features of Debategraph, while also having the freedom to investigate social issues in which you are interested. There are not too many steps needed to complete this assignment. In the few following pages, each step of the assignment is outlined.

The US House of Representatives debates many issues every year. The representatives that make up this decision-making body cast votes that are supposed to represent the interests of the constituents from their respective districts. Communicating with your representative is an important civic responsibility. A well thought out and constructed request could sway his or her vote on an important piece of legislation.

Where To Find Topics

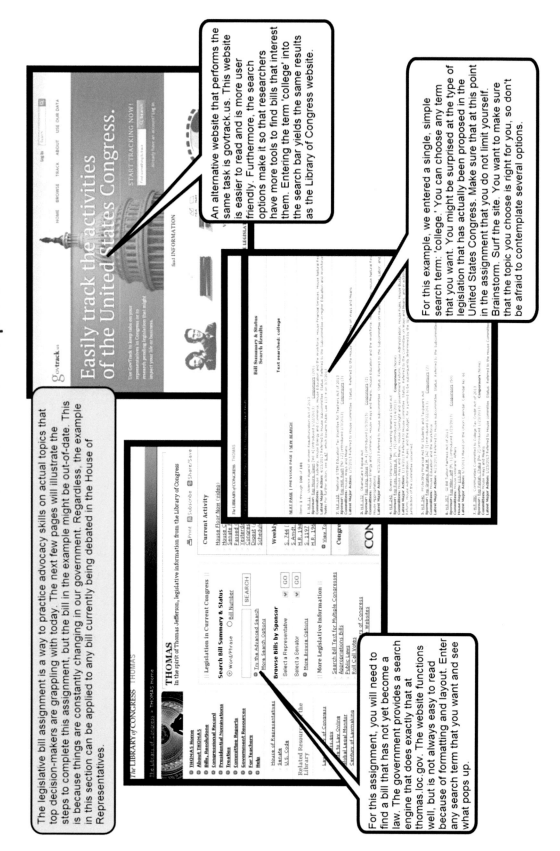

The legislative bill assignment is a way to practice advocacy skills on actual topics that top decision-makers are grappling with today. The next few pages will illustrate the steps to complete this assignment, but the bill in the example might be out-of-date. This is because things are constantly changing in our government. Regardless, the example in this section can be applied to any bill currently being debated in the House of Representatives.

An alternative website that performs the same task is govtrack.us. This website is easier to read and is more user friendly. Furthermore, the search options make it so that researchers have more tools to find bills that interest them. Entering the term 'college' into the search bar yields the same results as the Library of Congress website.

For this example, we entered a single, simple search term: 'college.' You can choose any term that you want. You might be surprised at the type of legislation that has actually been proposed in the United States Congress. Make sure that at this point in the assignment that you do not limit yourself. Brainstorm. Surf the site. You want to make sure that the topic you choose is right for you, so don't be afraid to contemplate several options.

For this assignment, you will need to find a bill that has not yet become a law. The government provides a search engine that does exactly that at thomas.loc.gov. The website functions well, but is not always easy to read because of formatting and layout. Enter any search term that you want and see what pops up.

Selecting a Topic

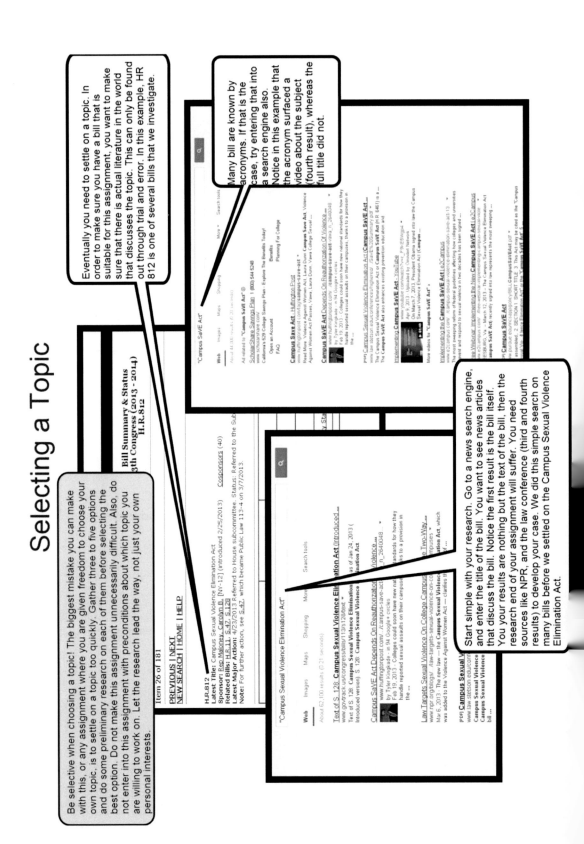

Be selective when choosing a topic! The biggest mistake you can make with this, or any assignment where you are given freedom to choose your own topic, is to settle on a topic too quickly. Gather three to five options and do some preliminary research on each of them before selecting the best option. Do not make this assignment unnecessarily difficult. Also, do not enter into this assignment with preconditions about which topic you are willing to work on. Let the research lead the way, not just your own personal interests.

Eventually you need to settle on a topic. In order to make sure you have a bill that is suitable for this assignment, you want to make sure that there is actual literature in the world that discusses the topic. This can only be found out through trial and error. In this example, HR 812 is one of several bills that we investigate.

Many bill are known by acronyms. If that is the case, try entering that into a search engine also. Notice in this example that the acronym surfaced a video about the subject (fourth result), whereas the full title did not.

Start simple with your research. Go to a news search engine, and enter the title of the bill. You want to see news articles that discuss the bill. Notice the first result is the bill itself. You your results are nothing but the text of the bill, then the research end of your assignment will suffer. You need sources like NPR, and the law conference (third and fourth results) to develop your case. We did this simple search on many bills before we settled on the Campus Sexual Violence Elimination Act.

Bill Summary & Status
113th Congress (2013 - 2014)
H.R.812

Item 26 of 181

PREVIOUS | NEXT
NEW SEARCH | HOME | HELP

H.R.812
Latest Title: Campus Sexual Violence Elimination Act
Sponsor: Rep Maloney, Carolyn B. [NY-12] (introduced 2/25/2013)   Cosponsors (40)
Related Bills: H.R.11, S.47, S.128
Latest Major Action: 4/23/2013 Referred to House subcommittee. Status: Referred to the Sub...
Note: For further action, see S.47, which became Public Law 113-4 on 3/7/2013.

Stock Issues

Once you have determined which bill you want as the topic of this assignment it is time to structure your advocacy. You are going to use the **Stock Issues** structure. Stock Issues are arguments that tend to recur for certain types of debate. For policy debate, which this assignment is, the stock issues are **Harms, Inherency,** and **Solvency.** This set of stock issues makes up an **Advantage.** An **Advantage** is a good thing or a set of good things that come from your plan or advocacy. Be sure to structure each of your **Advantages** with **Harms, Inherency,** and **Solvency.** Instructors sometimes have their own variations to stock issues that they like to teach their students. There is no one absolute set of **Stock Issues** that apply to all debates, they merely provided initial structure to the opening of the debate.

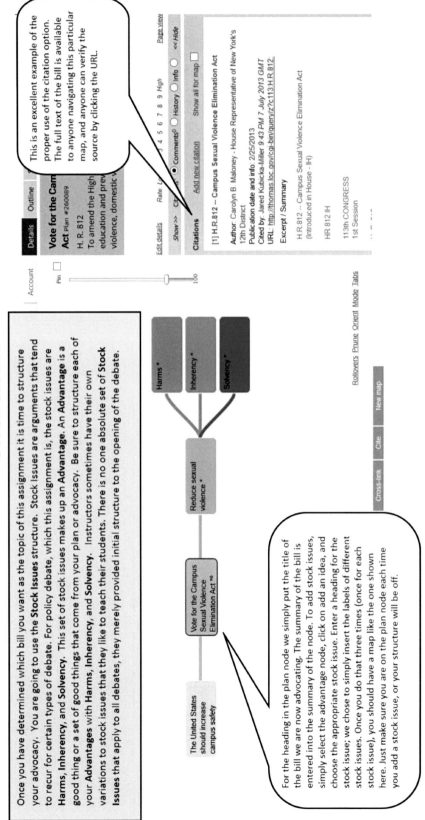

This is an excellent example of the proper use of the citation option. The full text of the bill is available to anyone navigating this particular map, and anyone can verify the source by clicking the URL.

For the heading in the plan node we simply put the title of the bill we are now advocating. The summary of the bill is entered into the summary of the node. To add stock issues, simply select the advantage node, click on add an idea, and choose the appropriate stock issue. Enter a heading for the stock issue; we chose to simply insert the labels of different stock issues. Once you do that three times (once for each stock issue), you should have a map like the one shown here. Just make sure you are on the plan node each time you add a stock issue, or your structure will be off.

Harms

The first issue we will explore is that of harms. Before you advocate a change to the status quo (i.e. 'the way things are'), you need to argue that there are problems that need fixing. If you fail to establish that there is anything wrong with the status quo, then your opponent could easily argue that it "if it ain't broke don't fix it." Harms can be established quantitatively-- through figures and statistics-- and qualitatively-- through real-life stories of people struggling with the status quo.

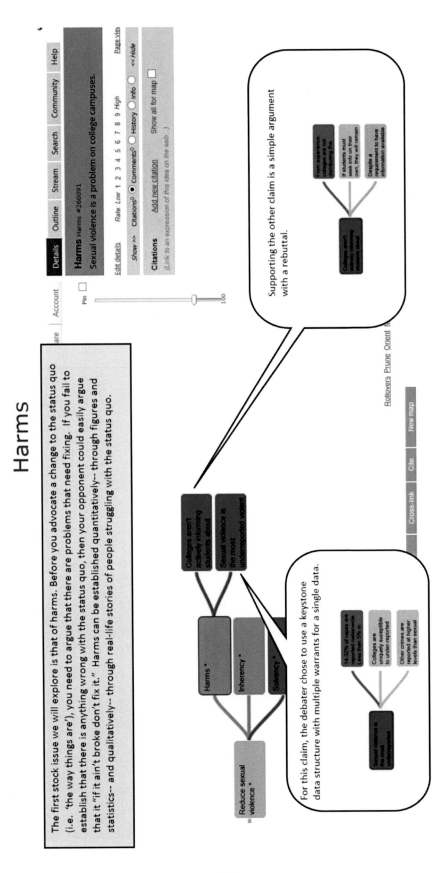

Supporting the other claim is a simple argument with a rebuttal.

For this claim, the debater chose to use a keystone data structure with multiple warrants for a single data.

Inherency

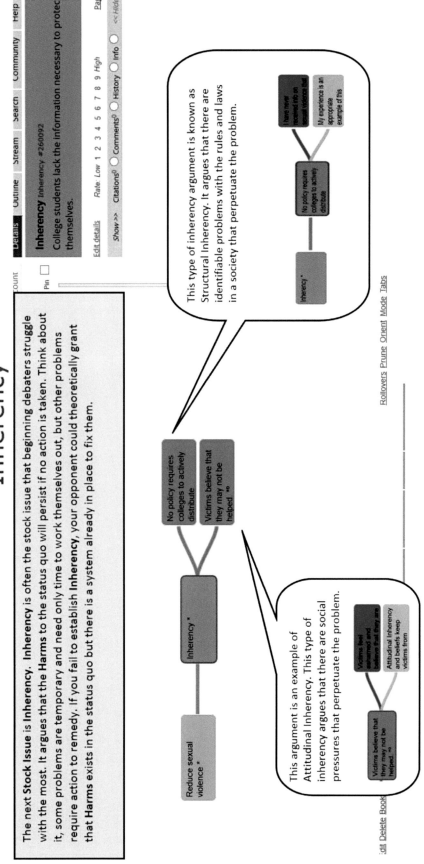

The next **Stock Issue** is Inherency. **Inherency** is often the stock issue that beginning debaters struggle with the most. It argues that the **Harms** to the status quo will persist if no action is taken. Think about it, some problems are temporary and need only time to work themselves out, but other problems require action to remedy. If you fail to establish **Inherency**, your opponent could theoretically grant that **Harms** exists in the status quo but there is a system already in place to fix them.

This type of inherency argument is known as Structural Inherency. It argues that there are identifiable problems with the rules and laws in a society that perpetuate the problem.

This argument is an example of Attitudinal Inherency. This type of inherency argues that there are social pressures that perpetuate the problem.

Rollovers Prune Orient Mode Tabs

Reduce sexual violence *

Inherency *

No policy requires colleges to actively distribute

Victims believe that they may not be helped *0

No policy requires colleges to actively distribute

I have never received info on sexual violence that

My experience is an appropriate example of this

Inherency *

Victims feel ashamed and believe that they are

Attitudinal inherency and beliefs keep victims from

Victims believe that they may not be helped. *0

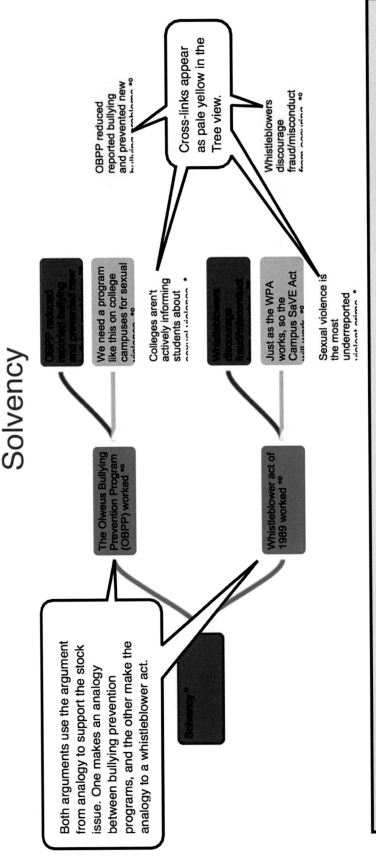

Solvency

OBPP reduced reported bullying and prevented new bullying problems *0

Whistleblowers discourage fraud/misconduct from occuring *0

Cross-links appear as pale yellow in the Tree view.

OBPP reduced reported bullying and prevented new bullying problems *0

We need a program like this on college campuses for sexual violence *0

Colleges aren't actively informing students about sexual violence *

Whistleblowers discourage fraud/misconduct from occuring *0

Just as the WPA works, so the Campus SaVE Act will work *0

Sexual violence is the most underreported violent crime *

The Olweus Bullying Prevention Program (OBPP) worked *0

Whistleblower act of 1989 worked *0

Solvency*

Both arguments use the argument from analogy to support the stock issue. One makes an analogy between bullying prevention programs, and the other make the analogy to a whistleblower act.

The final stock issue is Solvency. This argues that the proposed plan of action has a reasonable chance for success. Many students fail to realize that just because they found a plan to address the problem does not mean that plan is destined for success. Many well-intentioned plans are flawed and fail to deliver results. We suggest finding evidence of similar plans that have been enacted elsewhere in the world, or deal with similar problems, and were successful. You may also find expert opinions that vouch for the soundness of the plan.

Legislative Bill Final

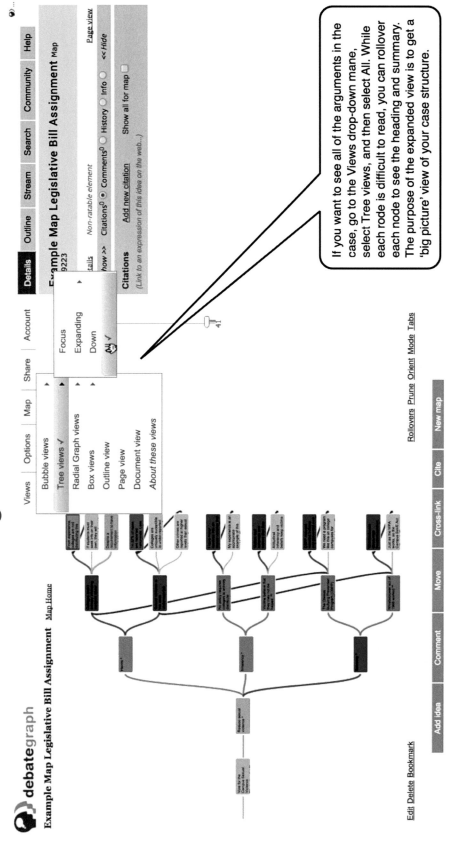

Alternative Views

You may want to use an alternative view for your case. Debategraph offers a wide variety for your work depending on which view suites you best

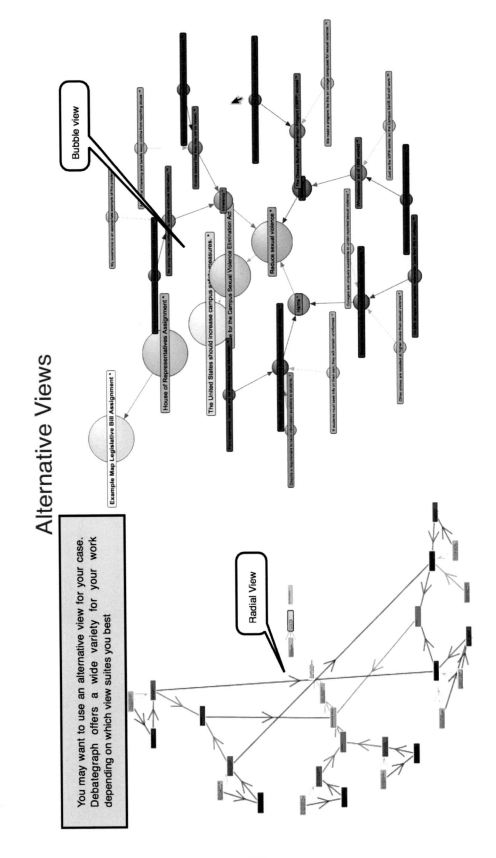

NOTES

NOTES

NOTES

NOTES

ABOUT THE AUTHOR

Jared Kubicka-Miller has been studying argumentation and debate for more than 15 years. He participated in the National Parliamentary Debate Association for 4 years and achieved second place at the 2003 National Parliamentary Tournament of Excellence. He received his M.A. from California State University Long Beach in 2006. He has been a professor and coach at Santiago Canyon College ever since.

Glossary

Abstract: The ability for language to refer to things that don't actually physically exist. There are levels of abstraction that communicators can use making their messages more concrete or more abstract.

Active listening: a communication technique that emphasizes concentrating on, responding to, and remembering a speaker's message.

Adherence: Arguers adhere to the arguments they are making when they take a position and offer an audience direction.

Adrenaline : Increases your blood pressure and your heart rate and to make you more alert generally and is literally preparing your body for a physical event that you might need to do.

Ambiguous: A single word or sentence could be interpreted multiple ways from multiple people.

Arbitrary: There's no inherent relationship between the object being referenced, In the sounds or letters that form the word for that object. This understood by recognizing that many different languages have their own words that sound very different from each other even if they are referencing the same object.

Argument: Any combination of propositions aimed at persuading an audience to a particular viewpoint, belief, or action; and, that particular conclusion is claimed to be supported by the other propositions.

Argument Fields: Describe different social spheres, each with individualized standards for judging good and bad arguments.

Attitudinal inherency: Type of inherency that argues that there is a common behavior or attitude that perpetuates the harms.

Backing: Any additional information or evidence that is used to supply or support the data or the warrant in Toulmin Model.

Burden of proof: When arguing, it is the obligation to provide sufficient data and warrants for their arguments.

Channel: The medium, through which, a sender chooses to transmit a message. Messages must be sent through channels, sometimes multiple channels simultaneously. A channel is the medium that the sender choose to send the message through. It could be face-to-face, through the television, text, the phone, a billboard, skywriting, interpretive dance, and the list goes on.

Claim: The fundamental position (belief, viewpoint, or action) which arguers want an audience to accept according to Toulmin.

Communication Apprehension: Physiological factors at work when anyone experiences speech anxiety.

Communication Model: Models developed by theorists to help better explain how it is that human beings share information. Origins found in the linear model, to the development of the interactive model, and more recently of transactional communication.

Competition: In debates, it is the forced choice between plans and counter plans.

Controversy: Assumption about any argument is that the arguer is discussing an issue that has room for disagreement.

Cortisol: A hormone that influences your brain physiology. It has an effect on the prefrontal cortex and the hippocampus, which are the critical thinking parts of your brain and where learning happens.

Criterion: This stock issue functions as a weighing mechanism by which arguments can be judged throughout a debate.

Critical Affirmative: Affirmative prioritizes and puts a great amount of focus on ethics or morality for how a debate should be evaluated.

Data: Any research, evidence or other support that is presented in order to support the claim according to Toulmin Model.

Demographics: statistical data regarding characteristics of groups of people.

Enthymeme: Defined contemporarily as an 'incomplete syllogism', Aristotle defined enthymemes as a syllogism based on probabilities.

External Interference: Things that impede a message that originate from outside of the communicators, like the room temperature, loud noise, the weather, etc.

Feedback: Message sent by receiver delivered through channels and affected by noise and frame of reference.

Fiat: Latin for "let it be done," it is used as a technique in argumentation and debate to advocate for a plan of action by imagining that plan being adopted in a real-world situation.

Field contextual definition: The idea that a word of phrase has particular meaning, and ought to be defined, by referencing the field of study which it is used.

Field Dependency: The idea that certain elements of argument may be considered acceptable for one field, but unacceptable in another.

Field Invariant: Those components of arguments that are consistent across all fields.

Fight or Flight Response: The autonomic response affecting analytical parts of your brain. Inhibited by cortisol and adrenaline because your body, from an evolutionary standpoint, wants you to prepare yourself for some physical action: fight that danger or to take flight, to run away from it.

Glossophobia: Speech anxiety, or the fear of public speaking. A fear that is consistently rated as people's biggest fear.

Harms: An argument, or set of arguments that attempt to persuade an audience that there are problems with the status quo.

Inherency: An argument, or a set of arguments that argue that the problem will persist if no action is taken.

Interactive Model of Communication: Model of communication which identifies Sender, Receiver, Message, Channel, Noise, Feedback.

Instrumental Value: A value that leads to other values.

Internal Interference: Anything that impedes communication and originates from within the communicators, like a bad night's sleep, or communication apprehension.

Invention: An argument is made with the goal of creating new knowledge.

Language Acquisition Device: Noam Chomsky's most significant contribution is the theory that all humans are born with biological structures (a language acquisition device) in the brain that make us uniquely able to acquire language.

Language Games: One of Ludwig Wittgenstein greatest theoretical contributions to the study of language is the observation that people tend to learn and use language through what he called language games. This is contrary to the prevailing opinion at the time that language was somehow a reference to some external reality world. Language is an activity that forms relationships and generates behaviors. The best way to understand language is to look at how language is used rather than trying to unearth some sort of meaning.

Linear Model of Communication: An early theory developed by Claude Elwood Shannon and Warren Weaver in the 1950's. Primarily interested in communication through the telephone The model consisted of a sender, a message, a channel, and a receiver.

Link Story: Explanation for how the plan creates a series of effects.

Message: A message is anything that the sender communicates, intentionally or unintentionally.

Micropolitics: Suggests is that is possible for you to affirm the topic by simply identifying a micropolitical action, it usually understood as an individual action, a choice that any one of us would make in our lives.

Natural Arguments: Understanding the difference between formal and informal logic.

Net-benefits: Also known as cost-benefit-analysis or CBA. Debaters typically prefer the term net benefits, and the reason why is debatable, but CBA typically implies that everything is evaluated in monetary terms. Debaters tend to weigh arguments in more humanist terms, so net benefits allows for debaters to defend impacts that are not put into dollar figures.

Noise: In communication studies, anything that impedes the transmission of a message.

Non-unique: A response to a disadvantage which argues that the plan is not uniquely responsible for whether or not the impacts occur.

Opposition block: A phenomenon common in team debate where the last negative constructive is immediately followed by the first negative rebuttal, effectively giving the negative team back-to-back speeches.

Oxytocin: Sometimes called the "bonding hormone" or the "love hormone" because it's responsible for feeling a sense of community. In some ways, it helps to balance all of the distracting effects of Cortisol.

Permutation: in debate, it is the argument that there is no forced choice between the plan and counterplan because both could hypothetically coexist together.

Policy Criterion: It is considered the job of debaters to hash out the different impacts in the round. For this reason it is common for criteria to come from economic schools of thought. It is uncommon in a policy debate to declare a single thing to be valued unlike value debates.

Power Pose: A way of positioning one's body to increase their self confidence. With training, conditioning and discipline Amy Cuddy suggests by proactively engaging in power poses influences how your brain responds to stress.

Primary source: An original document where the research, and analysis is done by the author at the time of the study.

Qualifier: Toulmin's element of argument which modifies the strength of a claim.

Qualitative Harms: Type of harm data which rely on statistical data to articulate the extent of human suffering.

Quantitative Harms: Type of harm based on data of particular people and events.

Reason: Statements act as the rationale for the conclusion the arguer.

Rebuttal: Any response that offers further clarification in Toulmin's Model.

Receiver: Decoder of a message.

Scheme: In language, it is a figure of speech where the arrangement of words are modified for effect.

Sender: Encoder of a message.

Significance Argument: An explanation that you solve for a significant amount of your harms.

Solvency: An argument, or set of arguments that the proposed plan will solve the harms.

Stasis: The rest or halt which occurs between opposing arguments.

Stock Issues: The questions which occur with frequency in the course of argumentation.

Structural Inherency: Type of inherency which argues that there is a law, or policy that is creating the harms.

Syllogism: A method of reasoning where a conclusion is derived from two given or assumed premises. Comprised of three parts: a major premise, a minor premise, and a conclusion. Both premises are built upon prior observations. If both premises are true, then the conclusion is necessarily true.

Terminal Value: Something considered value in and of itself. Common terminal values are life, justice, and freedom.

Topicality: A standard argument in debate rounds whose central issue is whether or not the affirmative advocated a case that supports the resolution.

The Transactional Model: Model of communication has become very popular which does away with the sender/receiver and considers all members to simply be "communicators" that are encoding and decoding messages simultaneously.

Trope: a figure of speech that modifies the meaning of a word, phrase, or section of language for artistic effect.

Unintentional Messages: Message the sender does not intend to communicate especially nonverbal messages.

Uniqueness: Any argument, or set of arguments, that identifies a particular area of life that would otherwise be unaffected by the proposition advanced by the affirmative.

Utilitarianism: Popularized by John Stuart Mill utilitarianism argues that we should act in ways that provide the greatest amount of good for the most amount of people. Commonly used as a value criterion.

Utopian fiat: a type of fiat abuse where a debater advocates an impossible, or highly improbable plan and dismisses arguments about the practicality of the plan in question.

Value Criterion: Typically involves two things: the thing that is being valued, and the criterion itself that provides a mechanism for achieving the value.

Value Justification: Argument that the affirmative side warrants the value criterion in the debate.

Value Objection: This stock issue answers the question "In what ways does the negative side fail to meet the value?"

Warrant: The reason or logic connecting the data with the claim.

Amossy, Ruth. "The New Rhetoric'S Inheritance. Argumentation And Discourse Analysis." *Argumentation* 23.3 (2009): 313-324.

Andersen, Kenneth E. "The Rawlsian Argument For A Model Of Developing An Ethic." *Conference Proceedings -- National Communication Association/American Forensic Association (Alta Conference On Argumentation)* (1981): 1003-1013.

Aristotle. *Prior Analytics.* Trans A. J. Jenkinson. Amazon Digital Services, 2008.

Arnett, Ronald C. "The Responsive "I": Levinas's Derivative Argument." *Argumentation & Advocacy* 40.1 (2003): 39-50.

Bar-Elli, Gilead. "Wittgenstein On The Experience Of Meaning And The Meaning Of Music." *Philosophical Investigations* 29.3 (2006): 217-249.

Batt, Shawn. "Keeping Company In Controversy: Education Reform, Spheres Of Argument, And Ethical Criticism." *Argumentation & Advocacy* 40.2 (2003): 85-104.

Belt, Rabia. "Contemporary Voting Rights Controversies Through The Lens Of Disability." *Stanford Law Review* 68.6 (2016): 1491-1550.

Bennett, William H. *Varsity Debate.* Taos, New Mexico: CDE, 1996.

Benoit, Pamela J. "A Defense Of Argument As Disagreement." *Argumentation & Advocacy* 28.1 (1991): 35.

Benoit, William L., and Jayne R. Henson. "A Functional Analysis Of The 2008 Vice Presidential Debate: Biden Versus Palin." *Argumentation & Advocacy* 46.1 (2009): 39-50.

Bitzer, Lloyd F. "Aristotle's Enthymeme Revisited." *Quarterly Journal Of Speech* 45.4 (1959): 399.

Borden, Sandra L. "Mapping Ethical Arguments In Journalism: An Exploratory Study." *Mass Communication & Society* 10.3 (2007): 275-297.

Brodak, Geoffrey W., and Matthew Taylor. "Resolutions of fact: A critique of traditional typology in parliamentary debate." *Parliamentary Debate: The Journal of the National Parliamentary Debate Association* 7.1 (2002): 24-34.

Brownlee, Don. "Forensics Education And Ethics." *Conference Proceedings -- National Communication Association/ American Forensic Association (Alta Conference On Argumentation)* (1989): 468-471.

Burnett, Nicholas F. "Archbishop Whately and the Concept of Presumption: Lessons for Non-Policy Debate." *CEDA Yearbook.* 13 (1992). 20-24

Carney, Dana R., Amy JC Cuddy, and Andy J. Yap. "Power posing brief nonverbal displays affect neuroendocrine levels and risk tolerance." *Psychological Science* 21.10 (2010): 1363-1368.

Cartaginese, C. "Man-Made Global Warming: the Myth that Refuses to Die." *NewsRealBlog.com.* 25 Nov 2009. Web. https://newsrealblog.wordpress.com/2009/11/25/man-made-global-warming-the-myth-that-refuses-to-die/

Chomsky, Noam. *Aspects of the Theory of Syntax.* Cambridge: M.I.T., 1965 Print.

Christmann, Ursula, Christoph Mischo, and Jürgen Flender. "Argumentational Integrity: A Training Program For Dealing With Unfair Argumentative Contributions." Argumentation 14.4 (2000): 339-360.

Cox, J. Robert. "Postmodernity, Cryptonormativism, And The Rhetorical: A Defense Of Argument Studies." *Conference Proceedings -- National Communication Association/American Forensic Association (Alta Conference On Argumentation)* (1993): 8-12.

Crossman, Mark R. *Burden of Proof: An Introduction to Argumentation*. Mason, Ohio: Thompson, 2003.

Crosswhite, James. "Awakening The Topoi: Sources Of Invention In New Rhetoric's Argument Model." *Argumentation & Advocacy* 44.4 (2008): 169-184.

Dittus, James K. "Restraining Whately: An Examination Of The Role Of Presumption In Risk Analysis." *Conference Proceedings -- National Communication Association/American Forensic Association (Alta Conference On Argumentation)* (1993): 61-64.

Eminem, Obie Trice, 50 Cent, Jay-Z, Freeway, Xzibit, Macy Gray, Nas, Rakim, and Young Zee. Music from and Inspired by the Motion Picture 8 Mile. Shady/Interscope Records, 2002. CD.

Fahnestock, Jeanne. "Audience In The New Rhetoric And The Formal Appeals." *Conference Proceedings -- National Communication Association/American Forensic Association (Alta Conference On Argumentation)* (1995): 7-11.

Fisher, Walter R. "Technical logic, rhetorical logic, and narrative rationality." *Argumentation* 1.1 (1987): 3-21.

Follette, Charles. "Deep Rhetoric: A Substantive Alternative to Consequentialism in Exploring the Ethics of Rhetoric." *Dimensions of Argument: Proceedings of the Second Summer Conference on Argumentation*. Annandale, VA: Speech Communication Association, (1981). Eds. George Ziegelmueller, and Jack Rhodes.

Franken, Al. "Climate Change Speech." *Senate Floor Speech*. U.S. Senate, Washington D.C. 01 Aug. 2016. Speech.

Freely, Austin J. and David L. Steinberg. *Argumentation and Debate*. Belmont, California: Wadsworth, 2005.

Gallagher, Michael D. "Video Games Don't Cause Children to be Violent." *U.S. News and World Report*. 10 May 2010. Web.

Gardner, Bill. "From 'shrill' Housewife to Downing Street: The Changing Voice of Margaret Thatcher." *The Telegraph*. Telegraph Media Group, 25 Nov. 2014. Web. 01 Aug. 2016.

Gedney, Thomas R. "Argument of John Quincy Adams, Before the Supreme Court of the United States, in the Case of the United States, Appellents, vs. Cinque, and Others, Africans, Captured in the Schooner Amistad." 128 Fulton Street, New York. 1841. *The Avalon Project*. Web. 1 Aug. 2016.

Gladwell, Malcolm. *Outliers: The story of success*. Hachette UK, 2008.

Godden, David M., and Douglas Walton. "A Theory Of Presumption For Everyday Argumentation." *Pragmatics & Cognition* 15.2 (2007): 313-346.

Goddu, G.C. "Reasonable Doubt: A Note On 'Neutral' Illatives And Arguments." *Argumentation* 13.3 (1999): 243-250.

Goodnight, G. Thomas, and Gordon R. Mitchell. "Forensics As Scholarship: Testing Zarefsky's Bold Hypothesis In A Digital Age." *Argumentation & Advocacy* 45.2 (2008): 80-97.

Goodwin, Jean. "Perelman, Adhering, And Conviction." *Philosophy & Rhetoric* 28.3 (1995): 215-233.

Graham, Keith. "Preconditions For Normative Argumentation In A Pluralist World." *Argumentation* 15.4 (2001): 471-487.

Hansen, Hans Vilhelm. "An Exploration of Johnson's Sense of 'Argument'." *Argumentation* 16.3 (2002): 263-276.

Harpine, William D. "Stock Issues In Aristotle's Rhetoric." *Journal Of The American Forensic Association* 14.(1977): 73-81.

Harriger, Katy J. "The Federalism Debate In The Transformation Of Federal.." *Publius: The Journal Of Federalism* 27.3 (1997): 1.

Henkemans, A. Francisca Snoeck. "State-of-the-art: The structure of argumentation." *Argumentation* 14.4 (2000): 447-473.

Hicks, Darrin, and Ronald Walter Greene. "Conscientious Objections: Debating Both Sides And The Cultures Of Democracy." *Conference Proceedings -- National Communication Association/American Forensic Association (Alta Conference On Argumentation)* (2010): 172-178.

Hicks, Darrin. "Disagreement And Democratic Pluralism." *Conference Proceedings -- National Communication Association/American Forensic Association (Alta Conference On Argumentation)* (1995): 302-307.

Hitchcock, David. "The practice of argumentative discussion." *Argumentation* 16.3 (2002): 287-298.

Hollihan, Thomas A. and Kevin T. Baaske. *Arguments and Arguing.* Prospect Heights, Illinois: Waveband Press, 1994.

Hollinger, Robert. "Practical reason and hermeneutics." *Philosophy & Rhetoric* (1985): 113-122.

Johnson, Ralph H. *Manifest Rationality: A Pragmatic Theory of Argument.* Mahwah. NJ: Lawrence Erlbaum Associates, 2000. Print.

Johnson, Ralph H. "Manifest rationality reconsidered: Reply to my fellow symposiasts." *Argumentation* 16.3 (2002): 311-331.

Kant, I. *The Critique of Pure Reason.* Trans. J. M. D. Meiklejohn. Amazon Digital Services. 2011.

Katula, Richard A., and Richard W. Roth. "A stock issues approach to writing arguments." *College Composition and Communication* 31.2 (1980): 183-196.

Kauffeld, Fred J. "Presumptions And The Distribution Of Argumentative Burdens In Acts Of Proposing And Accusing." *Argumentation* 12.2 (1998): 245-266.

Kimball, Robert H. "What's wrong with argumentum ad baculum? Reasons, threats, and logical norms." *Argumentation* 20.1 (2006): 89-100.

Klien, Stephen A. "Defining "Public Character": Agency And The Ethical Criticism Of Public Argument." *Conference Proceedings -- National Communication Association/American Forensic Association (Alta Conference On Argumentation,* (1999): 341-350.

Klumpp, James F. "Freedom And Responsibility In Constructing Public Life: Toward A Revised Ethic Of Discourse." *Argumentation* 11.1 (1997): 113-130.

Kock, Christian. "Choice Is Not True Or False: The Domain Of Rhetorical Argumentation." *Argumentation* 23.1 (2009): 61-80.

Koren, Roselyne. "Can Perelman'S NR Be Viewed As An Ethics Of Discourse?." *Argumentation* 23.3 (2009): 421-431.

La Ban, Frank K. "Academic Debate: Can We Afford It?." *Association For Communication Administration Bulletin* 34 (1980): 73-74.

Legge, Nancy J., and James R. DiSanza. "Can You Make An Argument Without Being In An Argument? A Relational Approach To The Study Of Interactional Argument." *Journal Of The Northwest Communication Association* 21.(1993): 1-19.

Loxton, Daniel. "Flat Earth?! The Convoluted Story Of A Flatly Mistaken Idea." *Skeptic* 19.4 (2014): 65-73.

McDaniel, James P. "Responsibilities: Speculations On Rhetoric And The Ethico-Political In Postmodernity." *Conference Proceedings -- National Communication Association/American Forensic Association (Alta Conference On Argumentation)* (1993): 159-161.

McGee, Michael Calvin. "The Moral Problem Of Argumenium Per Argumenium." *Conference Proceedings -- National Communication Association/American Forensic Association (Alta Conference On Argumentation) (1985)*: 1-12.

Mehltretter, Sara Ann, and Dale A. Herbeck. "55. Looks Count: Newspaper Accounts Of The First Kennedy-Nixon Debate During The 2004 Presidential Campaign." *Conference Proceedings -- National Communication Association/American Forensic Association (Alta Conference On Argumentation)* (2007): 555-557.

Merz, Miwa Yamazaki. "The Effects Of Self-Construal And Perceived Control On Argumentativeness And Communication Apprehension." *Journal Of Intercultural Communication Research* 38.2 (2009): 59-75.

Miller, Robert Keith. *The Informed Argument: A Multidisciplinary Reader and Guide.* San Diego: Harcourt Brace Jovanovich, 1986. Print.

Nixon, Richard, and Nikita Khrushchev. "The kitchen debate." *New York Times* (1959): 1.

Norman, A.P. "The Normative Structure Of Adjudicative Dialogue." *Argumentation* 15.4 (2001): 489-498.

O'Keefe, Daniel J. "Potential Conflicts Between Normatively-Responsible Advocacy And Successful Social Influence: Evidence From Persuasion Effects Research." *Argumentation* 21.2 (2007): 151-163.

O'Keefe, Daniel J. "Two Concepts Of Argument." *Journal Of The American Forensic Association* 13. (1977): 121-128.

Peart, Neil. "Neil Peart Quotes." *BrainyQuote*. Xplore, 01 Aug. 2016. Web

Perelman, Chaïm, and Lucie Olbrechts-Tyteca. *The New Rhetoric: A Treatise on Argumentation*. Trans. John Wilkinson and Purcell. Notre Dame: University of Notre Dame, 1969. Print.

Rieke, Richard D., et al. *Argumentation and Critical Decision Making*. Boston: Pearson, 2005. Print.

Rowland, Robert C. "The Function of Presumption in Academic Debate." *CEDA Yearbook*. 13 (1992): 20-24.

Rowland, Robert C. "Purpose, Argument Fields, And Theoretical Justification." *Argumentation* 22.2 (2008): 235-250.

Rutledge, Skip, and G. L. Forward. "Presumption and Defending the Status Quo in Intercollegiate Debate: An Exploratory Survey of Judge Perceptions in Parliamentary & CEDA/NDT Debate Formats." *Journal of the National Parliamentary Debate Association* 10 (2004): 24-48.

Rybacki, Karyn C., and Donald J. Rybacki. *Advocacy and Opposition: An Introduction to Argumentation*. Englewood Cliffs, NJ: Prentice-Hall, 1986. Print.

Sommerville, Joseph A. "Experts in Moral Argument." *Spheres of Argument: Proceedings of the Sixth SCA/AFA Conference on Argumentation*. 1989.

Stroud, Scott. "Habermas And Debate Theory: A Putative Link Between The Theory Of Communicative Action And Traditional Resolutional Typologies." *Conference Proceedings -- National Communication Association/American Forensic Association (Alta Conference On Argumentation)* (1999): 325-333.

Sung, Minkyu. "Questioning The Neo-Liberal Architecture Of "Dromocratic" Regime: A Critique Of Governmental Rationality Of "Speed." *Conference Papers -- International Communication Association* (2007): 1.

Swift, Crystal-Lane. "Pre-Fiat Vs. Post Fiat Kritik Implications Debate, Cost Benefit Analysis Criterion, Or Just Water The House Plant?: National Parliamentary Tournament Of Excellence Judging Paradigms." *The Forensic of Pi Kappa Delta* 92.2 (2007): 27-32.

Tindale, Christopher W. "A Concept Divided: Ralph Johnson's Definition Of Argument." *Argumentation* 16.3 (2002): 299.

Toulmin, Stephen. *The Uses of Argument*. Cambridge: Cambridge UP, 1999. Print.

Turner, Monique Mitchell, et al. "Do Lay People Prepare Both Sides Of An Argument? The Effects Of Confidence, Forewarning, And Expected Interaction On Seeking Out Counter-Atitfudinal Information." *Argumentation & Advocacy* 46.4 (2010): 226-239.

Walton, Douglas. "Enthymemes, Common Knowledge, And Plausible Inference." *Philosophy & Rhetoric* 34.2 (2001): 93-112.

Wenzel, Joseph H. "Ethical Proof: A Reexamination Of Aristotelian Theory." *Conference Proceedings -- National Communication Association/American Forensic Association (Alta Conference On Argumentation* (1983): 43-53.

Whaley, Bryan B. "Evaluations of rebuttal analogy users: Ethical and competence considerations." *Argumentation* 12.3 (1998): 351-365.

Whately, Richard. *Elements of Rhetoric.* Delmar, NY: Scholars' Facsimiles & Reprints, 1991. Print.

Wikipedia. "HitRecord." Wikipedia. Wikimedia Foundation, 01 Aug. 2016. Web. 01 Aug. 2016.

Wittgenstein, Ludwig. *Philosophical Investigations.* Oxford: Blackwell, 1967. Print.

Wooten, Victor. "Music as a Language - Victor Wooten." *TED-Ed.* TED-Ed, 13 Aug. 2012. Web. 01 Aug. 2016.

Zarefsky, David. "Moral Argument In Political History: The Case Of The Lincoln-Douglas Debates." *Conference Proceedings -- National Communication Association/American Forensic Association (Alta Conference On Argumentation)* (1983): 201-212.

Zarefsky, David. "The role of causal argument in policy controversies." Journal of the American Forensic Association 13 (1977): 179-191.

Made in the USA
San Bernardino, CA
23 August 2016